Business Firms and the Common Law

Business Firms and the Common Law

The Evolution of Efficient Rules

Paul H. Rubin

PRAEGER SPECIAL STUDIES • PRAEGER SCIENTIFIC

Library of Congress Cataloging in Publication Data

Rubin, Paul H.
  Business firms and the common law.

  Includes bibliographical references and index.
  1. Business enterprises--United States. 2. Common
law--United States. 3. Law--Economic aspects--United
States. 4. Government litigation--United States.
I. Title.
KF1366.R8   1983   346.73'07   83-11028
ISBN 0-03-063914-X   347.3067

Published in 1983 by Praeger Publishers
CBS Educational and Professional Publishing
a Division of CBS Inc.
521 Fifth Avenue, New York, New York 10175, USA

3456789 052 987654321

Printed in the United States of America
on acid-free paper

To *Joe*, *Sabrina*, *Alex*, and *Rachel*

Acknowledgments

This book represents the culmination of research which took place over several years. Many people had helpful comments on that research. I would like to thank Gregory Alexander, Louis deAlessi, Walter Hellerstein, Richard Higgins, Carl Jordon, Ellen Jordan, James Kau, Edmund Kitch, William Landes, Henry Manne, George Priest and Mario Rizzo, for such comments. Special thanks are due to Richard Posner and Gordon Tullock for many useful suggestions, and for providing the intellectual paradigm within which this book has written. Part of the research was financed by grants from the Liberty Fund. Thanks are also due to *The Journal of Law and Economics* and *The Journal of Legal Studies* for permission to reprint parts of articles which appeared there.

Chapter 5 was originally coauthored with Peter Shedd, and Chapters 6, 7, and 8 were coauthored with Ellen Jordan; I would like to thank them for permission to reprint that material here. However, these chapters have been sufficiently rewritten so that I absolve Professors Shedd and Jordon of any responsibility for remaining errors.

Introduction

In 1973, in the first edition of *Economic Analysis of Law*,[1] Richard Posner proposed that the common law could be understood as an attempt to achieve economic efficiency, defined as the mimicking of what market transactions could have achieved had such transactions been possible. This was an extremely powerful insight, and has led to substantial amounts of research by lawyers and economists who have attempted to defend or refute this hypothesis. Even if the claim turns out to be incorrect it will have served a very important scientific function, for incorrect hypotheses that provide clues for testing are more useful than are no hypotheses; without some hypothesis the scientific enterprise is paralyzed.

A major weakness in Posner's claim was the absence of a mechanism that could be expected to have generated the observed efficiency. Posner argued that judges consciously sought efficiency since they were isolated from any self-interest in decisions by the institutions of the judiciary itself. Therefore, since this isolation existed, judges felt that efficiency was as good a goal as any to pursue, and did so. This argument was rather weak, and led those who did not believe in the efficiency of the common law to claim that this mechanism was in fact insufficient to guarantee that efficiency would be achieved. Moreover, this claim was especially questionable since it occurred at a time when many economists[2] (including Posner himself)[3] were arguing that statute law was the product of special-interest forces and had nothing to do with a desire for efficiency. Though William Landes and Richard Posner attempted to relate the interest group theory to the theory of efficient common law rules,[4] nonetheless, a question remained as to whether the forces for efficiency were sufficiently strong to lead to the result which Posner observed.

In 1977 I proposed a mechanism that would lead to efficiency independent of the desire of judges to achieve this goal (or any other goal).[5] This mechanism was based on the self-interested behavior of disputants; it showed that in some circumstances, parties to disputes would have greater incentives to litigate inefficient rules than efficient rules. If this were true, then there would be a greater chance of overturning inefficient rules than of overturning efficient rules and therefore the law should, over time, evolve toward greater efficiency. This result has been extended and criticized in the literature, and the issue is by no means settled. (Much of this criticism is addressed in Chapter 2.) Nevertheless, there are some tentative conclusions that can be reached about the process of common law evolution.

First, many parties have agreed that there are certain tendencies that should be identified in the law. Most specifically, it seems that parties with substantial ongoing interests in a legal rule should be able to achieve that rule. Such parties will engage in litigation and relitigation until desired rule is achieved. They will also be able to spend more on such litigation than will parties without such an ongoing interest. Other mechanisms are available to parties with continuing interests.

Second, the rules achieved by such parties will, in certain circumstances, be efficient. If the parties represent the interests of all potential disputants with interests in that rule, then the rule will turn out to move toward efficiency. Conversely, if the parties do not represent such interests, then there is no mechanism that will lead the rule toward efficiency. Thus, the focus shifts from an examination of the nature of the rules to an examination of the nature of the disputants. The evolutionary theory then predicts that, given the right sort of disputants, the law should evolve toward efficiency. The nature of this process is discussed in more detail in Part I.

This creates a strong interest in firms as litigants. Firms have exactly the sort of interests that have been identified as leading to efficiency. In a dispute involving two firms, both may be expected to view themselves as potential litigants in future cases and both may view themselves as being likely to be on either side in future disputes. Therefore, in disputes involving two firms we might expect efficiency to prevail. Moreover, in disputes involving firms and employees or customers, we might also expect efficiency to occur since the contractual relationship involved means that the parties should internalize any benefits from efficient rules. Therefore, the focus in this book is on the firm as a litigant. The arguments deal with the predicted behavior of firms as disputants with ongoing interests in legal rules and with the types of rules sought by firms.

The plan of this work is as follows: Part I deals with the mechanisms of rule change and with the forces leading toward or away from efficiency in this process. The predictions of this section are that in many cases firms as litigants will seek and achieve efficient rules. Part II examines some rules dealing with firms and finds that, indeed, there are efficiency explanations for these rules. This part is not a proof, in that the evidence is not statistical evidence; it is primarily suggestive. (Chapter 6 provides stronger evidence than in the other chapters; here, all cases dealing with a particular rule and the effects of the rule are more carefully examined.) Part III deals with litigation decisions by government agencies in their dealings with firms and with the responses of firms. The theory would predict that such agencies would have even stronger interests in precedents than would the firms with which they are dealing, and that therefore rules derived from this process would tend to favor the agency, independent of any interest in efficiency. This part also examines some responses by firms to this process, and concludes that firms are beginning to organize in order to litigate and achieve favorable decisions with respect to such agencies. Certain "legal foundations" (essentially, business oriented public interest law firms) seem to be the agents of firms in this organization. Finally, Part IV examines the implications of legal rules for decision making. In Chapter 9, it is argued that if rules are economically efficient, then decision making for the firm is relatively inexpensive, since in this circumstance firms will not need to know what the law is, but will be able to make decisions based on costs and benefits (since this is what the law will also consider).

The last chapter summarizes the argument and presents policy implications. The basic argument is that firms will in most cases achieve efficient outcomes if left alone. Interference with firms, either through statutes or through litigation by regulatory agencies, will generally lead to inefficient outcomes. In those cases where firms will not reach desirable solutions (such as cases where property rights are ill-defined, as in pollution) an optimal solution may be to create property rights and vest these rights in private owners, for this solution will then again lead to efficient outcomes. It has long been known that giving private parties rights to scarce resources will lead to efficient utilization of these resources. In this book, the argument is carried one step further; it is argued that private parties will also seek and obtain efficient rules governing the use of resources. The firm as litigant seems to seek and generally obtain efficient legal rules.

NOTES

1. Richard A. Posner, *Economic Analysis of Law*, 2d ed. (Boston: Little, Brown, 1977).

2. Initially, George Stigler, "The Theory of Economic Regulation," *Bell Journal of Economics and Management Science* 2 (1971): 3-21.

3. Richard A. Posner, "Theories of Economic Regulation," *Bell Journal of Economics and Management Science* (1974).

4. William Landes and Richard Posner, "The Independent Judiciary in an Interest Group Perspective," *Journal of Law and Economics* (1975).

5. Paul H. Rubin, "Why Is the Common Law Efficient?," *Journal of Legal Studies* (1977): 51-61: Chap. 1 of the present volume.

Contents

Business Firms and
the Common Law

PART I

THE LITIGATION PROCESS

In this part, the litigation process is examined. The major conclusion is that when there are symmetries between the parties to disputes of a certain type, then the rules governing such disputes may be expected to be efficient. When such symmetries are lacking, then the expectation of efficiency is weakened or removed.

CHAPTER 1

Why Is the Common Law Efficient?

Posner, in *Economic Analysis of Law*,[1] argues persuasively that the common law can be best understood as an attempt to achieve economic efficiency. He is less persuasive in his explanation of why this is so—his argument is essentially that judges may as well decide in terms of efficiency, since they have no other criteria to use. To an economist accustomed to invisible hand[2] explanations of efficiency in the marketplace, this justification seems weak.

Of related interest is the analysis by William Landes,[3] John Gould,[4] and Gordon Tullock[5] of the decision to litigate a dispute rather than settle. All have concluded that, in general, parties will settle out of court. But, for the common law to remain efficient, it must change as conditions change; changes in the common law require that some cases be litigated. Does the rationality of the common law rest on irrational behavior of litigants?

In this chapter it is shown that these issues, the presumed efficiency of the common law and the decision to use the courts to settle a dispute, are related. In particular, this relationship will occur because resorting to court settlement is more likely in cases where the legal rules relevant to the dispute are inefficient, and less likely where the rules are efficient. Thus, efficient rules may evolve from in-court settlement, thereby reducing the incentive for future litigation and increasing the probability that efficient rules will persist. In short, the efficient rule situation noted by Richard Posner is due to an evolutionary mechanism whose direction proceeds from the utility-maximizing decisions of disputants rather than from the wisdom of judges.

Section I of this chapter contains an analysis of the framework that will be used to discuss pressures for efficiency. Section II contains the actual analysis, in which it is shown that efficiency occurs in situations where both parties to a dispute have an ongoing interest in cases, and that efficiency need not occur if one or both parties does not have such an ongoing interest. Section III contains some complications and extensions. The last section is a summary.

I. GENERAL FRAMEWORK

Throughout this chapter an example of accident liability is used to illustrate the arguments. The particular example does not matter, for, as Posner has shown, torts, property, and contract law can all be analyzed within the same framework.[8] Suppose there is a certain type of accident that costs X when it occurs. Parties of type B are the victims and parties of type A the defendants if the accident occurs. Liability may be placed on A or on B. If liability is placed on A, the optimal solution for A is to spend S_A on accident avoidance and allow N_A accidents to occur; conversely, if liability is placed on B, S_B will be spent on avoidance and N_B accidents will occur. Assume also that this is an either/or situation: the technology of avoidance in this case is such that there is no joint action that A and B could take to further reduce accident and prevention costs. For purposes of analysis, assume that it is efficient for liability to be placed on B, that is,

$$T_B = S_B + N_B X < S_A + N_A X = T_A \qquad (1)$$

where T_A and T_B represent total present value of accident costs plus prevention costs for parties A and B respectively. Equation (1) indicates that this total cost is less if B is liable than if A is liable.

Efficiency requires that A not be made liable for the accident for the most efficient solution is for B to spend S_B and there to be N_B accidents. Whether B will spend S_B on avoidance or A will spend S_A depends on the current liability assignment, that is, on the decision that the parties expect the courts to reach if there is an accident and litigation occurs. Courts are somewhat bound by precedent. Thus, if precedents favor B, then S_A will be spent and total accident costs will be T_A ; conversely, if precedents favor A. (Because the possibility of joint action is eliminated by assumption, one situation or the other will occur.)

Define R as the probability that B will win the suit if an accident occurs and the parties litigate. The value of R is defined by precedent: if $R > 0.5$, precedents favor B and B is likely to win if the case is litigated. If $R < 0.5$, precedents favor A. We assume throughout the chapter that both parties agree on the value of R. The current liability assignment is then efficient if $R < 0.5$. It is assumed throughout that judges are likely, but not certain, to decide on the basis of precedent. As shown below, it is the possibility of changing current precedents which sometimes makes litigation worthwhile and that will in some circumstances lead to efficiency.

The Coase theorem[7] indicates that placement of liability does not matter. If A were made liable, he would simply pay a bribe to B in order to induce B to avoid accidents; as indicated by (1), this would be the efficient solution. This will in fact occur if the costs of paying the bribe are sufficiently low; however, it is possible that the transactions costs will be greater than $(T_A - T_B)$, the saving from shifting liability to the efficient bearer. In this case, if he is liable, A will accept liability rather than paying B. Even if it is feasible for A to bribe B, there will be some transactions costs involved in paying the bribe. In Section II, it is assumed that paying a bribe is not feasible; in Section III the case of feasible bribery is examined.

II. ANALYSIS

Given the basic situation discussed above, there are some cases in which there will be pressure for the law to evolve toward efficiency. The crucial point is the interest that the parties have in decisions as precedents. Thus, some legal cases involve individuals with a one-time interest in the outcome, while other cases involve corporate bodies of some sort: government agencies, labor unions, firms, insurance companies. Such organizations would have an interest in legal cases as precedents as well as interests as litigants.[8] Insurance companies, for example, would be concerned with future liability cases as well as with a particular case. In analyzing the relation between efficiency and litigation, there are three basic situations that must be considered. In part A, the situation in which both parties have a substantial interest in the case as precedent is considered. Part B discusses the situation in which only one party is interested in the case as precedent. Part C considers the situation where neither party is interested in the case as precedent.

A. Both Parties Interested in Precedent

If both parties to a certain type of legal dispute have a substantial interest in future cases of this sort, then precedents will evolve toward efficiency, the common law situation posited by Posner. If rules are inefficient, there will be an incentive for the party held liable to force litigation; if rules are efficient, there will be no such incentive. Thus, efficient rules will be maintained, and inefficient rules litigated until overturned.

Substantial interest in precedent refers to a situation in which the party is likely to be in many such cases in the future. In effect, such parties are concerned with the entire stream of costs, T_A, or T_B, rather than with X, the damages from one particular accident. Start with an inefficient rule: A is held liable if accidents occur, so that A is now spending S_A on accident avoidance and $N_A X$ on damage payments for those accidents which still occur. An accident has just occurred so the parties must decide whether to settle or litigate.

If the case is litigated and B wins, he is paid X; if A wins, he does not pay X in this case, and, in addition, A saves T_A in the future, but B must begin to pay T_B. Court costs for each party are C. The value to A of a court setttlement is

$$V_A = R(-X) + (1 - R)T_A - C \tag{2}$$

and to B:

$$V_B = R(X) + (1 - R)(-T_B) - C . \tag{3}$$

The parties can settle out of court if

$$-V_A > V_B \tag{4}$$

which simply says that a settlement can be reached if the expected loss to A of going to court is greater than the expected gain to B. If this is so, there is room for negotiation. Conversely, if (4) is not satisfied, the parties will litigate. In this example, litigation will occur if

$$(1 - R)(T_A - T_B) > 2C . \tag{5}$$

Here, $T_A - T_B$ is the cost of the inefficient legal rule. As this becomes larger, litigation is more likely. Conversely, as R becomes larger (that is, as the inefficient rule is more entrenched) litigation is less likely. As court costs are higher, litigation is less likely. Finally, if the current rule were efficient (that is, if T_B were greater than T_A), (5) would never be satisfied, so that there would be no litigation.

What will happen? If the parties go to court, B will probably win, since both parties agree that $R > 0.5$. However, whenever this situation arises in the future A will again go to court. Eventually some court will find in favor of A; at this point, the law has been changed and is now efficient. From that time on, precedents will favor A in comparable cases. Since there is no deadweight loss to party B when he is forced to bear liability (i.e., no term comparable to $T_A - T_B$), B will not find it worthwhile to go to court when such an accident occurs: instead, B will spend S_B on avoiding such accidents and bear the cost $N_B X$ of those which do occur.

It is now possible to define precisely the meaning of substantial interest. A's interest in this sort of case is substantial precisely if T_A is large enough so that (5) is satisfied. As this problem has been defined, it is not relevant whether B has a substantial interest or not; however, as will be shown in the next section, both parties must have a substantial interest if efficiency is to be guaranteed.

What if both parties are insurance companies with ongoing interests as either defendants or plaintiffs? Then both A and B become interested in $T_A - T_B$, the efficiency savings from future cases. It can easily be shown that, if both parties are equally likely to be on either side of such cases in the future, (5) is unchanged so that the pressure for efficiency will be maintained.

We have thus shown that if rules are inefficient, parties will use the courts until the rules are changed; conversely, if rules are efficient, the courts will not be used and the efficient rule will remain in force. An outside observer coming upon this legal rule would observe that the rule is efficient, but this efficiency occurs because of an evolutionary process, not because of any particular wisdom on the part of judges. If judges decide independently of efficiency, we would still find efficient rules. Intelligent judges may speed up the process of attaining efficiency but they do not drive the process.

B. Only One Party Interested in Precedent

If only one party to a dispute is interested in future cases of this sort, there will be pressure for precedents to evolve in favor of that party that does have a stake in future cases, whether or not this is the efficient solution. This is because a party with a stake in future decisions will find it worthwhile to litigate as long as liability rests with him; conversely, a party with no stake in future decisions will not find litigation worthwhile.

Let us continue our example: an accident has happened to a certain B. As the law now stands A is likely to win the case, that is, $R < 0.5$, and both parties agree on the value of R. However, B has a stake in the result of this decision; A has no such stake. That is, this type of case is an ongoing case for B, but a one-time case for A. If B goes to court and wins, then in the future he will save S_B per period. T_B is the present value of the stream of accident costs to B as long as he is liable. Thus, if the courts are used and B wins, he receives X from A as a result of this accident; in addition, he saves T_B in the future. On the other hand, if A wins, he does not pay X; A is, by assumption, not interested in future decisions. The value of A of a court case is:

$$V_A = R(-X) - C \tag{6}$$

and the value to B is:

$$V_B = R(X) + R(T_B) - C. \tag{7}$$

In this case, A will be willing to pay $R(X) + C$ to avoid a court settlement and B will be willing to accept $R(X) + R(T_B) - C$. Therefore, there will be no settlement if

$$R(T_B) > 2C. \tag{8}$$

From (8) we see that unless R is very small (that is, unless precedents are extremely clear and unfavorable to B), or unless court costs are large, B will find litigation worthwhile. Moreover, each time such an accident occurs, B will go to court again rather than settling. As such behavior continues, at some point some court may rule in B's favor. Then the rule favors B, and B will therefore cease taking precautions to avoid accidents. Rather party A will begin spending S_A on accident avoidance. When such accidents occur again, the A who is involved will pay X to B, rather than litigate, since A has no future interest in the case.

This same argument could be turned around: if A has an ongoing interest in this type of case and B does not, then A will go to court until a favorable ruling is obtained. From this time on, precedents will favor A and this rule will persist, since no B will find litigation worthwhile. Thus, when one party has an ongoing interest in a type of case there is a tendency for cases to be litigated until a precedent is established that favors this party. There is no tendency for efficiency in this situation.

This case appears to describe the evolution of nuisance laws in the nineteenth century.[9] By the end of that century, those causing nuisances were largely factories, which would have ongoing interests in liability rulings; conversely, those suffering from nuisances were mainly individuals with no such interests. (Factories were concerned with T_B, but individuals were indifferent to T_A.) The evidence indicates that nuisance laws did, in fact, largely favor factories and firms rather than individuals.

C. No Interest in Precedent

If neither party is interested in precedents then the current rule will persist, whether it is efficient or inefficient. That is, if neither party has an ongoing interest in cases of this sort, then neither will force use of the courts. All such cases will be settled on the basis of the current rule, whatever it might be. Since cases will not go to court, there will be no pressure to change this rule.

Again, begin with the situation in which an accident has occurred. A certain party of type B has lost X and is considering suing the party A who is liable. Both parties agree that the probability of B winning is R. If there is no interest in precedent, then the exact value of R is irrelevant for our purposes. We assume risk neutrality since, as indicated below, risk aversion would complicate the analysis without changing the results.

Clearly, if this is the entire problem, the parties would settle. To A the expected value of a court settlement is

$$V_A = -RX - C \tag{9}$$

and to B it is

$$V_B = RX - C. \tag{10}$$

The parties can settle out of court if (4) is satisfied; this becomes

$$RX + C > RX - C \tag{11}$$

which is obviously met. Thus, rather than going to court, A can pay some amount L to B, where

$$RX - C < L < RX + C \tag{12}$$

and this will be better than a court settlement for both parties. This is the essence of the argument as to why most cases may be expected to be settled out of court. If the parties are risk averse, we replace terms in (9) and (10) with their utility equivalents. For risk averse individuals, the utility of a lottery is less than the utility of the expected value of the lottery; thus, in (4) the left side becomes relatively larger and the right side relatively smaller. Risk aversion makes out-of-court settlements relatively more likely.

In this situation, the courts will be used only if the parties disagree about the value of R. However, there is no reason to assume that such disagreement is related to the efficiency of current rules. Thus, as long as there is agreement about the probability of decisions, the legal rule will not change, and if there is disagreement and consequent pressure for rule change, there is no presumption that changes would be in the direction of increased efficiency. This situation is presumably that which exists when disputants are individuals with little ongoing interest in solutions. Furthermore, disputes would ordinarily be settled in accordance with current legal rules. It would be unusual for such cases to go to court, and there is no presumption that rules in such cases would be efficient. However, to the extent that the types of legal cases involving individuals are the same types of cases as those involving corporate bodies, this conclusion must be modified for, as we have seen, there is pressure for efficiency in the latter type of case, whereas individual disputants will accept the existing rule, whether it is efficient or not.[10]

III. SOME COMPLICATIONS

This section considers in turn: situations in which bribery is feasible; costs of out-of-court settlements; public good problems; situations in which different types of parties are interested in the same type of case; and some applications to statute law.

A. Bribery

Assume again that liability is currently inefficiently assigned, that is, A is liable. As mentioned in Section I, it may be possible in this case for A to bribe B to take precautions, rather than taking precautions himself. As before, define T_A and T_B as the present value of the stream of costs if liability is placed, respectively, on A or B; from (1) we know that

$$T_B < T_A . \tag{13}$$

Define T_N as the present value of costs to A of bribing B to take precautions. T_N would include normal aspects of transactions costs: costs of finding the relevant B, of actually making the payments, of monitoring B's behavior, etc. A will find it worthwhile to bribe B if

$$T_N < T_A - T_B , \tag{14}$$

that is, if the cost of paying the bribe is less than the saving from taking efficient precautions. Even in this case, however, there is a deadweight loss—an efficiency loss caused by the actual cost of paying the bribe, T_N.

Even with the bribe, there will still be an N_A accidents per period. One of these accidents has occurred. A is now liable to pay X to the injured B. As above, A must decide whether to pay or to litigate. If A settles out of court or loses the case in court, he must then spend $T_N + T_B$ and he must continue to negotiate with parties B and pay the accident costs of these parties. If B loses, then he must pay T_B, that is, in the future A will not be liable if this type of accident occurs, so that B will spend S_B on avoiding such accidents. In addition, if B loses, he will not be paid X, damages in the accident that have already occurred. Thus, there is a $(1 - R)$ chance of B losing T_B. For A, the expected value of going to court becomes

$$V_A = R(-X) + (1 - R)(T_B + T_N) - C \qquad (15)$$

and for B

$$V_B = R(X) + (1 - R)(-T_B) - C. \qquad (16)$$

This occurs because, once A has won a case, the law is changed so that precedents now favor A, rather than B. This is the essence of judge-made common law.

The parties will again settle out of court if (4) is satisifed, but this now becomes

$$(1 - R)T_N < 2C. \qquad (17)$$

They will go to court if (17) is reversed:

$$(1 - R)T_N > 2C. \qquad (18)$$

The parties will go to court if the expected present value of the costs to A of negotiating with B in the future to have B take precautions is greater than the total court costs. What has happened is that T_N, the present value of these negotiation costs, is a cost to A but not a gain to B. The stakes in the case are asymmetrical, so that there is less possibility of a settlement between the parties. Notice also that T_N is, in this situation, the present cost of the inefficient legal rule.

The situation above is again one in which both parties have an ongoing interest in decisions. It is likely that this will be the only relevant situation for bribes for if B does not have such an interest it is probable that B will be unidentifiable in advance. In this case it is likely that the cost of A bribing B would be prohibitive, and the analysis used in Section II–B would be relevant.

Notice also that there is no relationship between court costs and bribery (transactions) costs. The decision as to whether or not to bribe B is made before the accident occurs whereas the decision to go to court or not is made after the accident has happened. Our argument is that A is likely to go to court to save future transactions costs. Of course, as shown in (18), if court costs are high enough relative to the present value of transactions costs, the case will be settled; but this simply says that if court costs are greater than the costs of the inefficiency imbedded in the current rule, it is not worth changing the rule.

B. Settlement Costs

Throughout, we have ignored the costs of settling the dispute out of court. This action will have some costs, and as these costs increase, the probability of going to court increases. Formally, such costs can be included in the analysis simply by redefining C everywhere as net court costs—the difference between court costs and settlement costs. The level of net court costs is itself an important parameter in the models. As can be seen from (5) and (18) the courts are more likely to be used in overturning inefficient rules as court costs are smaller. John Gould[11] has argued that high court costs have the desirable effect of reducing inefficient litigation. It must be pointed out, though, that such costs also have the undesirable effect of reducing efficient litigation, that is, litigation aimed at overturning inefficient rules.

C. Different Types of Parties, Same Type of Case

In Section II we saw that when only one party has an ongoing interest in a type of case, precedents could be expected to evolve in favor of that party. Conversely, when both parties have an interest, precedents should evolve toward efficiency. However, it is possible that some cases of a certain type will involve only one party with an ongoing interest, while other cases of the same sort will involve two such parties. In this situation a conflict could easily arise as when only one party has an ongoing interest, the inefficient solution may be favored, while when both have such an interest the efficient solution may be favored.

It is possible that cases of this sort would be continually litigated. However, if this were to happen, parties would observe that precedents would not be binding, and this would reduce the incentive for litigation. A more likely solution is for parties to differentiate the cases, so that one sort of precedent would govern cases with one coporate body and a different set of precedents would govern cases with two corporate bodies. The law would then be inconsistent, but no litigant would have an incentive to capitalize on this inconsistency, and therefore it would continue to exist.[12] This explanation for legal inconsistency would seem to be a fruitful area of research for scholars trained in the law.

D. Public Good Problems

Once a decision is reached in a case, the decision is a public good.[13] It affects all parties of type A and B. Thus, a party of type A may decide not to litigate a case, even if such litigation would be efficient, in the hope that some other A may do the litigating and save the original A court costs. However, equations (5) and (18) are not particularly stringent: In many cases, court costs are not prohibitively high. Nonetheless, we might expect some free-rider problems. Our model would predict, for example, that large companies would be involved relatively more in litigation than would small companies.

Statute law is often inefficient.[14] However, in some cases lobbying for passage of statute law can take the place of deciding to litigate in the model.[15] Thus, if some law were proposed benefitting one well-defined small group at the expense of another well-defined small group, and if the group that would lose would lose more than the gaining group would gain (i.e., if the law were inefficient), then the potential losers would be able to outspend the potential gainers, so that we would not expect the law to be passed. Thus, we would expect that inefficient statute laws would correspond to our analysis of the situation in which only one party has an interest in precedent, that is, such laws would be passed at the expense of large groups that would not be able to effectively lobby against their passage because of free-rider problems.

IV. SUMMARY

We have shown that the efficiency of the common law, to the extent that it exists, can be explained by an evolutionary model—a model in which it is more likely that parties will litigate inefficient rules than efficient rules. If decisions are made randomly, there will be a movement in the direction of efficient laws. The same model provides an explanation for using the courts to settle some disputes, rather than relying on out-of-courts settlements.

The evolutionary pressure comes from the behavior of litigants rather than of judges. We therefore found it useful to study behavior of potential litigants, classified according to their interest in cases as precedents. We found that when neither party is interested in precedents, there is no incentive to litigate, and hence no pressure on the law to change. When only one party is interested in precedent, that party will litigate until a favorable decision is obtained; so the law in these cases will favor parties with such an ongoing interest. When both parties have an ongoing interest in a type of case, there will be pressure toward efficiency. When different types of parties have an interest in the same type of case, we would expect inconsistencies to exist in the law.

Finally, we would predict that the evolution toward efficiency, in those cases where there would be such an evolution, would be faster as current rules are more inefficient, as net court costs (court costs less settlement costs) are lower, and as inefficient rules are less soundly entrenched.

NOTES

1. Richard A. Posner, *Economic Analysis of Law* (Boston: Little, Brown, 1972).

2. For a general discussion of invisible hand explanations, *see* Robert Nozick, *Anarchy, State and Utopia* (1974).

3. William M. Landes, "An Economic Analysis of the Courts," *Journal of Law and Economics* 14 (1971): 61.

4. John P. Gould, "The Economics of Legal Conflicts," *Journal of Legal Studies* 2 (1973): 279.

5. Gordon Tullock, *The Logic of the Law* (1971).

6. Posner, *Economic Analysis*, pp. 98–102.

7. Ronald H. Coase, "The Problem of Social Cost," *Journal of Law and Economics* 3 (1960): 1.

8. Richard A. Posner, "The Behavior of Administrative Agencies," *Journal of Legal Studies* 1 (1972): 305, discusses the interest of agencies in settling cases for use as precedents.

9. *See* Joel Franklin Brenner, "Nuisance Law and the Industrial Revolution," *Journal of Legal Studies* 3 (1974): 403, for a discussion that is consistent with this argument.

10. *See* sec. III–C.

11. Gould "Economics of Legal Conflicts," p. 296.

12. It might appear that the inconsistency would lead some disputants to litigate in the hope of capitalizing on the inconsistency. However, both parties would be aware of this possibility, and thus there would be no asymmetry. Our analysis rests on assuming that litigation occurs only when there is an asymmetry between parties.

13. *See* Gordon Tullock, "Public Decisions as Public Goods," *Journal of Political Economy* 99 (1971): 913.

14. Paul H. Rubin, "On the Form of Special Interest Legislation," *Public Choice* 21 (1975): 79.

15. This point is due to Gordon Tullock, made in private correspondence; *see also* Chap. 2 of the present volume.

CHAPTER 2

Common Law and Statute Law

I. INTRODUCTION

Those concerned with the economic analysis of law often make a distinction between common law and statute law. Posner, for example, claims that the common law is, by and large, economically efficient (wealth-maximizing) while statute law is more concerned with redistribution, generally toward special interests.[1] He argues that the distinction between the effects of the two types of law is caused by the nature of the arguments allowed in the legislative forum as compared with the judicial forum. Legislators consider the particular individuals involved and the impact on these individuals of the decisions reached; moreover, individuals and groups are allowed to petition the legislators for favors. Judges, on the other hand, are explicitly forbidden from considering the deservingness of the individual litigant, and must render their decisions on the basis of more objective criteria. The distinction between these processes would, according to Posner, lead to the greater concern with efficiency that he finds in the common law than in statute law. Friedrich Hayek has also emphasized the difference between common law and statute law, or command, though in his case the basis for the distinction is somewhat less clear than the efficiency-inefficiency dichotomy emphasized by Posner.[2]

More recently, interest in the explanation for common law efficiency, where such efficiency exists, has shifted from a Posnerian view, that efficiency is a result of the wisdom of the judges in reaching decisions, to other explanations. In particular, there is now a literature arguing that the observed efficiency is a result of evolutionary processes in which inefficient rules are more likely to be litigated and overturned than are efficient rules.[3] One of the key results of this literature is that there will be some tendencies for laws to evolve toward efficiency but that this evolution will, for various reasons, not be complete. Since the theories do not predict complete efficiency in all areas of the common law, some who believe that the law is efficient everywhere have rejected the theories. However, one argument of this chapter will be that in fact the theories, at least in some of their variants, do have useful descriptive predictions. It will be argued that the law is efficient in those areas where some of the evolutionary theories indicate that it should be efficient, and inefficient in areas where the theories would also predict this.

In addition to the theory of Chapter 1, the evolutionary theories that are emphasized here are those of William Landes and Richard Posner, and John Goodman. In the first two of these theories, parties with an interest in precedent are likely to litigate inefficient rules (or, in the Landes-Posner variant, efficient but not completely efficient rules) until these rules become efficient. In the Goodman model, those with interest in precedents are likely to spend more on litigation if the current rule is inefficient. In either case, the model is driven toward efficiency by decisions of litigants and efficiency is achieved if, and only if, litigants represent the set of future potential parties to disputes involving the rule under consideration. That is, for efficiency to result from these models, parties to particular disputes must represent symmetrically all future interests in such disputes. If this condition is not satisifed, then the models indicate that the law will not be driven toward efficiency. Rather, the law will come to favor those parties that do have future interests in cases of the sort under consideration, whether or not it is efficient for such parties to be victorious. Jack Hirshleifer makes essentially the same point when he argues that in order to study forces leading to change in the law, it is necessary to determine the factors that make it more or less difficult to mobilize support from members of groups or potential groups with interests in changing the law.

The models discussed above apply to the litigation process. The arguments are that those with stakes in the outcome of the case, and particularly in the precedential value of the case, will spend more on litigating and thus be more likely to win. However, Gordon Tullock has raised an important point in connection with this analysis.[4] He argues that spending on lobbying by special interest groups with an interest in particular statutes is exactly analogous to spending on litigation by these same interest groups. That is, if spending on litigation drives the common law toward efficiency, then, in the same way, spending on lobbying should drive statute law toward efficiency. The fact that we observe (or seem to observe) efficiency in one area but not in the other would then be inconsistent with these theories. We are then either driven back to Posner's wise-judges explanation for the pattern of common law efficiency or else we must reexamine the evidence about the relative efficiency of common versus statute law.

This chapter provides such a reexamination. In particular, it is argued that what appears to be a statute-common law distinction is actually a distinction between, essentially, pre–1930 law and post–1930 law. (The exact cut-off date is obviously arbitrary.) That is, in the early period most law was efficient and was mainly common law. In the later period, most law was inefficient and was mainly statute law. Observers looking at the law and concluding that common law is more efficient than statute law are then confounding an effect due to time with an effect due to efficiency. Part II of this chapter provides some evidence that the relevant distinction is based on time rather than on the type of law. Part III provides an explanation for the change in efficiency of rules based on changes in costs of organizing interest groups. It is argued that the movement toward inefficiency, in both statute and common law, is a result of technological change in the costs of organizing interest groups. Part IV applies the analysis to an issue raised by Posner at several points—the issue of class actions. To anticipate the conclusion, it is argued that greater reliance on class actions and other methods of judicially-aggregating claims has no necessary implication about efficiency. The last part is a summary.

II. IS COMMON LAW NECESSARILY MORE EFFICIENT THAN STATUTE LAW?

This section briefly examines three bodies of law that are partially statutory and partially common law. The claim is, at least in these cases, that common law is not necessarily more efficient than statute. The laws considered are: property law in the nineteenth century; unconscionability in the twentieth century; and law dealing with monopoly.

A. Statutes in the Nineteenth Century: Property

Property law is one of the common law areas viewed by Posner as being essentially economically efficient. However, deeper examination of the basis for contemporary American property law indicates that much of the foundation of the law, including the efficient aspects of this law, rests in nineteenth-century statutes, rather than in common law. In fact, the form of contemporary property law is a result of a combination of statute and common law rulings, and it is not obvious that either type of ruling has been more efficient than the other.

The three criteria given by Posner for efficiency in property rights are: universality, exclusivity, and transferability. Modern American property rights systems in land fulfill all of these requirements to a substantial extent. However, this system is due to statute as much as to common law. In particular, the basic type of land tenure in the United States, fee simple, does allow free transfer of land. But this form of land tenure was itself imposed by statute, rather than by common law.[5] Thus, it was statutes, such as those passed in New York in 1827–28, that simplified the old common law feudal land tenures. As Lawrence Friedman says, "Statute and practice worked hand in hand to simplify land remedies."[6]

Other statutory changes dealt with the ability of women to transfer land. A 1787 Massachusetts statute allowed women deserted by their husbands to petition for the right to sell land. Moreover, the change in the status of women from a situation in which " . . . her legal existence and authority in a degree lost or suspended, during the continuance of the matrimonial union"[7] to a situation in which women could buy and sell land was brought about primarily by the various Married Women's Property Acts, statutes, rather than by common law decisions. Moreover, the institution of "dower", which allowed a wife to claim one-third of land owned by the husband, even if the land were sold, (thus placing a cloud upon title) was also overturned by statute.[8] Thus, in these cases, transferability of property was greatly increased by statutes, which essentially overturned the old feudal common law methods of transferring property.

Another feature of efficient property systems is universality. Everything must be owned for efficiency (at least to the point where enforcement of title is more expensive than the value of ownership). In the case of American land, the relevant fact was that the government owned most of the continent. It was the various Homestead Acts—statutes—that gave title of government-owned land to private individuals.[9] It was also statutes that created property rights in intellectual capital, in the form of patents and copyrights.

It is not claimed that the common law of the nineteenth century was inefficient, nor is it claimed that statutes in this period were always efficient. The point is rather that in many cases both common law and statutes worked "hand in hand" to achieve efficiency, and that our current feelings that statutes are less efficient than common law rules may be based on current situations, rather than on universal principles. To further explore this argument, common law rules in the twentieth century are briefly explained and it is shown that in many cases common law rules are no more efficient than are statutes.

B. Common Law in the Twentieth Century: Unconscionability

Many of the inefficient statutes of the twentieth century are those that interfere with freedom of contract. Economists are fond of citing minimum wage laws and rent control laws as examples of such inefficient interferences. Other interventions are various product safety laws that forbid consumers from purchasing particular products if some agency such as the Consumer Product Safety Commission or the National Highway Traffic Safety Administration forbids such purchase. These are examples of statutory interferences with freedom of contract, and also examples of economically inefficient laws.

However, there are many common law interferences with contract that are equally inefficient. Many of these common law interferences are cases in which freely agreed upon contractual terms are invalidated because they are held to be "unconscionable".[10] This doctrine, according to Richard Epstein, is partially of common law creation; and, even when it is based on statutes, Epstein claims that the statutes are so loose that a substantial part of the doctrine occurs because of judicial interpretation. Thus, when contracts are overturned because of unconscionability, we are observing inefficiencies in common law cases.

A detailed examination of cases in which unconscionability has been used in court cases to overturn efficient private contractual agreements will not be undertaken for Epstein has performed such an examination. He gives several types of contracts that have been overturned as being unconscionable and provides reasons as to why such rulings have been inefficient.[11] The types of cases he lists are: add-on clauses, waiver-of-defense clauses, exclusion of liability for consequential damage, due-on-sale clauses, and termination-at-will clauses. In all cases, reasonable grounds are indicated as to why consumers would be willing to enter into contracts with such clauses, and in all cases courts have overturned these clauses. These rulings by common law judges are as inefficient as statutory rules that deny consumers other types of contracts, as discussed above. Again, the point of this section has not been to demonstrate that all common law rules are currently inefficient, but rather to indicate that both statutes and common law rules are currently likely to be inefficient.

C. Monopoly

It is sometimes argued that the common law was opposed to monopoly and that monopolies were generally created by statute. If this claim were true, it would be inconsistent with the arguments made here since the evolutionary process would not be expected to operate in such a manner as to remove monopoly. This is because any one consumer of a monopolized product or potential entrant into a monopolized industry would have less of an interest in eliminating the monopoly than the monopolist would have in maintaining his position. Thus, the models of legal evolution that depend on relitigating inefficient rules or on spending being greater by parties with interests in efficiency would predict that the common law should favor, not oppose, monopoly. In fact, however, the claim that the common law was opposed to monopolies is probably incorrect. Robert Ekelund and Robert Tollison have argued, convincingly, that the apparent favor shown by seventeenth- and eighteenth-century common law courts toward competition in England was actually the result of a conflict over rights to issue monopoly grants between Parliament and the Crown, rather than any attempt to promote competition.[12] Morton Horwitz, in his discussion of the conception of monopoly and competition in nineteenth-century American law, indicates that competition was as likely to come out of granting of additional charters by legislatures as from court rulings, and that judges sometimes gave chartered corporations more monopoly protection than the legislatures did.[13] Moreover, the antitrust laws themselves are statutory, rather than common law, creations. That these statutes currently are enforced in an inefficient manner is not inconsistent with the theory developed here. The major party with an ongoing interest in the enforcement of antitrust laws are the enforcers, the Justice Department and the Federal Trade Commission. These parties would have no particular desire for efficiency; thus, it is not surprising that the law has not evolved toward efficiency.[14]

III. INTEREST GROUPS IN THE LEGAL PROCESS

Is there an explanation for this change from relative efficiency in both statute and common law in the last century to their relative inefficiency now? The hypothesis is that there is such an explanation, which is an implication of forces identified in the Rubin and Goodman models of litigation discussed above. Recall that in these models the important determinant of the outcome of the litigation process is the nature of the litigants. In the Goodman model, the factor that decides the nature of case law is the expenditure by litigants on litigation; more spending is associated with a higher probability of victory. In the model of Chapter 1 (and, to a lesser extent, in the Landes-Posner model) the determining factor is the interest of the litigant in the case viewed as precedent. Thus, both of these models have essentially the same implications for efficiency and for the nature of the outcomes. Efficiency results if each party to the litigation represents the entire set of social interests on the same side in future disputes of this type. That is, if the party that has the most to gain from a victory is representative of all gainers and the party with the least to gain is representative of all losers, then these models predict that the litigation process will lead to efficient outcomes. Conversely, if the parties are, for whatever reason, not typical of all potential parties involved in such disputes, then there is no presumption that the models will lead to efficiency.

Chapter 1 discussed the nature of the litigants and the implication for the outcome of the nature. Two possible situations were identified. A party could have a "substantial interest in future cases of this sort" or not. The results of the model were the following: 1) If both parties did have such an ongoing substantial interest, then the common law litigation process would likely lead to efficiency. This is because an inefficient rule would lead to deadweight losses, which could not be bargained away, and thus the inefficient rule would be more likely to be litigated. A similar result would follow from Goodman's model, where the party that expected to benefit from an efficient outcome would spend more on litigation than would the other party, and would thus again provide an incentive for efficiency. 2) If neither party had an ongoing interest, then there would be no incentive for litigation at all and the law would remain as is; there would be neither an incentive for efficiency nor for inefficiency. 3) If one party had an ongoing interest and the other did not, then precedents would come to favor the party with the ongoing interest, independent of efficiency. That is, the party that is "in the market" would spend more on litigation or would continually relitigate until favorable precedents were obtained. If the party that is in the market is the party that should win (from an efficiency standpoint) then the law will evolve toward efficiency. If the party that is in the market should not win, then the law will evolve away from efficiency. That parties with such ongoing interests do tend to win at litigation has been shown by Marc Galanter,[15] who, however, did not discuss the efficiency implications of his work.

On this view, then, disputants who are in the market will tend to litigate until they reach a favorable decision. They may achieve such a decision by spending more on litigation, by relitigating cases whenever issues arise until a favorable decision is reached, by choosing cases to litigate until a particularly apt case for establishing precedent occurs, or by using other techiques aimed at obtaining favorable precedents which are discussed most throughly by Galanter. For such parties, the distinction between common law and statute law may not be definitive. When they are unable to obtain favorable decisions at common law (for reasons discussed below) they may simply turn to the legislature and attempt to obtain desirable outcomes there. For any given litigant, however, the decision to use either the courts and achieve favorable common law rulings or to use the legislature and achieve favorable statutes should be a purely instrumental decision, depending solely on which type of ruling would be most profitable. This view of the process does not lead to a prediction of greater efficiency in common law than in statute law.

While it is not the purpose of this chapter to address the issue of types of rulings that may be sought in each type of arena, a brief discussion of likely distinctions between common law and statute law is in order. This is especially true since the models of legal evolution discussed above have some implications for this issue. In Chapter 1, it was argued that litigants must decide whether to litigate for favorable precedents based on the costs and benefits of such litigation and on the probability of victory. As the current rule becomes more entrenched, the probability of overturning this rule becomes lower, so that the payoff from litigating becomes smaller. Landes and Posner modify this argument by suggesting that litigation of undesirable rules (i.e., rules that the party with the continuing interest does not like) may actually make such rules more firmly entrenched, and so is even less likely to occur than in the model of Chapter 1. It was assumed there that the precedent will govern or not, while Landes and Posner allow for marginal changes in the probability of a precedent determining a case, where the probability is a function of past decisions using this same precedent. Thus, in either of these models, it is possible to reach a situation where a rule that a party dislikes is so firmly entrenched in the common law that further litigation will be unlikely to change the rule and may even strengthen it. (In the models referred to, the discussion is in terms of efficient and inefficient rules, but the same point applies to any rule that the party with the continuing interest favors.) Parties will then attempt to obtain favorable statutes, rather than favorable court rulings, when the position that they advocate is so far from current strongly entrenched rules that common law litigation is unlikely to reach a favorable outcome. If, as will be argued below, the structure of litigants was such that, in the nineteenth century, rules were generally efficient and if now there are pressures from groups that favor other outcomes, then we would expect greater reliance now on statute since the efficient common law rules would be difficult to overturn—not because they are efficient, but merely because they are well established.

The claim of this chapter is that, in the past, costs of organization were sufficiently high to preclude formation of potential interest groups into litigating or lobbying groups, so that the prime actors in the legal process (both statute and common law) were individuals. Conversely, it has now become less expensive to organize interest groups and therefore the recent patterns of law are such as to reflect group interests.[16] There are no necessary theoretical implications from this process for efficiency; whether it leads to efficiency or not is an empirical matter. However, it is inconsistent to argue, as Posner does, that group litigation is more efficient than individual litigation and that group lobbying is less efficient for there is no necessary distinction between the two. To illustrate the points made above, three types of law will be considered. They are cases where there are contractual interests between the parties, cases where there are no contractual interests but the parties are symmetrical, and cases where there are no contractual interests and the parties are asymmetrical.

A. Contractual Interests

As long as courts are willing to enforce mutually agreeable contracts, then the form of the law dealing with cases where there are contractual interests is almost irrelevant. If the law should be inefficient in some context, some costs will be imposed since parties will be forced to add extra provisions in their contract. However, if courts will enforce these provisions, then the additional costs of inefficient principles of contract law will be relatively unimportant. As an example, consider landlord-tenant law. As evolved in the nineteenth and early twentieth century, this body of law seemed to favor landlords.[17] However, there are contractual agreements between parties. Therefore, economic theory would suggest that the parties to the agreements would derive the most efficient terms since any gains from efficiency would easily be capitalized into the price; that is, if there were profitable changes in the terms of the contracts, the parties would be able to internalize these potential gains. Moreover, there is some evidence of the efficiency of this branch of law. Werner Hirsch has empirically studied the effects of statutory changes in landlord tenant laws, which have essentially mandated warranties of implied fitness in housing, and he concludes that these changes have led to deadweight losses borne by consumers.[18] Sam Peltzman's demonstration that laws mandating increased safety in automobiles have not saved any lives is also evidence of the efficiency of relatively unregulated markets where there are contractual agreements between parties.[19] Thus, in situations where the parties have contractual agreements, theory would indicate that the contractually agreed upon terms would be efficient, and the evidence that we have is consistent with this theoretical prediction. Chapters 3, 4, and 5 deal in more detail with cases of this sort, and demonstrate that contractual provisions are generally efficient.

B. No Contract, Symmetric Interests

In cases of this sort, the evolutionary models would predict efficiency in the law. That is, if parties have symmetric interests in cases and precedents, then there should be incentives to litigate inefficient rules (or to spend more on such litigation when the rule is inefficient) so that we would expect rules in such cases to evolve toward efficiency. Moreover, in such cases, if the rules do not evolve toward efficiency, then there would be substantial deadweight losses imposed, since the absence of a contract between parties indicates that transactions costs would be sufficiently high so that parties would be unable to negotiate around the law. Two examples of situations in which there are symmetric interests but no contracts are automobile accidents and business torts.

In the case of automobile accidents, it is clear that individuals have no incentive to litigate since no individual expects to be in many accidents. However, almost all automobile drivers have insurance. Insurance companies would expect to be involved in numerous cases, and thus would have interests in precedents. Moreover, any one insurance company would expect to be on either side of any given type of case in the future (i.e., a company that insures the plaintiff in one case would expect with equal probability to insure the defendant in future cases of the same sort) and in this situation the models predict convergence toward efficiency in precedent. This situation is interesting since there are those who claim that litigation costs are so large in the case of automobile accidents that other forms of insurance, such as "no-fault" insurance would be better.[20] Recently, Elizabeth Landes has studied the effect of adoption of no-fault insurance on accident rates and has found that this policy leads to significantly increased accident rates.[21] While this evidence does not prove that the liability system in effect before the adoption of no-fault was efficient, it does at least suggest that one alternative proposed by many was probably less efficient than the system evolved by the common law, presumably driven by insurance companies with symmetric interests in precedents.

Another area in which there are no contractual relationships but in which we would expect symmetric interests and therefore efficient precedents is the area of business torts. Here, the wrongs at interest are those committed by one business against another. Since both parties are business firms, we would expect both to be interested in future cases of the sort under dispute. We would also expect either party in one case to be equally likely to be on the other side in future cases. Thus, the theory would predict the same sort of evolution toward efficiency in this situation as in the situation involving automobile accidents. One example of business torts that has been subjected to economic analysis is the law of false advertising.[22] Here, except for "passing off" (mislabeling products), the common law allowed virtually no relief for one business when another misrepresented its product. Many commentators felt that this law was inefficient, and the Lanham Act, a statute, was passed in order to give firms greater grounds for redress. Chapter 6 examines the impact of this law by examining all cases in which a claim was made under the Lanham Act; the conclusion of this exhaustive study of cases was that the statute made virtually no difference. That is, in almost all cases the Lanham Act claim merely replaced a potential common law claim for passing off, and where the Lanham Act claim did not replace the common law claim (a trivially small number of cases) there was no gain in efficiency from the Lanham Act claim.

C. Asymmetric Interests, No Contract

In this case, there is no presumption that the law will have any connection with efficiency. As is generally true, we assume that each party attempts to maximize its own self-interest. However, in this case there is no connection between self-interest and efficiency, that is, there is no presumption that maximizing self-interest will lead to efficient outcomes. An example of this situation is Joel Franklin Brenner's discussion of nineteenth-century nuisance law.[23] At the beginning of the nineteenth century, nuisance law seems to have been efficient, in that remedies were easily available when one party imposed nuisance on another. This is consistent with the theory, since in general parties to nuisance actions at that time were symmetric. That is, they were generally landowners with similar rights and therefore similar interests. The ease with which litigants could obtain injunctions was probably efficient since low transactions costs between parties meant that negotiation could occur and rights could flow to their highest valued uses.

By the end of the century the parties in nuisance actions were polluters, who were generally industrial firms, and victims, who were either individuals or landowners. In this case, the polluter would have a more substantial interest in being able to pollute than any one individual would have in stopping the pollution. Given this situation, the theory would indicate that precedents would come to favor the party with the ongoing interest—the industrial polluter. In fact, this seems to be what did occur. Although there were some statutes passed aimed at alleviating problems of pollution, it appears that in fact these statutes had little effect, again as the model would predict. Whether the situation in industrialist England was efficient or not is difficult to say; Brenner indicates that citizens might have been willing to tolerate the pollution in return for the benefits of industrialization. However, it does seem consistent with the argument proposed here that the party with the ongoing interest was the party to prevail in obtaining favorable court rulings and also favorable legislation (or the lack of effective unfavorable legislation.)

Thus, the evidence cited above is consistent with the claim that precedents will come to favor parties with ongoing interests. Precedents will also be efficient if parties with ongoing interests are symmetrically distributed on both sides of particular cases, but the efficiency is a by-product of the litigation process aimed at maximizing the wealth of the litigants. If costs of organizing groups should change, then the types of litigants observed should also change. This would then be expected to lead to changes in both common law decisions and statutes.

In fact, this does seem to be what has occurred. In statute law areas, it is clear that organized interest groups are able to influence legislatures in significant ways. James Kau and Paul Rubin provide substantial amounts of empirical evidence on this point.[24] Moreover, one of the major groups that influences legislation in several ways are labor unions. It is common for representatives from districts with many union members to vote in ways favorable to union interests. Also, unions contribute money to candidates who vote in ways that are desirable from the union standpoint. Candidates who receive contributions from unions are likely to change their voting in ways that support union desires. Furthermore, with respect to the issues of interest in this book, it is true that unions, as important organized political groups, did not exist before 1935, the year of the first passage of the National Labor Relations Act. Thus, in the area of statute law, we find that it has been fairly recent changes that have created interest groups with substantial lobbying ability.

In the case of common law, the evidence is less firm. However, it does seem likely that many recent inefficient common law rulings have not been achieved by a process of two party litigation; rather, in many of the cases some third party or set of third parties has been involved. Many of the recent rulings affect poor persons who would not themselves be able to hire counsel. In many of these cases counsel has been provided by government agencies or volunteers with interests beyond the case at hand. For examples, Epstein lists six cases in his discussion of unconscionability. In four or these cases the court record identifies *amici* briefs, indicating that the parties to the disputes were not the sole parties involved in the litigation. (The cases in which *amici* briefs were filed were: *Williams v. Walker-Thomas, Unico v. Owen, Tucker v. Lassen Savings and Loan Association,* and *Coast Bank v. Minderhout.*) Epstein also discusses the issue of termination-at-will clauses in franchise contracts, where one important party has been automobile dealers' associations. As Stewart Macaulay demonstrates, these associations have been active both as litigants and as lobbyists.[25] That such contracts were efficient before the intervention is shown in Chapter 3.

Thus, we observe that changes in both statute and common law can be explained, at least in part, by changes in the nature of litigants and lobbyists, and that these changes are caused by increased activity of groups in attempting to change the law. These changes themselves have probably been caused by various technological changes in the cost of organizing: increased urbanization leading to reduced communication costs, increased literacy, telephone and television, and perhaps increased mobility caused by automobiles. These changes in costs of communicating and organizing have thus led to the formation of groups for lobbying and litigating with consequent results in changing the law.[26]

There is no *a priori* reason why this process of increased group activity in seeking legislation should be inefficient. In fact, we may identify at least one area in which there were probably net gains from such increased activity. This is the area of environmental legislation. The form of environmental laws, which mandate particular standards rather than simply charging polluters fees based on the amounts of pollution, has generally not been efficient. Many such laws have probably gone beyond the point where marginal cost equals marginal benefit. Yet it is probably true that, net, such laws have increased welfare. This is because, as discussed above in the example of nineteenth-century nuisance law, polluters probably had a more substantial ongoing interest in their rights to pollute than those suffering from pollution had in their right to be free of pollution. Therefore, when organization costs were high, polluters probably dominated the law in an inefficient manner. This would be a case where interests were asymmetric and there was no contractual arrangement between the parties, and in which there would therefore be no expectation of efficiency. It is also possible that some recent "deregulation" in industries such as air transportation, motor carrier transportation, and communication has been brought about by increased organization ability of customers of these industries. Such deregulation has provided clear economic benefits, since the regulation that has been repealed generally served to cartelize the regulated industries.

IV. CLASS ACTIONS

At several points, Posner argues for class action suits as alternatives in areas that are now regulated by statute or by direct government regulation.[27] His claim is that such suits would be more efficient than the current rules. These suits would allow individuals (or attorneys—the agent is irrelevant) to aggregate small claims that are not individually worth pursuing and thus have enough at stake to make prosecution of a case worthwhile. If, for example, many consumers each lose a small amount from a fraudulent claim about a product, no one consumer will have incentive to sue for redress, and thus firms may find it profitable to make such claims. One solution to this problem has been the Federal Trade Commission, which, however, has not been very effective in stopping this behavior.[28] An alternative solution would be a class action representing all defrauded consumers, so that, in aggregate, the claim would be worth pursuing and thus there would be costs imposed on firms that made such claims. Similar arguments could be applied to other areas of behavior where regulation has replaced litigation. Class actions would probably be a good substitute for the Environmental Protection Agency.

The inefficiency in not allowing class actions as discussed by Posner is inconsistent with the claim that the law is economically efficient because judges preferred efficient law. If this were so, then the judges should have been able to allow the optimal amount of class action suits. It is difficult to see why judges have not been convinced by arguments relating to aggregation of small claims and allowed class actions in cases where efficiency arguments could have been made for such claims. From the perspective advanced here, however, it is not difficult to see why even efficient class action suits would not have been allowed under common law rules. While the class, had it been organized, would have been able to outspend opponents in litigating (if the class interest were the efficient interest), the cost of organizing the class and of overcoming free rider problems may well have been too high in general for the class to form and litigate. Thus, the judicial distaste for class litigation is simply a result of the process discussed above: there was no party with sufficient stakes to invest in litigating until rules favoring classes came into being, and hence precedents evolved to oppose class litigation. The inefficiency in this area of law is explicable in terms of the interests of parties with substantial interests in litigating for favorable precedents. There was no such litigant with an interest in class actions.

But is Posner correct in arguing for broadened scope for such suits? Clearly, in some areas, such as pollution and small frauds that have already been discussed his claim would be correct. However, in other cases the argument would be just as clearly incorrect. In particular, if class actions were generally allowed, then we would expect the same types of agents to litigate as now lobby for statutes. That is, to the extent that the legal system allows class interests to litigate, then the common law system approaches the statutory system and the sort of inefficient legislation that has been statutorily established in recent years would occur instead through common law means. For example, if unions filed *amici* briefs for some low-paid workers, the issue of wages could have been litigated by arguing that wages below some minimum were "unconscionable" and hence, a minimum wage law would have passed by litigation rather than by statute. If this seems impossible, consider only that many of the regulatory laws passed since the 1930s were possible only because the Supreme Court reversed its earlier position and no longer overturned legislation on the basis of "substantive due process."[29] It presumably would have been possible to achieve the same result through legislation, in the form of a Constitutional amendment, but in fact the litigation process was sufficient. Posner errs in looking at particular areas in which class litigation would be efficient without considering the totality of situations in which such litigation would be expected to occur. When all such situations are considered, the presumption in favor of class actions is weakened

There is another implication of increased class actions. As we allow one set of interests to form and litigate (or lobby) we may expect that other interests would be formed to counterlitigate. This is merely an example of what Posner and Tullock have discussed as "rent seeking."[30] If, for example, we allow all victims of pollution to sue for redress, then we may at some point expect all polluters to form a lobbying or litigating group and oppose such litigation. Indeed, we may be observing such behavior now: the existence of pro market, or business oriented, legal foundations may be an example of counterlitigation. These organizations are discussed at some length in Part III. An example is the National Right to Work Legal Defense Foundation. This is a litigating group founded explicitly to counter the effects of labor unions in litigating in certain areas having to do with compulsory unionism. The issue of which side in these various disputes should win (in terms of efficiency) is not of interest here. What is of interest is the apparent proliferation of litigating groups, which serve merely to counter each other's power. In fact, the same thing may be happening in the area of lobbying; recent growth in business Political Action Committees may merely be a counter to the previous growth of labor union political activity.[31] Where the process ends will depend on relative costs of organizing for political and legal activity, and it is impossible to make any predictions about the potential efficiency or inefficiency of the result of this process. However, it is certain that the process itself is wasteful, as are all rent seeking competitions.

In the limit, of course, if all potential interest groups formed and perfectly sought their own interests, then efficiency would be achieved. However, this would require that all consumers organize as a lobbying group and have sufficient information to seek those property rights definitions that are truly in their interest (which does not seem to be true of the consumer-oriented interest groups that have been formed so far). This would require not only costless organization but also costless information. Absent these requirements, some but not all groups will form and there is no presumption about the ultimate implications of the process for efficiency.

V. SUMMARY

Many scholars draw sharp distinctions between statute and common law. In this chapter it is argued that this distinction is often overdrawn. It does appear that common law is preferable to statute, but this appearance is more a function of the time at which each type of rule dominated the legal system. Common law was important in the nineteenth and early twentieth centuries, when there were independent forces for efficiency. Statute law has dominated since the 1930s, when other forces that had no implications in favor of efficiency have prevailed. In particular, it is argued that the distinction is due to the nature of groups that have been able to form. In the early period, those favoring particular rules were mainly individuals, whereas in more recent times, various groups have been able to form and lobby for legislation or litigate for common law rules. So far, the inefficiency effects of the formation of these groups have probably outweighed their effects leading toward efficiency, but this is not necessarily true for all time. As other groups form, it is quite possible that there may be some movement toward efficiency. It may be argued that the environmental legislation of recent years, while incorrectly drafted, may nonetheless have created a bias toward efficiency on net. The recent deregulation in some industries may also be due to similar forces. It is not necessarily correct to argue, as does Posner, that class actions would be a movement toward efficiency, but it is not clear that there would not be such a move. All that is correct is that as more and more groups form and attempt to counter each other, there will be deadweight losses from the rent-seeking process itself.[32]

Finally, a word about policy. Posner's argument for class actions suits is a policy argument; that is, he is arguing that it would be good policy to allow broadened scope for such suits. The claim made in this chapter is that the nature of litigation that is allowed is an endogeneous factor within the system, determined ultimately by the technology of organization. To the extent that this is correct, those groups then will form for which costs of formation are less than benefits, and exhortations toward judges to change policy in various ways will have relatively little effect.

NOTES

1. Richard A. Posner, *Economic Analysis of Law*, 2d ed. (Boston: Little, Brown, 1977), particularly chaps. 13 and 19.

2. Friedrich A. Hayek, *The Constitution of Liberty* (Chicago: University of Chicago Press, 1960); and *Law, Legislation, and Liberty*, Vol. 1, *Rules and Order*, (Chicago: University of Chicago Press, 1973).

3. Paul H. Rubin, "Why is the Common Law Efficient," *Journal of Legal Studies* 6 (1977) 51: (see Chap. 1) George L. Priest, "The Common Law Process and the Selection of Efficient Rules," *Journal of Legal Studies* 6 (1977): 65; John C. Goodman, "An Economic Theory of the Evolution of the Common Law," *Journal of Legal Studies* 7 (1978): 393; William M. Landes and Richard A. Posner, "Adjudication as a Private Good," *Journal of Legal Studies* 8 (1979): 235; *see also* comments and discussion in vol. 8, pp. 285-398; Robert Cooter and Lewis Kornhauser, "Can Litigation Improve the Law without the Help of Judges?," *Journal of Legal Studies* 9 (1980): 139; Jack Hirshleifer, "Evolutionary Models in Economics and Law: Cooperation Versus Conflict Strategies," in *Evolutionary Theory in Law and Economics*, ed. Richard Zerbe, *Research in Law and Economics*, vol. 4, (Greenwich, Conn.: Jai Press, 1982).

4. Gordon Tullock, *Trials on Trial* (New York: Columbia University Press, 1980), also, discussion by Tullock in Zerbe, *Research in Law and Economics*, pp. 74-81.

5. The discussion of land law is largely based on Lawrence M. Friedman, *A History of American Law* (New York: Simon and Schuster, 1973); *see also* Jonathan R. T. Hughes, *The Governmental Habit* (New York: Basic Books, 1977).

6. Friedman, *A History of American Law*, p. 208.

7. James Kent, *Commentaries*, (1832), p. 106, quoted in Friedman, *A History of American Law*, p. 184.

8. Friedman, *A History of American Law*, p. 376.

9. For a discussion of the Homestead Acts, see Lance E. Davis and Douglass C. North, *Institutional Change and American Economic Growth* (London: Cambridge University Press, 1971), chap. 5.

10. The discussion of unconscionability is based on Richard A. Epstein, "Unconscionability: A Critical Reappraisal," *Journal of Law and Economics* 18 (1975): 293.

11. Ibid., sec. 4.

12. Robert B. Ekelund, Jr. and Robert D. Tollison, "Economic Regulation in Mercantile England: Heckscher Revisted," *Economic Inquiry* 18 (1980): 567.

13. Morton J. Horwitz, *The Transformation of American Law* (Cambridge, Mass.: Harvard University Press, 1977), chap. 4.

14. For discussion of the state of antitrust law emphasizing its current inefficiency, see Robert H. Bork, *The Antitrust Paradox* (New York: Basic Books, 1978), and Richard A. Posner, *Antitrust Law* (Chicago: University of Chicago Press, 1976). There is no explanation for the passage of the antitrust laws based on an interest group perspective, so that, in one sense, we do not really know why these laws were passed.

15. Marc Galanter, "Why the 'Haves' Come Out Ahead: Speculation on the Limits of Legal Change," *Law and Society Review* 9 (1974): 95.

16. Mancur Olson, *The Logic of Collective Action* (Cambridge, Mass.: Harvard University Press, 1965), defines the concept of "latent" group as a group that it does not pay to form. The argument here is that whether a group is latent or whether it actually forms will depend, at least in part, on the costs of organization; as these costs become lower, some groups which were latent will begin to form. The argument here is that whether a group is latent or whether it actually forms will depend, at least in part, on the costs of organization; as these costs become lower, some groups, which were latent, will begin to form.

17. For a discussion of the state of landlord tenant law and its recent changes, see, for example, Richard H. Chused, *A Modern Approach to Property: Cases—Notes—Materials* (St. Paul, Minn.: West Publishing Co., 1978), chap. 3.

18. Werner Z. Hirsch, *Law and Economics* (New York: Academic Press, 1979), chap. 3.

19. Sam Peltzman, "The Effects of Automobile Safety Regulation," *Journal of Political Economy* 83 (1975): 677.

20. See, for example, Jeffrey O'Connell, "Elective No-Fault Liability Insurance for all Kinds of Accidents: A Proposal," *Insurance Law Journal* (1973): 495. Reprinted in Henry Manne, ed., *The Economic of Legal Relationships* (St. Paul, Minn.: West Publishing Co., 1975).

21. Elizabeth M. Landes, "Insurance, Liability, and Accidents: A Theoretical and Empirical Investigation of the Effects of No-Fault on Accidents," (Working paper, University of Chicago, Center for the Study of the Economy and the State, 1980).

22. Ellen R. Jordan and Paul H. Rubin, "An Economic Analysis of the Law of False Advertising," *Journal of Legal Studies* 8 (1979): 527, see chap. 6.

23. Joel Franklin Brenner, "Nuisance Law and The Industrial Revolution," *Journal of Legal Studies* 3 (1974): 403.

24. James B. Kau and Paul H. Rubin, *Congressmen, Constituents, and Contributors* (Boston: Martinus Nijhoff, 1982).

25. Stewart Macaulay, *Law and The Balance of Power: The Automobile Manufacturers and Their Dealers* (New York: Russell Sage, 1966).

26. While we would generally expect such organized groups to favor the economic interests of their members, this is not necessarily the only purpose for which groups form. For example, Kau and Rubin, cited in note 24, show that one type of group that seems to have had influence on legislation is the so-called "public interest lobby," lobbying groups with primarily ideological interests. That study in general supports the view that ideological, as well as economic, interests may be influential in passing legislation. The original analysis of the (increasing) role of ideology in economic legislation is in Joseph A. Schumpeter, *Capitalism, Socialism and Democracy* (New York: Harper and Row, 1950).

27. Posner, *Economic Analysis of Law*, chap. 13.

28. Richard A. Posner, "The Federal Trade Commission," *University of Chicago Law Review* 3 (1969): 47; Jordan and Rubin, "Economic Analysis of Law of False Advertising," p. 527.

29. See, for example, Gerald Gunther, *Cases and Materials on Constitutional Law*, 10th ed. (Mineola, New York: The Foundation Press, 1980).

30. Richard A. Posner, "The Social Costs of Monopoly and Regulation," *Journal of Political Economy* 83 (1975): 807; Gordon Tullock, "The Transitional Gains Trap," *Bell Journal of Economics* 6 (1975): 671.

31. For a discussion of Political Action Committees, see Edwin M. Epstein, "The Emergence of Political Action Committees," in Herbert Alexander, ed., *Political Finance* (Beverly Hills, Cal.: Sage Publilcations, 1979).

32. Goodman, "An Economic Theory of the Evolution of the Common Law," pp. 405-06, discusses several reasons why the common law might no longer be expected to be more efficient than statute law. However, part of the argument of this chapter is that the factors that have changed common law have also changed statute law. Therefore, there is no particular reason to expect statute law to be preferable to common law either.

PART II
SPECIFIC LAWS

The argument of Part I was that when parties have symmetric interest in rules, then litigation pressures should lead to efficient enforcement of those rules. That is, where there are appropriate symmetries, then enforcement of rules should be efficient. In this part, some tests of this general hypothesis are provided. Several bodies of law that deal with symmetric relationships between firms are considered in some detail. It is shown that all of these bodies are in fact efficient; the predictions of the theory seem to be borne out.

CHAPTER 3

The Franchise Contract

I. INTRODUCTION

A question of perennial interest to economists is the question of the nature of the firm.[1] In Ronald Coase's terms, we might ask why some decisions will be made within firms by fiat and others between firms by market transactions. But implicit within the entire literature is the idea that there is a reasonably sharp distinction between transactions within firms and transactions between firms; that is, there is an assumption that the border of the firm is sharp.

There are many types of transactions that profit-seeking individuals might find worthwhile in the marketplace. Products and markets have sufficiently diverse characteristics so that a large number of arrangements might be profit maximizing. Thus, it would be surprising if there were in fact a sharp distinction between interfirm and intrafirm transactions; rather, we would expect hybrid cases where markets allow various types of optimal blends. In fact, we do observe such mixed cases. One such intermediate case, much studied by economists, is sharecropping,[2] while another type of hybrid is franchising. In this chapter, the nature of the franchise contract is examined, using the tools of the theory of the firm discussed in the articles cited in note 1.[3] Section II discusses the institutional structure of the franchise. Section III considers and rejects the standard explanation of franchising in terms of capital markets. In Section IV an alternative explanation, consistent with economic theory, is proposed. Section V considers some additional aspects of franchising, and in Section VI some antitrust implications of the theory are developed. The last section is a summary.

The franchise contract is a contract between two parties, the franchisor and the franchisee. Therefore, in its pure form, we would expect such a contract to be efficient. However, in recent times, both antitrust authorities and organized groups of franchisees have litigated to change the terms of the contract. The arguments given in Chapter 2 would imply that such litigation should reduce the efficiency of the franchise contract. Indeed, this is what is found.

II. INSTITUTIONAL STRUCTURE

A franchise agreement is a contract between two (legal) firms, the franchisor and the franchisee. The franchisor is a parent company that has developed some product or service for sale; the franchisee is a firm that is set up to market this product or service in a particular location. The franchisee pays a certain sum of money for the right to market this product.

Franchise contracts have several more or less standard clauses.[4] First, the franchisor may provide various sorts of managerial assistance to the franchisee. This assistance will usually include site selection; training programs, either on the job or institutional; provision of standard operating manuals; provision of ongoing advice; and miscellaneous assistance, such as design of physical layout of the plant and advertising. The extent of assistance varies from industry to industry; in some cases there is virtually none.

Second, the franchisee will agree to run the business in a manner stipulated by the franchisor. Control by the franchisor may extend over products sold, price, hours of operation, conditions of the plant, inventory, insurance, personnel, and accounting and auditing. (Some of these controls have been weakened or overturned by various antitrust rulings.)

Third, the franchisee will pay royalties, usually a percentage of sales, to the franchisor. In addition, the franchisee may be compelled to purchase inputs from the franchisor or from approved suppliers, though this requirement will vary from contract to contract.

Fourth, the contract will have a termination clause. Usually the franchisor will be able to terminate the agreement almost at will. Finally, there will be miscellaneous clauses, dealing with matters such as the right of the franchisee to sell the franchise, rights of heirs of the franchisee to inherit the business, and the right to open a competing business after ceasing to be a franchisee.

Although some of the ability of the franchisor to control the behavior of the franchisee has been limited by various antitrust rulings,[5] we will consider contracts in the form that they took before such rulings, on the assumption that unrestricted contracts would have been profit maximizing. Under such contracts, it is notable that the franchisor has almost complete control over the behavior of the franchisee; in fact, the relationship is almost that of a firm and an employee. This relationship is especially apparent when we consider the ease with which the franchise agreement can be terminated by the franchisor. In this sense, it appears that the definition of the franchisee as a separate firm, rather than as part of the franchisor, is a legal and not an economic distinction. In fact, part of the argument put forth is that there exists no meaningful economic distinction, that is to say, the economic concept of "firm" does not have clear boundaries.

III. CAPITAL MARKET EXPLANATIONS OF FRANCHISING

A common explanation for the franchising of independent firms, rather than reliance on expansion by wholly-owned subsidiaries, is that franchising is a method used by the franchisor to raise capital.[6] Thus, it is argued, the franchisor is able to expand his business more quickly than would otherwise be the case.

A consideration of this argument in the light of modern capital theory quickly indicates that it is fallacious. A franchisor will own outlets in many areas; a franchisee will, in general, own only one or a few outlets in the same area. Thus, the investment of the franchisee will be much riskier than the overall franchise chain. A risk averse franchisee would clearly prefer to invest in a portfolio of shares in all franchise outlets, rather than confining his investment to a single store.

This means, essentially, that the franchisee will require a higher rate of return on his capital if he is required to invest in one outlet rather than in a portfolio. Conversely, the franchisor, by forcing relatively large risk on the franchisee, will himself earn a lower rate of return. This argument thus appears to make sense only if we assume that franchisors are more risk averse than franchisees. But since franchisees commonly invest a large share of their assets in acquiring the franchise, it is unlikely that this will be the case.

Let us make, arguendo, the strongest possible case for the capital market argument. Assume that franchisors are unable to use normal capital markets for expansion. Therefore also assume that they want to rely on their store managers for a source of capital. (Stating these conditions immediately indicates their implausibility.) Even in this case, the franchisor would do better to create a portfolio of shares of all outlets and sell these shares to his managers. This would diversify risk for the managers, with no (capital) effect on the franchisor. Thus, it is clear that capital market agruments do not explain franchising.

IV. AN ALTERNATIVE EXPLANATION

The alternative explanation follows directly from the work of Armen Alchian and Harold Demsetz[7] and Michael Jensen and William Meckling[8] on monitoring and control within the firm. Specifically, franchising is usually undertaken in situations where the franchisee is physically removed from the franchisor, and thus where monitoring of the peformance and behavior of the franchisee would be difficult. In this situation, it pays to devise control mechanisms that give the franchisee an incentive to be efficient—to avoid shirking and excessive consumption of leisure. To the extent that such mechanisms can be devised, both the franchisee and the franchisor gain, for they have a larger amount to share in some way. In other words, the shirking that is avoided is shirking that both parties would find undesirable.

The simplest way to motivate the franchisee is to give him a share of the profits of the franchise. Then he will work as hard as is efficient, for any leisure he consumes will clearly be worth the true cost. Thus, we would expect the franchise contract to be written in such a way as to give the franchisee much of the profits in the operation.

But presumably there is a well-defined market for people with the ability to be franchisees, and franchisors would not want to pay more for these people than this amount. There is, however, no assurance that the present value of these salaries would be equal to the present value of the profits of the franchise. Thus, the franchise fee is simply the difference between these two present values. The franchisee pays for the right to run the business and collect some of the profits for some period of time. Presumably his payment is adjusted so that he will make a normal return on his time and on his investment in the business (that is, on the payment), with this return adjusted for risk.

Consider an example. Assume there exists some franchise that will pay $15,000 per year for 10 years. If the interest rate is 6 percent, the present value of this stream is approximately $110,000. Assume the wage of a person competent to run this firm is $12,000. Then the present value of his earnings is approximately $88,000. Thus, the franchisee would pay $22,000 for the franchise and would earn a normal return on his time.This explanation of franchising, while rather obvious, has not been pointed out in the literature, where the capital market explanation is universally held to apply.

The argument to this point would seem to imply that the franchisee would receive all of the profits of the enterprise. If he receives only a share of the profits, there will still be some residual shirking. We would expect the payment made by the franchisee, the franchise fee, to be equal to the expected present value of the stream of profits; there would then be no ongoing payment from the franchisee to the franchisor.

In fact, we do not observe this; rather, the franchisor usually gets a share of the proceeds of the business. (Generally, the share is either a percentage of sales or a fee from selling goods and services to the franchisee.) It might appear that this method is used because of uncertainty. With a royalty payment, if the franchise should turn out to be more successful than predicted, the franchisor will obtain some of the excess profits; if it should turn out to be less successful than expected, the franchisee will not bear the full cost of this lack of success in his fee. However, due to the inefficiency of the reduction of the franchisee's property rights in the profits of the enterprise, we would expect that another method could be evolved for risk sharing. Another possibility may have to do with capital markets. Franchisees are usually individuals with relatively small personal wealth, and it may be difficult for them to raise enough capital to pay the full expected value of the franchise profits. While we cannot reject this argument out of hand, reliance on imperfect capital markets as an explanation of behavior is generally not satisfactory.

The most plausible explanation seems to be that the franchisee has some incentive to motivate the franchisor to be efficient. Just as the franchisor desires the franchisee to run the operation efficiently, so the franchisee desires to give the franchisor an incentive to be efficient in those aspects of the relationship that require an ongoing performance by the franchisor. Some areas of such behavior are the ongoing managerial advice, which the franchisor is sometimes required to give the franchisee, and advertising by the franchisor.

It is unlikely that either of these aspects of control is important enough to justify the reduction in the franchisee's profits and the corresponding reduction in his incentives for efficiency. However, there is another area in which the franchisee would like to control the behavior of the franchisor. To understand this, we must consider what the franchisee is buying when he buys a franchise. The main item purchased is the trademark of the franchise. This is valuable because consumers have a good deal of information about price and quality sold by establishments with a given trademark. Consumers have this information precisely because the franchisor polices franchises and makes certain that quality standards are maintained. What is involved is a classic externality problem. If any one franchisee allows quality to deteriorate, he will still generate revenue because consumers perceive him as being of the same quality as other stores with the same trademark. Thus, if one franchisee allows the quality of his establishment to deteriorate, he benefits by the full amount of the savings from reduced quality maintenance; he loses only part of the costs, for part is borne by other franchisees. All franchises would lose something as a result of this deterioration in one franchise: consumers would have less faith in the quality promised by the trademark.

There are several aspects to this policing. First, the franchisor must be careful to grant franchises to those who are likely to be competent in operating them. Some screening of potential franchisees is important. Second, the franchisor must control the quality of products offered by the franchisees. We argued above that the franchisee could best run the day-to-day operations of the business. This is true in the sense that he can produce the desired good (including quality) at the least cost. However, it is relatively inexpensive for the franchisor to monitor the quality of the goods produced, as opposed to the method of production. This is the sort of monitoring that franchisors undertake. Third, errors will sometimes be made, and some franchises will not be profitable. Such businesses will operate in the short run if they are covering variable costs and will shut down in the long run, when capital has been sufficiently depreciated. But it is precisely this depreciation of capital that the franchisor wants to avoid. The franchisor wants to eliminate any operations not maintaining the quality of the franchise. Contracts calling for easy termination of franchises makes it possible to avoid the period of quality deterioration.

Because of the externality problem, all franchisees have an interest in having quality policed. Assume now that the franchisor sold the entire value of the profits to franchisees, that is, the franchisor obtained no royalty from current sales. If quality deteriorates, this would reduce his income because renewal fees would decrease, as would fees from sales of new franchises. In addition, profits of existing franchises would also be reduced, but this reduction would have no effect on the franchisor. He would bear only part of the cost of reduced quality, and thus would have an incentive to underinvest in resources used in policing franchisees.

Thus, giving the franchisee a large share of the profits of the operation creates an incentive for him to be efficient in that part of the operation he can most efficiently control; giving the franchisor a share of the profits of all franchises gives him an incentive to be efficient in those aspects of the enterprise under his control. Both parts of the contract can be understood as an attempt to give property rights to the parties to the transaction in those areas they can efficiently control.

In virtually all franchise contracts, the receipts of the franchisor depend on the revenue (not profits) of the franchise. In some cases, there is a payment of a percentage of sales to the franchisor, while in other cases, the franchisee is required to buy inputs from the franchisor at above market prices. Urban Ozanne and Shelby Hunt[9] claim that this type of contract is inefficient, in that it would be more efficient for the franchisor to share in profits rather than revenues. They claim that the reason sales, rather than profits, are used is because monitoring of sales is easier that monitoring of profits. But in fact, most contracts give the franchisor the right to order audits of the franchise, and it is not clear that monitoring would be that difficult. Rather, it seems likely that the element of control of the franchisor, the policing of franchises, is more closely related to sales than to profits; thus, the contracts seem to be written in such a way as to give the franchisor the correct incentives.

The analysis to this point has some additional implications. First, there is some evidence in the literature that franchisors are buying back franchises in urban areas.[10] If franchising is used because control of behavior of store managers is difficult, then we would expect the existence of several stores in an area to reduce this control problem for the franchisor could have an agent who would supervise several stores as a unit. (Of course, the problem of monitoring the monitor would remain, but this would be a reasonably straightforward employer-employee problem and would be less difficult than monitoring the behavior of a store manager.) If stores are geographically separated, on the other hand, this sort of supervision would be more expensive, for monitors would need to spend much time traveling from store to store. When a franchisor begins operations, he will not have many stores in any given area, but after some time, if successful, he will have many outlets in large urban areas. At this point, it becomes worthwhile to buy back the franchises. Thus, the existence of owned outlets in urban areas and franchised outlets elsewhere would be consistent with our hypothesis.

The argument also has some implications about types of contracts in different businesses. Businesses can vary in two relevant dimensions: the amount of discretion available to managers and the value to the business of the trademark. In those businesses where there is much managerial discretion, we would expect a higher percentage of the revenue of the franchisor to come from the initial fee and a relatively lower percentage to come from royalties. In businesses where there are relatively few managerial decisions to be made, we would expect more of the income of the franchisor to come from royalties. Second, where the trademark is more valuable, we would expect relatively more of the franchisor's revenue to come from royalties, for this would create an incentive for him to be efficient in policing and maintaining value. Thus, this theory has testable implications about the relationship between the nature of the industry and the franchise contract.

V. ADDITIONAL ISSUES

In this section, we discuss the behavior of the franchisee, the behavior of the franchisor, and some additional issues dealing with their interrelationship.

A. Franchisee Behavior

Perhaps the most important question to ask about the franchisee is why he would seek a franchise rather than operating an independent business. There appear to be four advantages of having a franchise. First, the trademark of the franchise and the product sold appear to be valuable, and the franchisee is willing to pay something to sell these commodities. Second, the franchisor often gives managerial advice to the franchisee. This advantage would appear to be minimal, since the market is easily able to provide such training and many types of franchises involve no such training. Third, the franchisor often makes capital availble to the franchisee in some form, either by cosigning for a bank loan or by actually buying the plant and leasing it to the franchisee. Presumably, franchisors are less risky borrowers than franchisees, and thus there can be a saving here. Finally, to the extent that franchisees are closer to being employees that entrepreneurs, they may simply lack the requisite human capital to open businesses without the substantial assistance of franchisors.

B. Franchisor Behavior

There are some aspects of franchisor behavior that we have not considered. First, franchisors often desire to closely control the behavior of franchisees. It appears that one major advantage of a franchise is the information it provides to consumers: when I take my family to a McDonald's I know what to expect, no matter where it is located. Thus, it would be worthwhile for McDonald's to spend a fair sum to maintain this situation and to curtail any local variation. This same sort of information control has been advanced as an explanation of the desire of manufacturers to maintain prices through resale-price-maintenance agreements.[11]

It was mentioned above that franchise contracts sometimes have clauses preventing the franchisee from opening a similar business for some period after termination of his franchise relationship. We would predict that this would be most common in those cases where substantial amounts of training are provided by the franchisor. Much of this training would be in the form of general human capital, and the franchisor might well desire to avoid having persons acquire this human capital for other uses.[12]

C. Interactions

George Stigler and Paul Rubin in their discussions of the firm develop the concept of "functions" or "activities" of a firm.[13] The argument is that different functions will reach their lowest cost level at differect levels. Stigler uses this argument as an explanation for vertical integration; Rubin uses it as the basis for a theory of firm expansion. However, this concept is also useful if we view the franchise as a hybrid between firm and market. In particular, we would argue that the franchisor will perform functions with costs that fall for a substantial level of output, while the franchisee will perform functions whose average cost curve turns up relatively sooner.

The most important function performed by the local franchisee is, of course, managing the day-to-day operations of the business. In fact, the entire justification for franchising turns on the fact that costs of this activity quickly become large (because of control problems), so that it pays to split this function off from the large firm (the franchisor) and to transfer it to the franchisee.

On the other hand, other management functions seem to have more substantial economies of scale. Thus, the franchisor sometimes provides for franchisees a detailed operating manual, training, and ongoing managerial assistance, as well as plant designs and site selection. In addition, the franchisor generally purchases advertising for the enterprise, although this advertising is paid for by the franchisces through an advertising fund. It therefore appears that the division of tasks between the franchisor and the franchisee can be explained in terms of the average costs of performing these different tasks.

VI. ANTITRUST IMPLICATIONS

Recently, various aspects of the franchise contract have come under the scrutiny of antitrust authorities, including decisions on the exclusivity of the sales agreement, tying sales, price and product control, and termination arrangements in the franchise contract. There are several grounds for criticizing this trend.

First, there are many possible franchisors. No individual who wants to become a franchisee is forced to sign with any one franchisor; the market for franchise operations is competitive, with the only monopoly element being the trademark. Thus, it is difficult to see why the courts would want to interfere at all in the franchisee-franchisor relationship. What is involved here is a general freedom-of-contract issue rather than a specific franchise issue.[14] Arguments that rely on the ignorance of the franchise or the bargaining-power advantage of the franchisor are as valid here as in any other context (which is to say, not very valid)

Part of the justification for antitrust intervention may be that, once the contract is signed, the franchisor is in a monopoly position relative to the franchisee. But this argument rests on a misinterpretation of the nature of the relationship between the two parties. Legally, the franchise is a firm dealing with another firm, the franchisor. This legal classification is apparently a result of the fact that the franchisee must pay for the franchise. But, as we have seen, the economics of the situation are such that the franchisee is in fact closer to being an employee of the franchisor than to being an independent entrepreneur. It would thus appear that the categorization required in the legal system leads to inefficiency when the courts behave as if this legal categorization had some economic validity. One of the major purposes of this chapter has been to point out that there is no clear-cut division between what is and what is not a firm.

Should the courts continue to interfere in the franchise contract, it is possible that franchisors will turn to wholly-owned stores rather than to franchises. However, the efficiency incentives in having the manager earn a share of the profits may be sufficiently large for firms to try to preserve this arrangement. An alternative would be the evolution of an entirely new institution, where it would be explicitly recognized that the manager is an employee of the company, paying some amount for the position and being compensated entirely out of profits. However, the evolution of major new legal institutions is expensive, and the franchising contract would probably have to be more inefficient than it is now before such a development would be worthwhile.

VII. SUMMARY

In this chapter, we have used the modern theory of the firm, relying on an analysis of property rights, incentives, and monitoring, to explain the nature of the franchise contract. We have argued that the franchise relationship is intermediate between a single firm and a market transaction, and have shown that economic theory can explain the precise nature of the payments made by each party. In particular, the structure of the contract is such as to give each party property rights in those aspects of the operation under his control.

Finally, we argued that application of antitrust law to franchising is erroneous, based on a confusion of legal categories with economically meaningful categories. This has occurred because franchisees have organized into lobbying and litigating groups and have sought rulings that, while inefficient, nonetheless serve to benefit existing franchisees, as discussed in Part I of the present volume.[15]

NOTES

1. *See* Ronald H. Coase, "The Nature of the Firm," *Economica* 4 (1973): 386, reprinted in *Readings in Price Theory*, ed. George J. Stigler and Kenneth E. Boulding (1952), p. 331; George J. Stigler, "The Division of Labor is Limited by the Extent of the Market," *Journal of Political Economy* 59: (1951) 185, reprinted in George J. Stigler, *The Organization of Industry* (Ill.: Richard D. Irwin, 1968), p. 129; Armen A. Alchian and Harold Demsetz, "Production, Information Costs, and Economic Organization," *American Economic Review* 62 (1972):777; Paul H. Rubin, "The Expansion of Firms," *Journal of Political Economy* 81 (1973): 936; and Michael C. Jensen and William H. Meckling, "Theory of the Firm: Managerial Behavior, Agency Costs, and Ownership Structure," *Journal of Financial Economics* 3 (1976): 305.

2. See, for example, Steven N. S. Cheung, *The Theory of Share Tenancy* (Chicago: University of Chicago Press, 1969).

3. Richard E. Caves and William F. Murphy II, "Franchising: Firms, Markets, and Intangible Assets," *Southern Economic Journal* 42 (1976): 572, discuss many of the points raised here. However, their discussion is primarily in terms of assumed monopoly power of the franchisor; the discussion here is in terms of maximizing joint profits of both parties. Since markets for franchisees and markets for franchisors are both competitive, monopoly arguments seem inherently weak.

4. Urban B. Ozanne and Shelby D. Hunt provide a statistical analysis of terms of franchise contracts. *See* U.S. Congress, Senate, Select Committee on Small Business, *The Economic Effects of Franchising*, 92nd Cong., 1st sess., (Comm. Print 1971). For a legal analysis, *see* Coleman R. Rosenfield, *The Law of Franchising* (1970).

5. Rosenfield, *The Law of Franchising*, has a discussion of antitrust implications of franchising.

6. Almost all sources assume that capital is the explanation for franchising. For example: Ozanne and Hunt, *Economic Effects of Franchising*,

p. 32, "Obviously these firms are in franchising because they do not (or did not) have the necessary capital to expand through company-operated units . . . "; Rosenfield, *The Law of Franchising*, p. 8, "Yet this new breed of entrepreneurs [the franchisors] found that capital demands soon exceeded their resources . . . "; Alfred R. Oxenfeldt and Donald N. Thompson, "Franchising in Perspective," *Journal of Retailing* 3, (Winter, 1968–69): 44, "Franchisors create these systems because they have too little capital to consider a wholly-owned chain . . . "; idem, p. 9; Caves and Murphy, "Franchising: Firms , Markets," p. 581, "For financing outlets the capital supplied by franchisees has no ready substitute."

   7. Alchian and Demsetz, "Production, Information Costs," p. 777.
   8. Jensen and Meckling, "Theory of the Firm," p. 305.
   9. Ozanne and Hunt, *Economic Effects of Franchising*, p. 46.
   10. Ibid., p. 81.
   11. This point is made in George J. Stigler, "The Economics of Information," *Journal of Political Economy* 69 (1961): 213, reprinted in Stigler, *The Organization of Industry*, p. 171.
   12. Gary S. Becker, *Human Capital*, 2d ed. (New York: Columbia University Press, 1975).
   13. Stigler, *The Organization of Industry*, p. 129; Rubin, "The Expansion of Firms," p. 936.
   14. Richard A. Epstein, "Unconscionability: A Critical Reappraisal," *Journal of Law and Economics* 18 (1975): 293.
   15. The process of seeking legal change by organized groups of franchisees is discussed in Stewart Macaulay, *Law and the Balance of Power* (New York: Russell Sage, 1966).

CHAPTER 4

Unenforceable Contracts

I. INTRODUCTION

That many aspects of the common law may be explained in terms of economic efficiency, defined as wealth maximization, is a proposition that now is well established. The work of Posner[1] and others has made this proposition a well-established argument, and arguments that partially explain why this is true are provided in Chapters 1 and 2. Thus, it is a puzzle when there is some legal rule that cannot be so explained. To date, one of the main anomalies in the economic explanation of common law is the rule against penalty clauses in contracts. That is, if two parties sign a contract that specifies a payment in the case of breach and if the courts determine that these damages are greater than the actual costs of the breach, the damages will not be allowed. Though there are some explanations in the literature for this behavior based on economics,[2] these explanations have not been fully convincing.[3] Another area in which the economic analysis has not been fully satisfying is the area of specific performance. Anthony Kronman[4] is able to explain some of the reluctance of the courts to order specific performance in the case of contracts, but he, too, is left with some puzzles.

This chapter provides an explanation for both of these aspects of the behavior of courts in refusing to enforce contracts. The argument is based on Lester Telser's recent discussion of the theory of "self-enforcing contracts."[5] If a contract is self-enforcing, then parties to the contract will not need to use the courts in enforcing the terms of the agreement, unless some unexpected event occurs. If a contract is not self-enforcing, the parties will rely on other mechanisms for enforcement. One such mechanism is the courts. Disputants do not pay the full costs of litigation, for society provides a subsidy for the use of the courts. Thus, parties may sign non self-enforcing contracts in the expectation that the courts will settle the disagreements that they expect to arise. Since the parties do not pay full costs of the court system, such agreements may be signed even when the total costs of enforcement are greater than the benefits, since the parties would not internalize all of the costs of the contract. It will be shown below that the two types of contractual provisions discussed here, penalty clauses and specific performance, are not self-enforcing in Telser's sense, and that, therefore, enforcement of such contracts by the judiciary might lead to an inefficient use of resources in the enforcement of the contracts.

There is a methodological point relevant here. The economic approach to law may be either a positive or a normative approach.[6] The positive argument is that economic efficiency can explain what the law is and the normative argument is that the law should seek economic efficiency. It is important to keep these arguments separate. But what seems to happen is that when the positive argument does not apply, the normative argument is introduced. That is, in the case of penalty clauses, we cannot find an economic explanation for the legal treatment of these clauses. This is essentially a falsification of the theory when the theory is treated in a positive sense. But rather than treat the behavior as a falsification, we instead begin to use the normative argument and claim that the courts should begin to enforce penalty clauses. It would appear intellectually more satisfying to explain why this rule exists than to decry the rule as being inefficient.

Moreover, there is also some danger here. If the courts begin to accept the economic arguments, then it is possible that the law will be modified in the direction of what is perceived as increasing efficiency. If students of the economic approach err in their analysis and conclude that certain legal rules are inefficient when they are in fact efficient, and if the courts accept the economic reasoning, then there is a chance that costs will be imposed on society. In other areas of behavior, decision makers have sometimes accepted principles advanced by economists that have later turned out to be wrong and have thus reduced welfare. Examples from macroeconomic policy are not difficult to find; there are also examples in antitrust law and in regulation. Thus, we should want to be very sure that some principle of law is in fact inefficient before we advocate changing this principle.

The plan of this chapter is as follows: Section II discusses the theory of self-enforcing contracts. Sections III and IV apply this theory respectively to penalty clauses and specific performance. The section on penalty clauses will receive the most attention since this is the area of law most puzzling to economists. The last section is a summary.

II. THE THEORY OF SELF-ENFORCING CONTRACTS

In Lester Telser's terms, a self-enforcing agreement is one that remains in force only as long as it is in the interest of both parties to the agreement to maintain it. Either party can otherwise terminate the agreement at will. If either party violates the agreement there are no penalties and no recourse for the other party except termination. No third party is involved in settling disputes that arise. Since no third party is involved, the legal system would never be called upon in the case of such agreements. Thus, the fact that society pays a subsidy to the courts would not be relevant in such agreements; parties would enter into the agreements only if the value of the agreement were greater than all costs of the agreement.

Thus, strictly speaking, no contractual agreement would be self-enforcing in Telser's terms, for the existence of a contract always implies a potential for litigation and hence outside enforcement. It is possible, however, to modify Telser's argument slightly to allow for contracts as well as agreements. Parties do not enter into self-enforcing agreements with the expectation of breaking such agreements. A breach only occurs if there is an unanticipated change in the conditions underlying the agreement. We may then think of an agreement as being "expectedly self-enforcing," but with provisions for external enforcement in the case of unanticipated changes. If such agreements are entered, the courts would become involved only if some unanticipated change occurred, and the role of the courts would then be to determine liability for the results of such changes. This is the result of the standard economic theory of contract law, where it is argued that the function of such law is to detemine what the parties would have bargained for if the unforeseen event had in fact been anticipated.[7] Thus, in the case of such expectedly self-enforcing agreements, the parties would enter the agreement expecting it to be self-enforcing, but with a possibility of external enforcement if unanticipated changes occurred.

If such changes did occur and the parties did rely on the courts for enforcement, then a subsidy would be received since disputants do not pay the full costs of the court system. Thus, there would be an external cost to society from the existence of such agreements. However, there would also be an external benefit. This is because courts not only settle disputes, but also promulgate rules based on disputes. If some unexpected event occurs once, then it may occur again. When the courts settle a dispute between two parties based on unexpected occurrences, then other parties, who read the courts' decisions, are forewarned about the possibility of such events occurring and are able to make allowances for the event in their own dealings. They may do so either by relying on (now modified) contract law or by negotiating around contract law by including a provision in their contracts regarding the event. In either case, however, the courts have provided an external benefit to third parties, which explains the willingness of society to partially subsidize the dispute resolution process.

Consider now a third class of disputes—those which are not expectedly self-enforcing. These would be agreements into which parties would enter with the full expectation that third parties would be relied upon to settle the agreement, even in the absence of unexpected changes. Since such outside settlements would be expected, the parties would not enter into the agreement unless the expected benefits to them were greater than their anticipated costs including the expected litigation costs. However, since the parties would not pay the full costs of litigation, such agreements might be entered even when their total costs were greater than their total benefits. This is because of the subsidy paid by society to the court system.

Moreover, in the case of such agreements, there would be no external gain to society from resolving the dispute. The dispute did not arise as a result of an unexpected change in some condition, for it was an integral part of the agreement. Thus, the terms on which the court settled the dispute would provide no useful information to future parties in similar situations. Such parties would still have incentives to draw up contracts that would rely on the courts for enforcement, even knowing what terms would be imposed by the courts.

It is true that courts do sometimes settle disputes that do not have precedential value. Most torts cases are probably of this sort, absent significant technological changes that might change efficient liability assignments. Here, however, there does not seem to be any way for parties to avoid the use of the courts for there does not seem to be any alternative method of dispute resolution. (Landes and Posner,[8] for example, indicate that contractual agreements that use arbitrators are not feasible in tort cases where the parties have no preaccident dealings with each other.) Moreover, there is occasional technological change so that efficient rules may sometimes change and, without court settlements, there would be no way of communicating this change to interested parties. (In regard to automobile accidents it may also be that traffic laws are aimed at reducing the amount of accidents and hence the amount of subsidized litigation that would result from driving an automobile.[9]) But if there were enforcement of contracts that were entered into with the expectation of legal enforcement, parties would voluntarily be placing themselves in situations in which litigation would be likely to occur, and it is not surprising that courts will discourage such behavior.

It may sometimes pay for parties to enter into agreements with the expectation of litigation, for the benefits from such agreements may outweigh the costs. The only way to be certain of this value would be to have the parties themselves agree to pay all costs of settlements. This can be done in the case of arbitration agreements where the disputants will pay the full costs. Thus, if contracts that are not expectedly self-enforcing are signed and include clauses that require commercial arbitration in the case of dispute, we may infer that such contracts are efficient.

In summary, then, the argument is that all contracts signed by two parties must be value-maximizing vis-a-vis those parties. If the courts refuse to enforce such agreements and if there is an efficiency explanation for this failure to enforce, it must be in terms of effects of the contracts on third parties. The argument here is that such contracts impose burdens on the court system, which would lead parties to sign such agreements even if they are in sum not value-maximizing, and that, moreover, the litigation that would result from enforcement of these contracts would provide no useful information to other potential disputants. It is now demonstrated that this argument may apply in the particular cases in which the courts refuse to enforce contracts.

III. PENALTY CLAUSES

It is possible to write a contract that includes a clause specifying the amount to be paid by the performing party in the event of breach. However, this payment cannot be more than the cost to the paying party of the breach. If the payment is specified as being larger than this cost, the courts will generally hold that the payment is a penalty and will not enforce the agreement.

The failure of courts to enforce penalty clauses is clearly a puzzle to economists. Economists generally believe that any voluntary contract between two parties is efficient, for parties do not enter into agreements that do not benefit them. There are various reasons that would explain the willingness of parties to enter into agreements that specify penalty clauses. Charles Goetz and Robert Scott[10] show that penalties are efficient in the case of a buyer with idiosyncratic wants and that penalties might also be efficient forms of insurance. Posner[11] argues that sellers (particularly new firms) might want to prove that they are reliable and thus contract to pay penalties for nonperformance. There may be other reasons why parties might specify penalties; the general argument is that, if the parties voluntarily agree to a clause, it must be value-maximizing with respect to the parties.

The difficulty of devising an economic argument that would imply efficient nonenforcement of a voluntary contract is demonstrated by Kenneth Clarkson, Roger Leroy Miller, and Timothy Muris.[12] The argument here is that the paying party would benefit from nonperformance of the contract by the performing party if there were a penalty clause. Thus, the paying party would have an incentive to interfere with the performing party and make performance difficult. This effort would use resources (be inefficient). Also, the performing party would be forced to use resources to monitor the behavior of the other party and stop this behavior. Thus, the existence of a penalty clause will lead to wasteful use of resources by both parties and would be inefficient.

As Anthony Kronman and Richard Posner[13] point out, this argument is essentially paternalistic. That is, the effects identified by Clarkson et al. are purely two party effects that can be foreseen before the contract is signed, and the price negotiated by the parties should take into account these factors. The factors that they identify might mean that parties would be reluctant to sign such contracts unless there were substantial gains from the penalty clauses; these factors do not mean that the courts should fail to enforce the contracts once they are signed. The explanation, which has been given in the literature to date, is that the courts are being paternalistic and are protecting the performing party from signing a clause that is not in his best interest.

This argument is difficult to defend. The general principle of enforcement of contract law is that almost anything that parties agree upon will be enforced. Contracts are unenforceable as unconscionable, but (at least until recently) unconscionability has been interpreted in an extremely narrow framework. Moreover, if the courts wanted to interfere to protect parties from their own errors (the essence of paternalism) it would seem that a more obvious place to interfere would be in the case of the amount of the contract. But in fact, while courts will require consideration before enforcing a contract, it is an old and well-settled principle that courts will not question the amount of consideration. If paternalism were a part of contract law, one would expect it to occur here, rather than in the nonenforcement of penalty clauses.

There is another reason why the nonenforcement of penalty clauses, if nonenforcement is economically inefficient, is surprising. The rule seems to be quite an old principle of contract law.[14] The evolutionary models of legal efficiency discussed in Part I argue that, even if inefficient rules are promulgated, they will be litigated until they are overturned. While there are some doubts about these models,[15] they may be expected to apply in situations where both parties have symmetric and ongoing interests in cases of the sort under dispute. Thus, these models should be able to explain efficiency in commercial law in general and especially in contract law. The mechanism postulated in these models also seems to apply in the case of penalty clauses; cases in which the courts are asked to determine if a liquidated damage clause is a penalty are common legal occurrences, and if the nonenforcement of penalties were inefficient, we would expect the principle to have been overturned as a result of private litigation. The long term persistance of this clause, and the lack of paternalism in other areas of contract law, thus create at least a *prima facie* case that there is some economic efficiency basis for the behavior of the courts.

The situation then is that there is a strong presumption that principles of commercial and contract law—especially long established principles—are economically efficient. The rule against penalty clauses is such an established rule, so the presumption must be that it is economically efficient. But any voluntary agreement between two parties can also be assumed to be efficient with respect to the two parties. Is there any way out of the dilemma?

An argument, which can reconcile this paradox, is that while penalty clauses are efficient vis-a-vis the two parties involved, they have effects on third parties that serve to make them, net, inefficient. In particular, contracts with penalty clauses are often not even expectedly self-enforcing, in the sense defined above. That is, when contracts have such clauses, parties may expect attempted breach, and consequent litigation, even if circumstances do not in fact change. The argument rests in part on the insight of Clarkson et al , that is that in many cases the paying party will have an incentive and an ability to retard the performing party in performing its contractual obligations, for such behavior by the paying party would lead to a payment greater than the damages suffered. The performing party would anticipate this behavior, and would charge accordingly. It is not argued that the legal system is correct in disallowing such contracts to avoid these costs, as do Clarkson et al. The argument is rather that such behavior would lead to disputes and would therefore be inefficient in the use of judicial resources.

Consider some agreement between two parties with a liquidated damage clause, but no penalty clause. For an example, assume A has promised to deliver 1,000 widgets to B. If A does not deliver the widgets, B will lose $5,000; the contract is written with $5,000 as the amount of liquidated damages. If A delivers, B will accept delivery and there will be no dispute. A will presumably deliver unless there is some change in circumstances that was not anticipated. If A does not deliver, then the potential of being sued will force A to pay the $5,000; the contract is expectedly self-enforcing.

Now consider the same contract with a penalty clause—if A does not deliver, he must pay $10,000. A now delivers the widgets. What incentives face B? Contractual terms are in general rather complex: A has promised to deliver widgets of a certain type and grade by a certain date and in a certain condition. It is always possible for B to claim that A has in fact violated the contractual terms. Moreover, it is in B's interest to make this claim, for if he can prove that A did not honor the terms of the contract, he is $5,000 better off than if A did fulfill his contract. Thus, this contract is not self-enforcing in the sense that the contract is without the penalty clause. Even if both parties exactly fulfill their contractual obligations, one party has an incentive to try to get out of the contract, or to claim that the other party has violated it. In fact, Telser discusses at some length the possibility of false claims that exist when contracts are not self-enforcing.[16] Presumably, A considered this possibility when contracting, and the price that he has charged is higher to compensate. But there is still a social cost of the contract in terms of the extra judicial resources that will be used in resolving this dispute, and hence the agreement is possibly inefficient.

Moreover, the litigation which would result from this dispute would not be the sort of litigation that the public should subsidize. As discussed above, litigation serves two separate functions—dispute resolution and rule creation. The public subsidy to litigation is due to the rule creation aspect of ligiation. In litigation of penalty clauses, no rules are promulgated. In the example used, A claims that the widgets were delivered as specified and B claims that they were substandard. There is no policy issue here, for the courts would merely look at normal standards for widgets and determine if this particular set met those standards. The decision would have little future value as precedent, since, with penalty clauses, buyers would always have incentives to claim that defective widgets were delivered. Thus, in this type of case, disputes would be purely factual and would have no value to third parties. It is of course true that most such disputes would be settled rather than litigated. The class of transactions would, nonetheless, lead to substantially more disputes than in the case of normal contracts, and would thus create more instances of potential disputes, and hence potential litigation.

In fact, many disputes involving penalty clauses are penalties for late performance. A promises to perform some action by a certain date and to pay some amount for each day after this date on which he has not completed his promised action. However, this does not change the basic form of the argument. B has an incentive to claim that in fact the action was not completed on time, even if it was. Again, when we consider that many transactions are complex, it is plausible that there is room for disagreement about the exact date on which some action was performed. A builds a house for B and it is ready on the promised date, except that the lawn has not yet been planted. Is this part of the required agreement needed or not? A dispute here (or about other, subtler matters) can always arise and, if there is a penalty clause, incentives for such disputes will exist.

IV. SPECIFIC PERFORMANCE

In general, in the case of contract breach, courts will not require specific performance. Rather, money damages will be ordered. An exception seems to be the case of unique goods. In the example used by Anthony Kronman,[17] if A promises to sell you the original manuscript of Hobbes' *Leviathan* and then A attempts breach, he will be forced to comply exactly with the contractual terms. Conversely, if A promises to deliver a batch of ball bearings, the courts will not order such performance but rather will order only damages. In cases of personal service and contracts, such as a promise to build a house, specific performance will not be required.

While Kronman is sometimes able to justify the legal treatment of such contracts, he ultimately concludes that specific performance should be allowed in some situations where it is not now permitted. But the theory advanced here is completely consistent with the case law (as summarized by Kronman). The courts seem willing to enforce those specific performance contracts that are, in the terms used above, expectedly self-enforcing, but are unwilling to enforce contracts that are not self-enforcing.

Consider first the difference between the manuscript of *Leviathan* and 100 ball bearings. In each case, A has promised to deliver some goods (the manuscript, the ball bearings) to B and now wants to be free of the contract. Assume that the court forces specific performance. Then A delivers the manuscript. He cannot perform less than promised; there is only one manuscript, and if it is delivered then the transaction is over. Since the good is unique, A must deliver exactly what is promised and B, upon acceptance, is satisfied. A cannot debase the quality of what he delivers and B cannot claim such debasement. Similar arguments would apply to any unique good, such as a piece of land. A, if forced to deliver, must deliver exactly what was promised and, upon delivery, the contract is settled.

Such is not the case if the promise is to deliver 100 ball bearings that have not yet been manufactured. (If they have been manufactured, then presumably they are unique and specific performance will be ordered.) A now wants to be out of the contract, that is, he would prefer to pay damages and avoid delivery. A is forced to perform. What incentive does A have? His incentive may be to make 100 shoddy ball bearings so as to minimize the cost of fulfilling the contract. The existence of the dispute is evidence that this contract is no longer self-enforcing. If A can make shoddy bearings sufficiently cheap, then he will have delivered as ordered by the courts. B might now claim damages. A might settle, since he did not want to fulfill the contract anyway. However, there is again a dispute between A and B and again the possibility of litigation. Thus, specific performance when one party controls the terms of the performance leads to a nonself-enforcing contract with the attendant possibilities for litigation, and the possibilities for waste of the resources devoted by society to the courts. In the case of unique goods, this possibility does not exist, and it is therefore consistent for courts to enforce specific performance in one case but not in the other.[18]

V. SUMMARY

In this chapter, two types of contracts that are not enforceable were considered—contracts with penalty clauses and contracts for specific performance. Economists have been unable to explain the unwillingness of the courts to enforce penalty clauses, and have argued that such unwillingness was inefficient. The argument of this paper is that all contracts of these types are nonself-enforcing, and that therefore such contracts would lead to substantial numbers of disputes. Parties pay some but not all costs of disputes, and the litigation that would result from these contracts would not create any useful precedents for third parties. Therefore, the behavior of the courts toward these contracts may be an efficient way of utilizing judicial resources, and may not be inefficient. At the least, we might want to devote more research to this issue before advocating substantial changes in judicial behavior regarding these contracts. Finally, it may be useful in future research to determine the effects of various rules on potential litigation and to consider the external effects likely to be created (or not created) by such potential litigation.

In this chapter, certain arguments have been advanced that may explain the behavior of the courts as being economically efficient. Whether these arguments are correct depends not only on the existence of the forces discussed, but also on their magnitude, an issue that has not been addressed. Thus, the arguments advanced here must be considered as speculative and the case as unproven. Similar questions have been raised in the literature about the general applicability of economic analysis to questions of legal efficiency.[19] Until specific empirical testing of the theory has been performed, such questions are legitimate.[20] However, before such testing can be carried out, it is necessary to identify factors that can, at least potentially, explain the shape of the law in terms of economics, so that we know which factors should be measured in order to test the theory. This chapter may be viewed as an attempt to specify such factors in the case of certain unenforceable contracts.[21]

NOTES

1. Richard A. Posner, *Economic Analysis of Law* (Boston: Little, Brown, 1977).

2. Kenneth W. Clarkson, Roger Leroy Miller, and Timothy J. Muris, "Liquidated Damages v. Penalties: Sense or Nonsense?," *Wisconsin Law Review* (1978): 351-90.

3. Anthony T. Kronman and Richard A. Posner, *The Economics of Contract Law* (Boston: Little, Brown, 1979), p. 224.

4. Anthony T. Kronman, "Specific Performance," *University of Chicago Law Review* 45 (1978): 351.

5. Lester G. Telser, "A Theory of Self-enforcing Agreements," *Journal of Business* 53 (1980): 27.

6. Richard A. Posner, "Some Uses and Abuses of Economics in Law," *University of Chicago Law Review* 46 (1979): 281-306.

7. Posner, *Economic Analysis of Law*, chap. 4.

8. William M. Landes and Richard A. Posner, "Adjudication as a Private Good," *Journal of Legal Studies* 8 (1979): 235.

9. Donald Wittman, "Prior Regulation Versus Post Liability: The Choice Between Input and Output Monitoring," *Journal of Legal Studies* 6 (1977): 193.

10. Charles J. Goetz and Robert E. Scott, "Liquidated Damages, Penalties, and the Just Compensation Principle: Some Notes on an Enforcement Model and a Theory of Efficient Breach," *Columbia Law Review* 77 (1977): 554.

11. Posner, *Economic Analysis of Law*, p. 93.

12. Clarkson, Miller, and Muris, "Liquidated Damages v. Penalties," p. 351.

13. Kronman and Posner, *The Economics of Contract Law*, p. 224. However, Muris has recently argued that the failure by the courts to enforce penalty clauses is not due to paternalism; he argues that the parties to legal agreements would themselves sometimes choose to have the courts not enforce penalty clauses when one party had behaved opportunistically. See Timothy J. Muris, "Opportunistic Behavior and the Law of Contracts," *Minnesota Law Review* vol. 65 no. 4, (April 1981), pp. 521-90.

14. Clarkson et al., "Liquidated Damages v. Penalties," p. 351, indicate that the principle dates from at least the 17th century.

15. Robert Cooter and Lewis Kornhauser, "Can Litigation Improve the Law Without the Help of Judges?," *Journal of Legal Studies* 9 (1980): 139.

16. Telser, "A Theory of Self-enforcing Agreements," p. 43.

17. Kronman, "Specific Performance," p. 224.

18. Alan Schwartz, "The Case For Specific Performance," *Yale Law Journal* 89 (1979): 271, argues that in some cases specific performance should be ordered, and that the courts should appoint special masters, to be paid for by the contracting parties, in order to monitor such specific performance. If this were done, then the parties would be paying for the monitoring, and the argument raised in this paper would no longer be relevant. However, this is not now commonly done.

19. For examples, see Mario Rizzo, "Law Amid Flux," *Journal of Legal Studies* 9 (1980): 291; and Gordon Tullock, "Two Kinds of Legal Efficiency," *Hofstra Law Review* vol. 8, (1980), pp. 659-69.

20. For a futher discussion of this point, see Paul H. Rubin, "Predicability and the Economic Approach to Law: A Comment on Rizzo," *Journal of Legal Studies* 9 (1980): 319; chap. 10, below.

21. Martin Perry has pointed out that gratuitous promises would not be self-enforcing in the sense that the term is used here, since the promisor would have no incentive to carry out the promise. This is an additional reason, in addition to those suggested by Richard Posner, "Gratuituous Promises in Economics and Law," *Journal of Legal Studies* 6 (1977): 411, for the reluctance of the courts to enforce such agreements.

CHAPTER 5

Covenants
Not to Compete

I. INTRODUCTION

The common law generally does not enforce contracts in restraint of trade. An exception is made, however, for certain restrictive covenants. One class of such covenants are those signed by an employee who agrees not to compete with his employer for some period of time after termination of employment. Common law judges seemed to view these contracts as creating some monopoly power that is, however, justified by other interests. George Stigler[1], in his analysis of such covenants, also assumes that monopoly power (of masters, in master-apprentice contracts) is the relevant feature. It will be the argument of this chapter that such contracts were not based on monopoly power, but served different functions. In particular, in some circumstances, restrictive covenants were, and are, necessary to lead to efficient amounts of investment in human capital. Moreover, we will examine the behavior of courts in enforcing such contracts in order to ascertain if in fact enforcement may be viewed as being efficient, in the sense that much of the common law may be considered efficient. Since these are contracts between two parties with symmetric interests, the theory discussed in Part I would predict that they should be efficiently enforced.

In his seminal work on human capital, Gary Becker[2] has distinguished between "general" and "specific" on-the-job training. "General training is useful in many firms besides those providing it."[3] "Training that increased productivity more in firms providing it will be called specific training."[4] The concept of human capital has been one of the most fruitful innovations in economic theory in recent times;[5] moreover, on-the-job training is empirically very important in explaining observed patterns of earnings.[6] However, there are situations in which a basic result of the Becker model—that employees will pay for general training—will not hold because of peculiar features of training markets. One source of information about the functioning of real world labor markets is an examination of labor contracts. An examination of these contracts and of the legal treatment of labor relationships should be useful in understanding labor markets; conversely, an examination of the economics of training markets may shed light on the legal behaviors involved. Such an examination will be the purpose of this chapter. Section II discusses the general nature of the relevant contracts. Section III considers the economics of training markets in more detail. Sections IV and V discuss the way in which the law has dealt with the labor relationships. Section VI considers covenants not to compete ancillary to the sale of a business. The last section is a summary.

II. THE NATURE OF THE CONTRACTS

Throughout this chapter, we will be concerned with situations where a contract serves to restrict the activities in which an employee may engage after termination of employment. For various reasons, discussed in more detail below, an employer might want to constrain an employee to work for him for a certain period of time. However, it is an old and well-established principle of law that, in general, courts will not order specific performance—that is, a contract that requires that one continue to work for a firm for some period of time will not be enforced. The reason given for this refusal is generally in terms of avoiding involuntary servitude; indeed, part of the reluctance may stem from constitutional and statutory bans on indentured servitude. However, an alternative explanation is also available. It may simply be true that enforcement of such contracts would be very expensive for the courts, as discussed in Chapter 4. Such enforcement would require that the courts, or their agents, monitor the performance of employees and ascertain the amount of effort that was being provided. It does appear to be true that, in cases where performance is easily checked due to the unique characteristic of the item involved, such as in contracts for the sale of real estate, the courts will, in fact, order specific performance.[7] However, we need not concern ourselves with the reason for the court's reluctance to enforce such agreements but begin with the situation in which both parties are aware of this reluctance.

There is an alternative method of enforcing compliance by employees. This is to limit in the employment contract alternatives for the employee. If firm *A* spends money and resources training an employee to be a skilled basket weaver, this skill is valuable to any firm that hires basket weavers. However, if the employee has signed an enforceable agreement promising not to engage in basket weaving for five years after leaving the employment of firm A, then the employee has effectively agreed to work for firm A or to cease weaving baskets for five years. If he is much more valuable as a basket weaver than in any other trade, then he will continue to work for A. Thus, restrictive covenants in a labor contract effectively enable parties to contract for long periods of time. An example of such a covenant, taken from a recent contracts casebook,[8] is:

> Restrictive Covenant. The parties agree that Employer's talent packaging business is nationwide in scope and would suffer serious damage and loss of goodwill if Employee entered into direct competition immediately after termination of this agreement with the same customers and based in the same techniques and information used by Employer.
>
> For a period of two years after the termination of this agreement, the Employee therefore convenants that he will not in New York City or Los Angeles, California, directly or indirectly, own, manage, operate, control, be employed by, participate in, or be connected in any manner with the ownership, management, operation, or control of any business similar to the type of business conducted by the Employer at the time of the termination of this agreement.

We have not yet discussed explicitly the reason for desiring to so constrain employees. Presumably, since both parties voluntarily sign the agreement, it must serve to increase the value of resources. In the next section, we discuss the nature of employment relations and show how such agreements may be value maximizing.

III. TYPES OF HUMAN CAPITAL

Specific human capital and general human capital are the polar opposites of markets for types of training. Thus, if training is specific, there is only one firm that can employ the trained worker. After training, the worker is worth more to this firm than to any other potential employer. The employer, knowing this, will pay the worker more than any other employer in order to retain the worker and recoup his investment. However, in order to pay this higher wage, the employer will require the worker to pay for part of the specific training. Thus, employers and workers will share the cost and the gain from specific training. In the case of general training, the trained worker faces a competitive market. There will be many bidders for his talent. Thus, the employer knows that he will be required to pay the full market price for the trained worker, and hence the employer will not pay for any training. Conversely, the worker knows that he will receive the full value of his training and therefore the worker will be willing to pay for any such training.

In both of these market structures, prices are determinate. Thus, both parties to labor transactions can be certain about the future value of any training that is received, and can plan their investments accordingly. There is no uncertainity in either case (except for the normal uncertainty about future changes in demand or technology). Training in both cases will be efficient, in the sense that money will be spent on training to the point where the cost of the training will be equal to the present value. Moreover, notice that there has been no mention of labor contracts. Such contracts would have no relevance in the market structures considered. If training is truly specific, the employer needs no assurance that the worker will continue to work for him, for there is no other market in which the employee can sell his skill. If training is truly general, the employee knows that he can recoup his investment by quitting the current employer and going to work for any of a number of other firms. There is no value to either party of a long-term contract.

Thus, in the two cases analyzed by Becker, there is no need for any contractual term limiting the future market behavior of the worker; market forces will serve to generate solutions without such contracts. But in fact we observe that many employment contracts do contain clauses that limit the future behavior of employees, and that such contracts are common sources of legal dispute[9]. Therefore, there must be some aspects of real world labor markets that Becker's analysis does not fully capture. As we will argue more fully below, the lacuna in the Becker analysis is in terms of types of general training. In particular, there are some types of general training for which the worker will not pay. Assume, for example, that it takes a firm one day to teach some worker the details of a trade secret, which is valuable to many other firms, and is worth $100,000. In this case, the value of the information is so great that the worker cannot pay for it by accepting reduced wages. Moreover, because of difficulties in borrowing with human capital as collateral, there may be no other way in which the worker can finance the acquisition of human capital with sufficient high value.[10] If the worker borrows the money needed to finance the acquisition of the capital, then the lender has as security for his loan only the human capital of the worker. However, the inability of the worker to sign a binding contract, which creates the difficulty for the employer, also creates the same problem for the lender. Human capital cannot serve as collateral for loans because of the impossibility of compelling specific performance, In this circumstance, the firm would want the worker to sign a noncompetition clause, for such a clause would indicate that the worker could not use the training acquired anywhere else. Thus, covenants not to compete would be signed by workers who received general training with value sufficiently high so that the worker could not finance the acquisition of this training by accepting reduced wages.

Once the worker has received this training, however, an incentive for opportunistic behavior is created.[11] The worker has an incentive to try to violate the contract and profit from his training—either by going to work for himself or by going to work for another firm, which will pay him a premium because of the value of his training. In this situation, the worker is attempting to appropriate for himself the value of training for which he did not pay. If workers were able to do this, then the incentive for firms to invest in acquiring valuable information would be greatly reduced, for firms would not be able to protect such valuble information. We are specifically dealing here with cases where information cannot be protected by patent, and where therefore trade secrets are used.

Another inefficiency could be created if firms were not able to contractually require workers not to use valuable information elsewhere. If information is not protected by contract, then firms might spend resources in other ways to protect this information; this point is made by Posner in his discussion of privacy regulation.[12] For example, if some process requires three steps, and the process is secret, there are two potential methods of protecting the secrecy. One is to allow one employee to undertake all three steps but to bind this employee by a contract not to use the acquired information elsewhere. An alternative is to teach each of three employees only one of the three steps, so that no one employee will know enough to compete with the firm. It is possible, however, that the production process will be more costly if the second method of protection is used. (If not, then the second method would always be used and the law is irrelevant.) Thus, if the noncompetition clause is not binding, firms will be forced to use more costly methods of production in some circumstances in order to protect their proprietary information.

The argument so far is that firms will use noncompetition clauses in contracts when employees acquire certain types of general training in the course of employment, and that it is worthwhile for the courts to enforce such clauses in order to lead to efficient levels of investment in new technologies and to economize on unneccesarily expensive ways of protecting such information. Moreover, workers would have an incentive to behave opportunistically, to try to violate such contracts and capture for themselves the value of the information acquired. However, there may be a symmetry here; that is, firms would also have an incentive to behave opportunistically and to try to pay workers less than the full value of their marginal product, even after adjusting for human capital investments.

Assume that the courts will enforce all covenants not to compete in labor contracts. Some types of employment relationships will involve both types of general training—general training for which the worker will pay in the normal manner, by accepting reduced wages,and general training for which the worker cannot pay because of its high value. If the worker signs a covenant, then he would be unable to use any of the training in alternative employments. Presumably, then, the employer would be forced to finance all of the investment, since it would all be specific. However, if the worker then left this place of employment, some of his training would be valuable to many firms and its use would not cost the original employer anything, and yet the worker would be constrained from using this training; that is, there is a cost to not using general training (absent trade secrets). Thus, the covenant not to compete should ideally apply only to those types of training that involve trade secrets of the employer.

It may, however, be difficult or impossible to draft a contract with sufficient specificity to include in the covenant only the training that the employer desires to protect.The employer may not know in advance for exactly what sort of work a particular employee is best suited, and thus may not be able to specify contractually which information is to be protected. Moreover, the nature of trade secrets is often such that the details cannot be written down; the secret may consist of a series of actions involving a particular process.[13] Of course, even when the secret can be written down in a contract, the actual act of writing will itself seriously compromise the secrecy of information. Thus, the contract not to compete will, of necessity, involve some ambiguity. The employer may have an incentive to behave opportunistically and underpay the worker relative to the value of that part of the general training that the worker has financed, if the employer believes that the existence of the covenant will reduce the worker's mobility. There would thus be an inefficiency in enforcing all restrictive covenants, just as there would be an inefficiency in enforcing none of them. In such circumstances, the courts, in enforcing covenants not to compete, may have a useful function to perform. Specifically, when disputes about the terms of contracts arise the courts may attempt to determine just what sorts of information were expected by the parties to be included in the covenant, and to enforce the contract accordingly. This is consistent with the view that, in the case of ambiguous contracts, the role of the courts is, in general, to determine what the parties would have done had they predicted the apparently unforeseen circumstance.[14]

In summary, then, we have the following situation. Workers will be unable to pay the full value of some training that they will receive from firms, and will therefore sign contracts with clauses banning the workers from competing with former employers. Once the contracts are signed and the workers trained, then both workers and employers may have incentives to behave opportunistically: employees will have incentives to attempt to violate the contracts and sell the information acquired; employers will have incentives to underpay workers for general training for which the workers have themselves paid. If the courts are to be economically efficient in enforcement of contracts with these clauses, they must attempt to separate the two types of behavior.

Our explanation of covenants not to compete is in terms of human capital. We argue that such clauses are needed in order to lead to efficient levels of investment in training in circumstances where the person receiving training is unable to pay for the human capital by accepting reduced wages. An alternative explanation may be that such contracts serve to smooth out lifetime earnings of employees. Employers might choose to pay employees more than their marginal product in early years of employment and less than their marginal product later; this would provide employees with a smoother income pattern than payment according to marginal productivity would provide. If this were done, then at some point marginal products of employees would become greater than earnings, and employees would have an incentive to seek work in other firms where they could be paid their full marginal product. If employers did pay employees in this manner, then they would want contractual guarantees to prevent the employees from leaving. If this explanation were correct, we would expect to observe contracts with covenants not to compete in virtually all industries, for we might expect all workers to prefer such smoothing and thus all firms to provide it. However, this is not what is observed. Rather, as will be indicated, contracts with such covenants occur almost entirely in industries and situations in which training is important, and litigation over the contracts invariably involves determination of types of information acquired. Thus, a theory based on income smoothing does not seem to accord with the empirical observations, which indicate that such contracts always involve information acquisition. Therefore, the theory proposed here seems superior to the alternative. (It is, of course, possible that the litigated cases are a biased sample of all situations in which noncompetition contracts are signed; we have no evidence on the incidence of the contracts except the litigated cases. However, *a priori*, this does not seem likely.)

IV. LEGAL ANALYSIS: GENERAL CONSIDERATIONS

As is commonly the case, the language used in the legal decisions is not fully consistent with the underlying economic rationality. (As is also commonly the case, this inconsistency in language does not mean that the legal decisions are themselves inconsistent with the economics, for the latter proposition must be independently tested.) Litigation about contracts not to compete is generally between the employer, who is seeking enforcement of such a contract, and a former employee who has allegedly violated the contract. Thus, the courts seek to balance the interests of the employer and the employee, as well as to make sure public policy is not violated.[15] The legal language, which conflicts with the economic analysis, indicates that contracts will be enforced if their provisions are not "overly harsh" or do not create "undue burdens," remembering always that employees probably have insufficient bargaining power and are often forced to sign contracts of adhesion (standard form contracts) or seek employment elsewhere.[16]

The economic theory of contracts would indicate that all of these considerations are irrelevant. At the time a contract is signed, both parties must prospectively expect to benefit from the agreement, independent of their respective bargaining power. If an employer places a restrictive clause in an employment contract, he will reduce the supply of potential employees and thus will pay a higher wage to those persons who choose to work for him. Thus, employers will not put clauses in contracts unless the gain to the employer from including the clause is greater than the cost in higher wages that the contract will entail.

At the time when the contract is signed, the employee expects to benefit from the agreement. The common situation is one in which the employee is given some training that is valuable. If he signs the contract, then he must anticipate that, over the life of the agreement, his wages will be sufficiently increased as a result of the contract so that, net, it is worth signing. This increase in wages will occur for two reasons: first, because the contract makes the human capital that the employee will acquire specific to the firm providing the training (since the employee has contracted not to use this human capital elsewhere), the firm will pay the employee while he is acquiring the human capital;

in general, firms will pay for the acquisition of specific human capital. Second, once the employee has acquired the human capital, he is worth more to the firm than he would otherwise have been worth, and his salary will therefore be higher as a result. It will, however, not be as high as his marginal product to the firm after training, for part of the increment in productivity will have already been used in paying for the training. Thus, if the emloyee could appropriate for himself this additional human capital, he could earn more than the firm will pay him after training. By assumption, the training is specific only as a result of the contract; then, if the contract could be breached, the worker could increase his earnings above what the training firm would pay. As a result, workers have an incentive to challenge clauses that bind them not to compete after they have received training from the firm. This incentive is no different from the incentive of any party to a contract to get out of a contract after the other party has completed his obligation and before the initial party has completed his. The apparent desire of the court to protect the worker from harsh contractual terms is misplaced.

The other party to the dispute is the employer, who generally argues that his business will be harmed in some way if the employee is allowed to compete with the firm. But firms do not have rights to be free from competition, from former employees or from anyone else. In competitive industries, one more firm entering the market would have no effect on any competitor; in imperfectly competitive industries, the public (and hence economically efficient law) should encourage additional entry. Thus, arguments by firms based on intuitive (and misleading) notions of "fairness" are as economically misdirected as arguments by workers based on "unequal bargaining power." Moreover, firms would also have incentives to attempt to change retroactively the terms of the initial agreement. Assume, for example, that some employee receives some general training from the firm. Presumably, the employee has paid for this training through receiving lower wages during the term of the training. If this training is truly general then the employee might well choose to enter the business in competition with his former employer, or to work for another firm that will pay for the training; presumably the employer considered this possibility in deciding the wage to pay the employee during the training period. However, once the training is given, the employer would have an incentive not to pay the worker the full value of his marginal product. In this circumstance, it would be efficient to deny the employer the right to restrain the employee from competing. We thus have a situation in which neither party to a particular dispute has any incentive to make economically relevant arguments, and it is therefore not surprising to find that the language used by the courts in deciding cases involving clauses not to compete is not couched in the terms that an economist would use to analyze the decisions. As mentioned earlier, failure to use the language of economics does not mean that the decisions are economically incorrect, for one of the major advances of the literature applying economics to law has been to demonstrate that often the economic logic underlying the law is implicit[17] rather than explicit, and so might be the case here. In Part I it was shown that it is sometimes possible for the legal system to reach economically desirable outcomes independent of the knowledge of economics possessed by parties to disputes.[18]

V. LEGAL ANALYSIS: SPECIFIC RULES

Though the terms and ideas expressed in the legal cases are not the terms of economics, the cases do in fact seem to follow closely the arguments already given; that is, a close reading of the cases involving competition between employers and former employees indicates that the economic analysis can explain the decisions reached in the cases. Evidence indicates that there are two types of information most commonly at issue: customer lists and trade secrets. We will consider each in turn. The cases cited are primarily examples of the points discussed. They are representative, not exhaustive, of the pertinent case law.

A. Customer Lists

In many businesses, the list of customers is a valuable commodity. For example, many businesses require salesmen to call on customers periodically. It is then possible for these salesmen to develop close relationships with these customers and to learn their demands. If the salesmen leave the business and go into business for themselves or for a competitor, they may then solicit business from these customers. Judging from the number of cases involving this practice, it seems to be common. Moreover, disputes regarding customer lists can arise in situations in which there is no contractual prohibition on competition by past employees as well as in cases where there are agreements not to compete. How does the law handle such disputes?

In general, the legal results are quite close to what the economic analysis would predict. The most important distinction in law is the amount of effort required to develop customer lists. If the list of customers is simply a list that generally is available to firms engaged in some business or is a list of one-time customers, then the courts have refused to protect the firm's property in this list. Courts have held as unreasonable a covenant not to compete signed by a real estate salesperson[19] and one signed by a desk clerk for a car rental agency.[20] These covenants were declared unenforceable since the courts found that these employees had no special knowledge about the employer's past, present, or potential customers. Furthermore, in the real estate and car rental industry, the customers tended to be transient rather than repeaters. If a customer is not likely to seek the employers' services or products a second time, there is an insufficient reason to restrain potential competition from former employees. Thus, forbidding past employees from competing would not create any useful incentives.

Conversely, if a firm can show that it spent time and resources in developing its customer list, then a past employee who has signed an otherwise reasonable covenant not to compete generally will be banned from using this information.[21] If resources are required to establish a list of customers and if the list is not protected, then there will be an incentive to invest too few resources in developing lists of customers. Thus, this rule seems economically efficient. Moreover, it seems to be the main rule used by the courts in determining whether to afford protection to an employer. Many other criteria are mentioned by the courts (one is, that if an employee has memorized a list of customers, he may solicit these customers, but if he has copied the list in writing he may not[22]) but in fact a close reading of the cases indicates that it is almost always the effort spent by the firm in acquiring the customer list that will govern.

Another area of interest is the geographic scope of restrictive covenants. The legal analysis is in terms of the "reasonableness" of the scope of the covenant. However, a reading of the cases again indicates that the underlying rationale is fully consistent with the economic analysis. When the information acquired by the employee is simply information about customers, then the allowed geographic scope of the restriction is the area that contains these customers. For example, a contract may forbid an employee to compete in a geographical area (city, state, nation), but the employee may have dealt with customers only in one part of that area. Under this circumstance, the court will void the contract not to compete.[23] Restricting potential competition is reasonable only to the extent that a former employee has learned information from the employer that was costly to acquire. If an employee knew the employer's customers in the northeastern part of a city but had no knowledge of the employer's customers elsewhere, there is no reasonable basis for restraining this employee's future competition in the areas other than the northeastern part of the city.[24]

An employee dealing with customers in situations under discussion will learn two things. First, he will learn the nature of the business and, perhaps, some interpersonal sales skills. This training will be general, in the sense that any firm that requires dealing with customers would pay for the same skills. Second, the employee will learn the particular desires and habits of the customers of this particular firm. This training is also general, in that any other firm in the same business would find the information valuable. However, to the extent that the firm spent resources in acquiring this information, then it is likely to be of the sort that is too valuable for the employee to pay for. If this is so, then the information should be protected. Thus, the courts, in looking at the expense required for the firm to have developed the information in the customer lists, are probably correctly separating the areas of the employment relationship in which the covenant was meant to apply. Similarly, in the geographic cases, by forbidding competition with former customers the courts are probably forbidding the salesman from using capital for which he did not pay. By allowing competition with customers in other areas, the courts are allowing the salesman to utilize the general skills that he acquired during his employment and that were not considered in the noncompetition covenant. Thus, the analysis in the customer list cases seems quite consistent with the economic discussion presented in the earlier part of this chapter.

B. Trade Secrets

In general, trade secrets are given substantially more protection than customer lists. The common law had made it unlawful for an employee to disclose details about the employer's trade secret whether or not a covenant not to compete exists. Therefore, often the critical issue is the existence of a valid trade secret. It is not always clear whether important information, which has been developed by the employer, attains trade-secret status. One way an employer can be assured of protection is to have the employees with access to this confidential information sign reasonable agreements not to compete.[25]

Moreover, courts have allowed employers to place a much broader geographical scope on restricting the use of trade secrets than on the use of customer lists. The crucial issue is whether the employer needs this expansive protection or whether the covenant not to compete is unduly harsh on the employee's ability to secure gainful employment. When considering the employer's confidential information, such as trade secrets, many courts have decided in favor of the employer's protection despite a very broad territorial limitation. For example, in a Georgia case involving the well-known Orkin Exterminating Company,[26] the State Supreme Court discussed a restrictive covenant that applied a noncompetition limitation to the entire geographical area where the company was in business. In essence, this restraint amounted to a nationwide ban on the employee's right to participate in the pest control industry. Since the employee had obtained knowledge about Orkin's secret processes and since the company could have sent the employee anywhere to work, the Georgia Supreme Court held that the broad geographical restriction remained reasonable and enforceable. The following states the court's logic:

> The mere fact that while the employer does business in the entire territory, the employee did not work all the territory, would not render it unreasonable to bar the employee as provided in the contract (cite omitted). It is shown by this record that the employee had access to business information, data, technical developments and other restricted information belonging to the employer. Thus it is shown that the restriction is necessary to protect the employer. The evidence shows that this business is highly competitive and secret, which requires continued changes in engineering and technical skill. This employee is shown to have had access to such information, and he was given courses of training which could be used against the employer. In the light of this undisputed evidence, the fact that the employee did not actually work in all the territory embraced in the restriction is immaterial. His knowledge of the employer's business as thus acquired could be effectively used to the detriment of the employer throughout the territory embraced since the employer was doing business in that entire area. The employee was trained for the kind of work carried on throughout the area covered by the restriction and under the contract he was subject to be sent to all parts of that area. We hold that the restrictive covenant upon which this action is brought is legal, valid and enforceable.[27]

Restrictive covenants have been enforced in order to protect an employer's investment of time and money in developing expertise in the pest control[28] and in the wet shave razor industries.[29] However, courts have refused to enforce covenants not to compete based on protecting the employer's confidential information in the car rental business,[30] the real estate sales business,[31] and the travel agency business.[32] These latter cases involved companies that did not possess specialized information. Indeed, the courts held that what the employees had learned during their employment could have been learned from any similar company. If an employer argues for enforcement of a noncompetition agreement based on confidential information and fails to distinguish between confidential information and information available to the general trade, the covenant not to compete likely will be an unreasonable and unenforceable restraint on competition.[33]

Even though a company may actually have information that is subject to protection, covenants not to compete will not be enforced automatically. Of course, such agreements must not be overly burdensome as to the activity, time, and geographical restraints. Furthermore, the employer must be thorough in restricting those employees who have had access to the confidential information from competition. In other words, the employer must be careful to indicate the importance of this information by taking steps to assure its secrecy is maintained.[34]

Employers will sometimes attempt to restrain employees who have learned no special knowledge from their employment. As argued above, if all human capital provided is general capital, then we would expect the employee to pay for this capital by accepting reduced wages. The employer might, nonetheless, have an incentive to attempt to restrain such an employee from competition in order to reduce wages after training has occurred. The courts are, in general, unwilling to allow such restraint to occur, as would be consistent with economic efficiency.[35]

VI. SALE OF BUSINESS

When a business is sold, a common clause in the contract of sale is a clause that binds the seller from competing with the buyer; clauses similar to those discussed above in connection with employment contracts. However, the courts are much more lenient in interpreting these contracts. That is, courts are much more likely to enforce contracts not to compete by sellers of businesses than by employees of firms. The explanation given by legal authorities for this greater leniency is generally in terms of the greater wealth and greater bargaining power of the seller of a business relative to a former employee. A typical statement of the legal reasoning is:

> The average, individual employee has little but his labor to sell or use to make a living. He is often in urgent need of selling it and in no position to object to boiler plate restrictive covenants placed before him to sign. To him, the right to work and support his family is the

most important right he possesses. His individual bargaining power is seldom equal to that of his employer. Moreover, an employee ordinarily is not on the same plane with the seller of an established business. He is more apt than the seller to be coerced into an oppressive agreement. Under pressure of need and with little opportunity for choice, he is more likely than the seller to make a rash, improvident promise that, for the sake of present gain, may tend to impair his power to earn a living, impoverish him, render him a public charge or deprive the community of his skill and training. The seller has the proceeds of sale on which to live during his period of readjustment. A seller is usually paid an increased price for agreeing to a period of abstention. The abstention is a part of the thing sold and is often absolutely necessary in order to secure to the buyer the things he has bought. Usually the employee gets no increased compensation for agreeing to the abstention; it is usually based on no other consideration than the employment itself.[36]

For reasons discussed above, it is clear that this argument is incorrect in economic terms. A party will not sign a contract unless he expects to gain from the agreement, whether he be an employee or a seller of a business. Whether it is efficient to enforce a contract is independent of the relative wealth or bargaining power of the signers.

A buyer would want, and be willing to pay for, a noncompetition clause because the seller may have particular knowledge which may mean that, should he compete, the value of the business to the buyer will be reduced. The types of knowledge are the same as in the employment contracts. Thus, the seller may have built up good will and contacts with customers such that, should he go into competition with the former business, he will capture most of the business. Second, he may have trade secrets that were sold with the business; should he begin competing, the value of these trade secrets to the buyer would be less than the bargained-for price. In these circumstances, if the seller is not able to enter into a binding noncompetition contract, the value of the business would be reduced, and less businesses would be sold. Thus, prohibition of covenants not to compete by sellers of businesses would impede the flow of resources into higher valued uses, since, absent such covenants, buyers would pay less for businesses and thus some would not be sold.

Why would the courts be more willing to enforce covenants ancillary to the sale of a business than covenants ancillary to employment contracts? In the discussion of employment contracts, we argued that either party to the contract, the firm or the employee, might have an incentive to behave opportunistically; the employee might attempt to capitalize on the information that he acquired but did not pay for, and the employer might attempt to use a covenant to avoid paying the employee for some training for which the employee did pay. Thus, since there were opportunities for both parties to cheat on the agreement, the courts were required to examine the behavior of both parties to the contract. However, this is not true in the case of the sale of a business. The seller of a business could behave opportunistically by opening a competing business in violation of the agreement; the courts will restrain this behavior. The buyer of the business, however, has no further obligations to the seller once the purchase is complete, so there is no chance for the buyer to behave opportunistically toward the seller. Since this is so, if there is a dispute after sale of a business, it is likely to be a result of opportunistic behavior on the part of the seller, and hence the courts are probably correct in being more willing to enforce these contracts than those involving the employment relationship.[37]

VII. SUMMARY AND CONCLUSIONS

In the model of human capital proposed by Gary Becker, there is no need for covenants ancillary to labor contracts that ban employees from competing with employers after termination of employment. If human capital is general, then workers will pay for training and employers will be indifferent as to the future use of this capital. If training is specific, then the training will be of use only in the firm providing the training and so workers will be unable to use this training elsewhere. In actuality, however, we observe that many employment contracts are written with covenants that forbid the employee from competing with the employer after the termination of employment. The existence of these contracts is evidence that the standard model of human capital is incomplete; there must be forms of human capital that are not considered.

The argument advanced here is that there are two types of general training. In some cases, the value of general training is sufficiently high so that the trainee is unable to pay for such training, especially by accepting reduced wages during the training period. When this is the case, a firm will commonly have the employee sign an agreement not to use this training in a competing business. If it were not for the possibility of signing such agreements, then firms would find their incentives for investment in valuable informa-tion reduced. However, the existence of such contracts means that there are incentives for both parties to the agreement to behave opportunistically. Employees have an incentive to violate the agreement by using the information in competing businesses; firms have an incentive to underpay employees who have acquired information for which the employee has himself paid, if the firm can claim that all information is covered by the covenant. The courts seem to have been successful in determining which types of contracts should be enforced. In the case of a contract restricting competition by the seller of a business, there is no chance for the buyer to behave opportunistically, and thus the greater willingness of the courts to enforce these contracts (relative to employment contracts) is also consistent with the analysis presented here.

This research may also have policy implications. Frank Kottke[38] and others[39] have recently argued that courts should be less willing to enforce covenants not to compete than has been true in the past in order to make entry into concentrated industries easier. However, the evidence, which we have adduced here, indicates that the courts have done a good job of determining which covenants should efficiently be enforced. If these suggestions were adopted, the major effect would probably be to reduce the incentive of firms to invest in acquiring economically valuable information and to increase litigation costs.

Covenants not to compete are a part of the law of "unfair competition," and deal with symmetric interests between parties. This chapter has provided evidence of the efficiency of one part of the law, whereas Chapter 6 provides further evidence on another aspect. However, this chapter may have served an additional purpose. It was demonstrated that the economic analysis of human capital as traditionally used is somewhat incomplete, and there are types of human capital other than those analyzed by Gary Becker. Thus, an analysis of the legal cases has enabled us to better understand the economics involved in training markets; the legal analysis and the economic analysis were complementary.

NOTES

1. George J. Stigler, "Restraints on Trade in the Common Law," in *Organization of Industry* (Ill.: Richard D. Irwin, 1968), p. 255.
2. Gary S. Becker, *Human Capital* (New York: Columbia University Press, 1964).
3. Ibid., p. 11.
4. Ibid., p. 18.
5. For a survey indicating the importance in economics of this concept, see Mark Blaug, "The Empirical Status of Human Capital Theory: A Slightly Jaundiced Survey," *Journal of Economic Literature* 14 (1976): 827.

6. See Jacob Mincer, *Schooling, Experience and Earnings* (Cambridge, Mass.: National Bureau of Economic Research, 1974).

7. Richard A. Posner, *Economic Analysis of Law* (Boston: Little, Brown, 1977).

8. Addison Mueller and Arthur I. Rosett, *Contract Law And Its Application* (Mineola, N. Y.: Foundation Press, 1971), pp. 567–68.

9. In addition to the cases cited below, see Harlan M. Blake, "Employee Agreements Not to Compete," *Harvard Law Review* 73 (1960): 625.

10. George J. Stigler, "Imperfections in the Capital Market," *Journal of Political Economy* 75 (1967), reprinted in Stigler, *The Organization of Industry*, p. 113.

11. Benjamin Klein, Robert G. Crawford, and Armen A. Alchian, "Vertical Integration, Appropriable Rents, and the Competitive Contracting Process," *Journal of Law and Economics* 21 (1978): 297.

12. Richard A. Posner, "The Right of Privacy," *Georgia Law Review* 21 (1978): 393.

13. For some examples, see Oliver E. Williamson, "Transaction-Cost Economics: The Governance of Contractual Relations," *Journal of Law and Economics* 22 (1979): 233; see also Edmund W. Kitch, "The Law and Economics of Rights in Valuable Information," *Journal of Legal Studies* 9 (1980): 683.

14. Posner, *Economic Analysis of Law*, chap. 4.

15. For a discussion of the balancing between the employer's and employee's interests, see *Gillette Co. v. Williams*, 360 F. Supp. 1171, 1174 (D. Conn. 1973); *Career Placement of White Plains, Inc. v. Vaus*, 77 Misc. 2d 788, 354 N.Y.S.2d 764, 772 (Sup. Ct., Westchester Co. 1974); and *Standard Register Co. v. Kerrigan*, 238 S.C. 54, 119 S.E.2d 533, 540 (1961). The needs of the "public" were discussed by the courts in *American Hot Rod Ass'n., Inc. v. Carrier*, 500 F.2d 1269, 1277 (4th Cir. 1974); *Lloyd Damsey, M.D., P.A. v. Mankowitz, M.D.*, 339 So.2d 282, 283 (Fla. App. Ct. 1976), cert. denied. 345 So.2d 421 (Fla. Sup. Ct. 1977); *Hefelfinger v. David*, 305 So.2d 823, 824 (Fla. App. Ct. 1975); and *C.G. Caster Co. v. Regan*, 43 Ill. App.3d 663, 357 N.E.2d 162, 165 (1976).

16. *Restatement of Contracts* (1932), sec. 514.

17. Posner, *Economic Analysis of Law*.

18. Paul H. Rubin, "Why is the Common Law Efficient?," *Journal of Legal Studies* 6 (1977): 51; see chap. 1.

19. *Vander Werf v. Zunica Realty Co.*, 59 Ill. App.2d 173, 208 N.E.2d 74, 77 (1965).

20. *Behnke v. Hertz Corp.*, 70 Wis.2d 818, 235 N.W.2d 690, 693 (1975).

21. See *House of Tools & Engineering, Inc. v. Price*, 504 S.W.2d 157, 159 (Mo. App. Ct. 1973); and *Cascade Exchange, Inc. v. Reed*, 278 Or. 749, 565 P.2d 1095, 1098 (1977). Even though a list of customers may not be secret, an employer may have an urgent need to prohibit a former employee from soliciting the customers he has dealt with when that employee was the sole contact between the customer and the business. A typical example of this situation involves the route salesperson who calls on the customers and delivers the products ordered. See *Miller v. Frankfort Bottle Gas, Inc.*, 136 Ind. App. 456, 202 N.E.2d 395, 398 (1964).

22. For a general discussion of these cases, *see* Annot., "Former Employee's Duty, In Absence of Express Contract, Not to Solicit Former Employer's Customers or Otherwise Use His Knowledge of Customer Lists Acquired in Earlier Employment," 28 A.L.R.3d 7, secs. 1415 (1969).

23. For examples of covenants not to compete that were overbroad on geographical terms, *see American Hot Rod Ass'n. Inc. v. Carrier*, 500 F.2d 1269 (4th Cir. 1974); *On Line Systems, Inc. v. Staib*, 479 F.2d 308 (8th Cir. 1973); *Rector-Phillips-Morse, Inc. v. Vroman*, 253 Ark. 750, 489 S.W.2d 1, 61 A.L.R.3d 391 (1973); *Britt v. Davis*, 239 Ga. 747, 238 S.E.2d 881 (1977); *Howard Schultz & Assoc. of the Southeast, Inc. v. Broniec*, 239 Ga. 181, 236 S.E.2d 265 (1977); *Fuller v. Kolb*, 238 Ga. 602, 234 S.E.2d 517 (1977); and *Trilog Associates, Inc. v. Famularo*, 455 Pa. 243, 314 A.2d 287 (1974), wherein the Pennsylvania Supreme Court wrote:

> The restrictive covenants have no limitation on territory and thus are broader than is necessary for the protection of Trilog. Famularo in effect promised not to practice his profession *anywhere for anyone* in developing a shareholders' record system . . . . Such covenants, unrestricted in territorial application, are not necessary to protect any valid interest of the former employer and are unreasonable restraints of trade. 314 A.2d 287, 294.

24. For a thorough discussion of this type of geographical restraint as well as others, *see* Annot.,"Enforceability of Restrictive Covenants, Ancillary to Employment Contract, as Affected by Territorial Extent of Restriction," 43 A.L.R.2d 94, secs. 108–152 (1955).

25. Ibid., 410 F.2d 163, 171, wherein the court held: "But since it may be difficult to determine, as a matter of law, what is a trade secret, the covenant not to compete is a pragmatic solution to the problem of protecting confidential *information.* (Emphasis added.)

26. *Orkin Exterminating Co., Inc. of South Georgia v. Mills*, 218 Ga. 340, 127 S.E.2d 796 (1962).

27. Ibid., 127 S.E.2d 796, 797, 798. Cf. *Welcome Wagon International, Inc. v. Hostesses, Inc.*, 199 Neb. 27, 255 N.W.2d 865 (1977), wherein the court limited a similar covenant not to compete to the territory where the employee had actually worked instead of the broader area where the employer transacted business.

28. *See Orkin Exterminating Co., Inc. v. Wilson*, 501 S.W.2d 408, 411 (Tex. App. Ct. 1973).

29. *See Gillette Co. v. Williams*, 360 F. Supp. 1171, 1177, 1178 (D. Conn. 1973),

30. *See Behnke v. Hertz Corporation*, 70 Wis.2d 818, 235 N.W.2d 690, 693 (1975).

31. *See Miller v. Fairfield Bay, Inc.*, 446 S.W.2d 660, 663, 664 (Ark. Sup. Ct. 1969).

32. *See United Travel Service, Inc. v. Weber*, 108 Ill. App.2d 353, 247 N.E.2d 801, 803, 804 (1969). For a thorough listing of cases involving the

enforceability of restrictive covenants with regard to occupations, *see* "Enforceability of Restrictive Covenants, Ancillary to Employment Contracts, as Affected by Territorial Extent of Restriction," 43 A.L.R.2d 94, secs. 2665 (1955).

33. *United Travel Service, Inc.* v. *Weber*, 108 Ill. App.2d 535, 247 N.E.2d 801, 803 (1969); *Frederick* v. *Professional Building Maintenance Industries, Inc.*, 344 N.E.2d 299, 301 (Ind. App. Ct. 1976); and *Crouch* v. *Swing Machinery Co.*, 468 S.W.2d 604, 605, 606 (Tex. App. Ct. 1971).

34. *See Servomation Mathias, Inc.* v. *Englert*, 333 F.Supp. 9, 14 (M.D. Pa. 1971). In this case the employer made a manual of secret recipes available to several employees. Some of these employees had signed agreements not to compete; some had not. The court denied enforcement of the restrictive covenants on the grounds that the employer had failed to sufficiently protect its confidential information. The result may well have been different if all the employees with access to the recipe manual had signed similar contracts not to compete.

35. Since sec. 1 of the Sherman Antitrust Act, 15 U.S.C.A. sec. 1, declares certain restraints of trade to be illegal and sec. 2 declares certain monopolies to be illegal, the issue of antitrust law's application to postemployment agreements not to compete has arisen. See Harvey J. Goldschmid, "Antitrust's Neglected Stepchild: A Proposal for Dealing with Restrictive Covenants Under Federal Law," *Columbia Law Review* 73 (1973): 1193; Henry H. Janssen, "Antitrust Considerations in Proceedings Against Former Employees Who Compete Against Their Former Employer," *Business Law* 31 (1975): 2063; Charles A. Sullivan, "Revisiting the 'Neglected Stepchild' Antitrust Treatment of Postemployment Restraints of Trade," 1977 *University of Illinois Law Forum* (1977): 621; and note, "Trade Regulations: Sherman Act: May Changed Circumstances Render a Post-Employment Restraint Unreasonable and Violative of the Sherman Act," *Oklahoma Law Review* 31 (1978): 759.

36. *H&R Block Inc.* v. *Lovelace* , 208 Kan. 538, 493 P.2d 205, 211, 50 A.L.R.3d 730 (1972), as quoted from *Arthur Murray Dance Studios of Cleveland* v. *Witter*, 105 N.E.2d 685, 703-704 (Ohio Com. Pl. 1952). And see *Davis* v. *Ebsco Industries, Inc.*, 150 So.2d 460, 463 (Fla. Dist. Ct. App. 1963). wherein the court wrote: "Further, the rule that covenants restraining from entering into certain employment will not be enforced where the services are not special, unique, or extraordinary does not apply where the restrictive covenant is made in connection with the sale of a business." For a discussion of this unique services principle as it applies to restrictive covenants in employment contracts, *see* Margaret N. Kniffin, "Employee Noncompetition Covenants: The Perils of Performing Unique Services," *Rutgers Camden Law Journal* 10 (1978): 25.

37. See Annot., "Enforceability of Covenant Against Competition, Ancillary to Sale or Other Transfer of Business, Practice, or Property, as Affected by Duration of Restriction," 45 A.L.R.2d 77 secs. 146–49 (1956); and Annot., "Enforceability of Covenant Against Competition Ancillary to Sale or Other Transfer of Business, Practice, or Property, as Affected by Territorial Extent of Restriction," 46 A.L.R.2d 119 secs. 160–62 (1956).

38. Frank Kottke, *The Promotion of Price Competition Where Sellers Are Few* (Lexington, Mass.: Lexington Books, 1978), pp. 115–18.

39. *See* sources cited in Note 35.

CHAPTER 6

The Law of
False Advertising

Disputes between competitors, characterized by the law as "unfair competition," would appear to be an area where the litigants would have the kind of ongoing interest that provides economic incentive to litigate to an efficient outcome. But in apparent contradiction to this expectation, the common law relating to false advertising has been criticized as being inefficient. Assume, for example, that firm A makes false claims about its product and, due to the deception, some consumers purchase the product. Although each consumer may well have a legal action against the seller, no one consumer is likely to have lost enough to make litigation worthwhile.[1] Competitors of firm A may also have lost sales because of the deception and might have enough incentive to seek redress in the courts. To the surprise of commentators,[2] however, the common law has generally discouraged such suits. Even Posner has argued that statutory law may have been necessary to correct the common law's mistake: "[I]n section 43(a) of the Lanham Trade-Mark Act Congress created a new right of action for competitors injured by misrepresentation that, although little utilized, may well have repaired any deficiencies of the common law in this area."[3]

If the common law treatment of false advertising is inefficient, even though the litigants fit the evolutionary models, then those models are thrown into question. The contention in this chapter is that, contrary to appearances, the common law outcome with regard to false advertising is indeed consistent with efficiency.

A straightforward application of the economics of information and advertising explains the common law position. Furthermore, a study of the effect of the "correction" by statute sheds additional light on the question. If the common law was in fact inefficient, the Lanham Act and other statutory interventions should have led to increased efficiency in resource allocation. Conversely, if the common law had arrived at optimal rules, the statutes should not have improved upon common law outcomes. In short, a reversal of the common law rule by statute provides a good test of common law efficiency. In Part I we will consider the economics of advertising, with particular reference to the models of Phillip Nelson. Part II discusses the legal treatment of consumer and competitor suits against misrepresentation. Part III provides some evidence about effects of changing the legal environment. Part IV summarizes the conclusions.

I. ECONOMICS OF ADVERTISING

Until recently advertising presented something of a puzzle to economic theory. Much advertising is patently uninformative: rational consumers should not care what sort of breakfast cereal is eaten by famous baseball players, nor should they expect any relationship between the cleanliness of their clothes and the catchiness of the tune used to advertise a wash powder. Nonetheless, advertisers spend large sums of money on these sorts of messages as well as many others of equal value as information. Rational consumers should not be influenced by such messages, and rational advertisers should not spend money on messages without influence. Economists, believers in rationality by both consumers and producers, were puzzled.

Phillip Nelson has offered an explanation for this behavior.[4] Nelson argues that there are two types of goods: search goods and experience goods. Search goods are those whose salient characteristics can be ascertained by presale inspection (e.g., the comfort of a pair of shoes); experience goods are those that must be consumed to be evaluated (e.g., the taste of a candy bar). Nelson has shown that this distinction can account for many otherwise puzzling aspects of market behavior.

The role of advertising differs depending on which type of good is involved. In the case of search goods, where the consumer can and will easily determine for himself whether the goods are what he wants, advertisers have little incentive to misrepresent the quality of their goods. Thus, advertisers simply urge the consumer to make the inspection, and their message should be largely informative and truthful.

Note, however, that the time and effort rational purchasers devote to search are directly related to the magnitude of the purchase.[5] If a mistake would not be very expensive, the cost of acquiring information is likely to exceed the cost of purchase error. If, on the other hand, a mistake would be very costly, it pays to invest in reducing the probability of error. In plain terms, one might throw away the wrong color of a dollar lipstick, but most people cannot view with equanimity buying another car if they don't like the first one. Consequently, sellers should provide considerable information on high-risk, big-ticket purchases, since consumers should be willing to pay for it.[6]

In the case of the experience good, the consumer can determine quality only by purchasing and using the good. The function of advertising, therefore, is to get the consumer to try the product. Here, advertisers might have an incentive to mislead and make false claims. For low-priced, often-purchased goods,[7] however, it would not pay to make such claims, since the consumer can be fooled by them only once. Hence, a seller of such goods (e.g., soaps, which are very heavily advertised) would appear to be wasting his money to mislead. Nelson argues that advertising of such products does serve an informative purpose: by his outlay, the advertiser demonstrates his confidence that the consumer will be satisfied with the good and will purchase it more than once. In this instance the truth of any information is irrelevant, since the message conveys confidence in the quality of the product and consumers come away with little else. At the other end of the sale, false claims for higher-priced experience goods may result in enough damage to raise a realistic threat of consumer lawsuits, which should adequately deter those falsehoods.

Market checks on the efficacy of false advertising break down in that vast range of purchases that produce losses too great to shrug off, but too small to sue about. In this area, however, the market does provide some protection for the consumer: reputation in and of itself is valuable as an indicator of responsibility and honesty, qualities likely to produce substantial future benefits to the firm. Conversely, false advertising is likely to provoke negative consumer response. Hence, advertising expenditures can be capitalized much the same as other investment expenditures. For example, positive brand recognition contributes to the present value of the firm, but misrepresentation is likely to diminish it.[8]

Where the individual item sought is not heavily advertised, the consumer may choose to trust an intermediary, such as a department store or travel agent, to insure the quality of what he buys. The department store, in particular, deals in diverse products, not only in the particular merchandise being advertised; thus it stands to lose a great deal by misrepresentation. In short, no matter what kind of goods or services are involved, a decision to advertise conveys information: that the advertiser is willing to invest in his reputation and stands to lose if the customer is unhappy.

This argument has especial force in another situation, identified by Michael Darby and Edi Karni.[9] Some goods or, more often, services have "credence" qualities, defined as characteristics whose quality cannot be monitored by the nonexpert, even after consumption. For instance, if an automobile repair shop sells a consumer a part that he does not need, he will probably not detect any fraud if his car now runs better, even if it would have run equally well without the part. (Similar examples may be drawn from repair to humans, for example, unnecessary surgery.) Thus, the nonexpert consumer relies on the reputation of the seller, and the seller who has invested in his reputation has more to lose by practicing deception than one who has not.[10]

With respect to advertising, then, the characteristics of goods and services form a continuum, from those in which it is very easy to detect the truth or falsity of advertising claims (search goods: the truth of the claim can be ascertained before purchase) through experience goods (where the truth of the claim can be detected only after purchase and use) through credence goods (where the validity of advertisements may never be determined). As we move along this continuum from search to credence characteristics, misrepresentation becomes relatively more profitable, since detection by consumers becomes more expensive. Conversely, if consumers are aware of this problem, as goods and services acquire more credence characteristics, consumers should begin to rely more heavily on specialized buyers and on brand names as assurances of quality[11] in order to avoid being defrauded. Nonetheless, it is in the case of credence characteristics that self-protection becomes most difficult and in which some legal remedy would seem most important.

Even if we assume that there is much advertising that is misleading, how much policing of false advertising would be likely if competitors were allowed to perform such policing? For theoretical reasons, we would not expect much. First, in a competitive industry no one firm would lose much from false advertising by competitors and therefore no firm would have much of an incentive to take legal action. Similarly, if a monopolist falsely advertises, there would be no firm that would lose much since, by definition, monopolists have no close competitors. It would only be in the case of oligopolistic industries that there would be any incentive for competitors to sue for false advertising, provided the advertising be about one particular firm's product. If there were false advertising about the merits of the good made by all of the oligopolists, there would again be no incentive for legal action.[12] Thus, even in an oligopolistic environment, there would be little gain from allowing policing of misleading advertising since firms have little incentive to undertake policing activities.

Moreover, because it would be harder for new entrants to document all claims and because such firms advertise more heavily than established firms,[13] we might expect that much of the policing that would occur would be by established brands against new entrants. If threat of suit is used as a barrier to entry, there might be costs of allowing such litigation. Although the data are not extensive, we will provide some evidence on this point in Part III.

To summarize, this section has considered the costs and benefits of allowing more private policing of advertising. First, the analysis indicates that all advertising is informative, and even though its informational content may be nominal, the fact that the advertising exists is information in its own right. If advertisers were subject to suit, they might restrict their advertising, which would serve both to reduce information and to decrease the incentive to acquire a good reputation. Second, producers of new products rely heavily on advertising in order to create a market share. Claims of new entrants are particularly difficult to prove (or easy to challenge as being misleading), since such firms have no past history on which to base their claims. Thus, we might expect that, if competitors' remedies for misrepresentation became easy, such remedies would be used disproportionately against new entrants into the market, thereby imposing substantial costs on consumers in the form of foregone opportunities for new and innovative products. In short, there appear to be few benefits and sizable costs from policing advertising, especially at the insistance of competitors.

II. THE COMMON LAW'S RESPONSE TO FALSE ADVERTISING

A. Consumer Remedies

If consumers are misled by advertising and choose a product because of a falsehood, they have suffered an injury and resources have been misallocated. Accordingly, the common law[14] afforded the consumer redress for his injury, predicated on somewhat overlapping theories of breach of contract and misrepresentation. Some recently enacted state and federal consumer protection statutes provide additional causes of action.

On the theory that the seller has failed to deliver what was promised, the buyer may assert a claim based on the contract of sale. Part of the seller's obligation is to deliver "conforming" goods, and the buyer may reject goods that are not as promised. If he has already accepted the goods, a substantial nonconformity entitles him to revoke his acceptance if his failure to reject was either induced by the seller's assurances or caused by a latent defect. The buyer, in either case, has an action for damages against the seller, computed by determining the amount it will cost him to obtain conforming goods, as well as so-called incidental and consequential damages, including personal injuries.

If the buyer elects to keep the goods or if he cannot meet the standards for revocation, he may notify the seller that the goods do not conform to what he was promised, and may claim the difference in value between the goods as promised and the goods actually delivered. He may be barred from any remedy if he fails to notify the seller of his objection within a reasonable time.

This scheme obviously hinges on determining what was, in fact, promised or warranted by the seller. The sales article of the Uniform Commercial Code recognizes that sellers often make express representations about the goods, but, in addition, protects buyer expectations by providing certain implied terms in sales of goods. In the case of false advertising, however, the complaint will normally be a breach of an express warranty if the goods do not correspond to the advertising claims made about them.

Several roadblocks may confront a plaintiff here. First, he must show that the falsehood in the advertising rose to the level of a warranty or promise. The law requires that the representation in question must become "part of the basis of the bargain," and hence seems to require some showing that the information was material in the purchase decision. Second, the seller is given considerable latitude to "puff" or extol the virtures of his goods in a general way without incurring warranty obligations. Third, if the advertising is sponsored by the manufacturer, as it often is, the buyer may have to overcome the objection that he is not in a contractual relationship with anyone but his immediate seller, who made no false representation. But this privity-of-contract defense seems to be crumbling, particularly when personal injury results, but also where the only loss is monetary.[15] Fourth, the consumer must give proper notice or be barred from any remedy.

A final and very important issue is whether the seller has attempted to limit his liability or restrict the buyer's remedies by their agreement, often the closely-printed form presented for the buyer's signature. The code recognizes that parties may wish to bargain over the risks of product defects and to reflect those risk allocations in the price term. Thus, the seller is permitted to sell without warranties, provided certain requirements are met. In the false advertising situation, the seller may attempt to cut back on the claims made by his advertising by offering a much more limited undertaking in his forms. The code insists that such limiting language must be consistent with any express warranty the seller has created, and refuses to give effect to attempts to mislead the buyer by promising much in ads but cutting enforceable rights through the forms. One important loophole in such buyer protection is the code's parol evidence rule, which allows seller and buyer to deny effect to representations made before the final agreement is signed. If buyer and seller in fact agree that the sum total of their understanding is what is on the paper they sign, the parol evidence rule causes no great injustice since, if a term is omitted, the signer should have objected before signifying assent. But where there is no negotiation at all and the buyer is unaware of the necessity to double-check the long, densely printed form, sellers may be able to exclude responsibility for very relevant point-of-sale representations.

The seller may also undertake to limit the buyer's remedies if a warranty has been breached, by offering a so-called "repair or replacement" guarantee. The code does seek to protect the buyer, too, providing that if such a limited remedy "fails of its essential purpose," the buyer can assert all the remedies the code otherwise affords.

If the buyer can establish that the advertising claim did amount to a warranty that was part of the enforceable bargain, his road to recovery is an easy one. The seller's liability is absolute and the buyer's fault, if any, is irrelevant, unless his own conduct and not the misrepresentation is the cause of his injury.

If, however, he stumbles on any of the contractual defenses just outlined, he may elect to sue for breach of duty imposed by law, the duty not to deceive. The law of torts has long offered a remedy for misrepresentation on which the plaintiff has relied to his economic detriment. To avoid a too-easy upsetting of transactions, however, this remedy is difficult to obtain and requires proof of the defendant's fault. In most situations, the purchaser must show that the defendant knew or should have known the falsity of his statement and that he intended to deceive. Furthermore, the plaintiff must demonstrate that he justifiably relied on the misrepresentation and establish the causal connection between it and his damages.[16] If the complaint is that the advertisement in question was only a half-truth, the problem becomes more complex since the seller's duty to disclose has traditionally been very limited.[17] If deceit can be proved, the buyer may choose to disaffirm the sale and get his money back, or sue for damages. In egregious cases, punitive damages may also be awarded.

Any or all of these remedies could be asserted by a consumer who thinks he has been "taken" for false or deceptive advertising.[18] All of the remedies, however, share a common, major disadvantage: the cost of resorting to the courts in many cases far outstrips the relief available, even if the consumer has an airtight case. Hence, excluding those cases where the falsity of the advertised claim results in personal injury, or the magnitude of the loss is large,[19] it is not surprising that there are very few cases where consumers have sued. Attempts to lower the barrier of the cost of suit by legislative action are evaluated in Part III.

B. Competitor's Remedies

1. False Claims

In addition to those consumers who are misled, competitors of the misrepresenting firm are also harmed, since some sales that they would have made have been diverted to the other firm. Moreover, we would expect such competitors to lose substantially more than individual consumers. Thus, efficiency considerations suggest that competitors should be permitted to sue for damages or injunctions when false advertising has occurred. This is precisely the point made elsewhere by Posner.[20]

But the common law did not allow such suits. In *American Washboard* v. *Saginaw Manufacturing Co.,*[21] the court held that misrepresentation did not, in fact, provide an action for competitors. This same opinion was upheld by the Supreme Court in *Mosler Safe Co.* v. *Ely-Norris Safe Co.*[22] In an earlier decision in the same dispute, Judge Hand explicitly stated that: "The Law does not allow him [the damaged competitor] to sue as a vicarious avenger of the defendant's customers."[23] This would seem a curious result, since it is unlikely that the customers would sue in their own behalf; thus, the decisions seemed to indicate that no legal penalty would be imposed on misleading advertisers.

What would be the effect of these decisions on consumer? Consumers could not assume that there was any presumption of truth in advertising; rather, they would be forced to rely on their own devices to determine which products to purchase. In the case of search goods, inspection would be relatively more intensive than otherwise. In the case of experience goods, perhaps more sampling would occur than if consumers could believe the accuracy of advertising. In the case of credence goods consumers would be forced to rely on reputation and intermediaries. Thus there would be some efficiency loss if advertising could not be believed. In an optimal world there would be no misleading advertising. As we have argued above, however, suits by competitors would probably have little real impact, except as a new barrier to entry. In disallowing such suits, then, the common law probably had little effect on whether or not advertising is truthful.

2. Claims about Competitors' Product

One form of misrepresentation consists of making unjustified claims about one's own product. An advertiser may also make unfavorable statements about competitors or their products. This latter claim may be characterized as either disparagement or defamation. Disparagement occurs when the claims refer to goods made by rivals; defamation refers to making claims about the personality or other characteristics of the competitor rather than his goods. This distinction is important:

> In most states if a statement is defamatory per se, no actual financial damage need be proved, injury being conclusively presumed; in an action for disparagement, on the other hand, only special damages can be recovered, and usually they must be alleged and proved with considerable specificity. This requirement has been particularly troublesome since injunctions classically have been unavailable against either disparagement or defamation. Other differences also tend to make disparagement the more difficult path to recovery: in disparagement the plaintiff must prove the defendant's statement false, whereas in defamation the defendant bears the burden of proving truth; in disparagement, unlike defamation, "malice" is a requisite to recovery.[24]

These distinctions have been puzzling to commentators on the law.[25]

Economic analysis, however, can explain the common law's greater solicitude for competitors who claim defamation rather than disparagement. If firm A claims that firm B is owned by a devil worshipper, this will cost firm B money (in foregone sales) if customers believe the claim and prefer not to do business with devil worshippers.[26] There may be no efficient way for consumers to ascertain the truth of the devil-worshipper claim, for it is a credence characteristic. In contrast, if firm A claims that the product of firm B will not work well, then consumers can presumably determine the truth of this claim for themselves. Thus the relative ease with which a plaintiff may make out a case for defamation as compared with making out a case of disparagment, which appears mysterious when considered in terms used by courts, may be explicable in terms of the ability of consumers to determine truth and, hence, discount disparagement more than defamation. It is at least arguable that this distinction makes sense in economic terms. Specifically, false claims about product quality are claims about search or experience characteristics where consumers will not be misled. Claims about personal characteristics of manufacturers, on the other hand, are claims about credence qualities, which cannot be verified and where the legal process may be the most efficient way to lay false claims to rest.

In cases where an action for disparagement has been permitted, there is some evidence consistent with this contention. In at least some of these cases, the disparaging statements were not of the sort that consumers could verify for themselves; rather, such statements often dealt with actions of some third party. In *Testing Systems, Inc. v. Magnaflux Corp.*,[27] part of the disparaging statement dealt with the product of Testing Systems, but in addition, it was alleged that the government had decided not to continue to use the product. While it may be argued that consumers should be able to determine for themselves the quality of the product, it seems less plausible that they would be able to determine what decisions the government had made about the product. Similarly, in *Black & Yates, Inc. v. Mahogany Association, Inc.*,[28] at least one of the disparaging statements made about "Philippine mahogany" by the association was that the Federal Trade Commission was about to rule that Philippine mahogany could no longer be called mahogany; again, consumers could probably not check the validity of this sort of statement.

3. Producer Identity

The argument thus far has been that misleading advertising will not have much of an effect, either because it can be checked by purchasers (in the case of search goods) or because the message contained in advertising is basically irrelevant (in the case of experience goods). Therefore the common law's reluctance to entertain actions based upon such advertising is explicable in economic terms. To further strengthen this argument, consider an area in which the common law has generally provided injunctions against misrepresentation. This is the area of "passing off"—of misrepresenting the manufacturer of goods. In cases where B sells goods and claims that they were made by A, then the courts have not hesitated to enjoin the action. The original common law of trademark was aimed precisely at this practice.

The economic value of identification of the manufacturer is obvious. A producer will not invest in gaining a reputation by producing high-quality goods unless he can be sure of capturing the value of the brand name.[29] Trademark identification, moreover, imparts useful information to the consumer, information whose falsity would be difficult to detect.

The name of the producer is perhaps the most important credence characteristic of a good. For example, when a consumer buys a pair of blue jeans marked "Levi's" he must rely totally on the truth of the label;

it is completely impossible for him to trace back the movement of the goods from retailer to wholesaler to the manufacturer and check this claim. The firm should be permitted to establish a property right in the brand name of the product inasmuch as that right will lead to efficient investment in quality and reliability. Presumably if firm A spends money in advertising its product, it is to tell consumers that products made by this firm are worth buying, information that is useless unless consumers are able to tell which products are in fact made by firm A. Therefore, efficiency considerations dictate that the law should protect trademarks as the common law has done.

Another interesting area is the protection of geographic designation. In *Grand Rapids Furniture Co.* v. *Grand Rapids Furniture Co.*,[30] the courts held that a furniture store could not advertise that its furniture was made in Grand Rapids when in fact it was not; this is consistent with other cases, such as *Pillsbury-Washburn Flour Mills* v. *Eagle Co.*[31] But in *California Apparel Creators* v. *Wieder of California*,[32] the court did not enjoin New York clothing manufacturers from using the name "California" in their business. The court distinguished these cases on the basis of the loss involved. In the Grand Rapids case, the Grand Rapids manufacturers had a tight trade association, and virtually all of them were involved in the case; thus the court reasoned that any business diverted by the misrepresentation would have otherwise gone to these manufacturers and that, therefore, they had a substantial interest in the injunction. In the California case, there were approximately 4,500 manufacturers in California, only a few of whom were represented in the suit. Here the court believed that losses were not significant enough to the plaintiffs to grant relief.

This reasoning does not make economic sense. If consumers are misled about the place of origin of goods and if the place of origin is relevant, then it should not matter whether there are five or 5,000 manufacturers who lose by the misrepresentation; efficiency would require an injunction in either case. However, though the reasons provided by the court are not useful, the decision is nonetheless probably correct. Consumers presumably care, not about the actual location of the manufacturing plant, but about the reputation of the firm or manufacturer. If there are few enough firms so that they can form a tight trade association and sue as a class, then there are probably few enough manufacturers so that they can self-police the use of the geographic name and thus insure the quality of the goods bearing this name. Conversely, when there are so many firms that they cannot all join in a class for the purposes of legal action, there are probably too many to guarantee that any level of quality can be maintained by the firms bearing the geographic name. Hence, when there are many firms suffering the supposed loss, consumers probably do not rely on the name as a proof of quality, and thus there is not any loss in not protecting the mark. This seems to be a situation where the law has reached the economically correct decision, though the judicial reasoning is couched in other terms.

There are other areas of the law of producer identity that are subject to economic analysis, if not to economic solution. For example, consider the law of "trade names." A trade name at common law was a name or descriptive word with some meaning in addition to its use to identify a particular brand. An example is given in *American Aloe Corp. v. Aloe Creme Laboratories, Inc.;*[33] here, a company that produced products derived from the aloe verde plant with names such as Aloe-Creme and Aloe-Ointment brought suit against a competitor producing products with names such as Aloe Essence. The issue was whether the name Aloe was subject to trademark-type protection; the courts ruled that it was not. The economic analysis is reasonably straightforward: the cost of maintaining "aloe" as a trademark or trade name would have been the lost information by consumers about ingredients in competing products, while the benefits would have been the relatively greater incentive of the first company to protect its reputation. Economic analysis indicates that protection should be given to the point where marginal cost equals marginal benefits, that is, to the point where the incremental value of the greater incentive to protect reputation would just equal the incremental value of the additional information possessed about ingredients by consumers. Economic theory alone merely states the question. Just as proof of facts is necessary to decide legal issues, concrete empirical data are required to estimate where this point lies. Therefore, it is not surprising that courts must consider each case on its facts, and have not derived clear-cut rules in this area. Similar issues arise in determining what symbols associated with a product should be protected as trademarks (e.g., the picture of a shredded wheat biscuit in *Kellogg Co. v. National Biscuit Co.*).[34] Again the courts seem to have recognized the economic issue involved and attempted to deal with it. It is impossible to determine how successful they have been.

III. SOME EVIDENCE

The argument has been that allowing competitors to sue for misrepresentation would have been inefficient, except in the case of producer identity. Conversely, if suits were permitted, gains would have been minimal, inasmuch as market forces substantially limit the likelihood that firms engage in false advertising. In addition, the increased danger of suit would increase the risk, and thus the cost, of truthful advertising. Finally, such suits may have been used to restrict entry by new competitors, thus creating a net loss in social welfare.

To bolster our conclusion that the common law perhaps struck the best balance, we have examined the results of various steps taken to remedy the "deficiencies" of the common law in this area. First, government has assumed responsibility for consumer protection from false and misleading advertising. Second, legislation has been passed to encourage purchasers and competitors to undertake policing of false advertising. Finally evidence is available from the German experience, where competitors are permitted to sue rather freely.

A. The Federal Trade Commission

Richard Posner has analyzed in detail Federal Trade Commission cases dealing with misrepresentation and false advertising for 1963, 1968, and 1973. His conclusion is " . . . that only a small fraction of the Federal Trade Commission's activities in the false-advertising area is consistent with a proper allocation of Commission resources, considering the character of the false-advertising problem and the limitations of the Commission's sanctions."[35] Posner blames this poor effort on the lack of a theory by the commission as to where intervention would be likely to prove valuable. However, an alternative theory, which is also consistent with his evidence, has been developed here: there is simply not much harmful false advertising that occurs; therefore, Commission intervention would be unproductive, no matter what rule it might apply. (In fact, this argument is consistent with Posner's other policy suggestion, which is that the Commission be given powers to enforce a federal antifraud law and that it confine its efforts to deliberate attempts to defraud.) The uselessness in economic terms of most FTC proceedings may be due to ineptness on the part of the Commission, but it may also be due simply to the small population of costly deceptions that occur.

Both the FTC and commentators have explained the FTC's poor performance by pointing out that the only sanction formerly available to the FTC, the cease-and-desist order, was not effective against consumer deception.[36] That problem has now been remedied, for the FTC has been granted vastly greater enforcement powers by the Magnuson-Moss Act of 1975.[37] In addition to validating FTC power[38] to promulgate regulation rules, which have the force of law, the Act provides stiff penalties for violations. The FTC may now sue and obtain an injunction, sue to exact a penalty for the violation of an existing cease-and-desist order by anyone (not merely the named respondent) who does so with actual knowledge that the act was unfair and unlawful, or sue for violation of an FTC legislative (as distinguished from interpretative) rule. Fines of up to $10,000 per day may be imposed for each violation. The Act also empowers the FTC to seek redress for competitors and consumers if it can show that the act or practice " . . . is one which a reasonable man would have known under the circumstances was dishonest or fraudulent."[39] The FTC may seek rescission, reformation, return of property, and damages as relief for competitors or consumers. Although no private suit may be brought for violation of the FTC Act,[40] several states have passed smaller-scaled FTC acts[41] or other laws against deceptive trade practices, which provide private actions for consumers or competitors, often offering incentives to encourage private enforcement.[42] It remains to be seen whether a more potent FTC will "cleanup" a marketplace in which false advertising has run rampant and unchecked.

B. New Remedies for Purchasers

Recognition that a rational person will not spend money for a lawyer, court fees, and whatever his own time is worth to collect miniscule amounts has led to a number of proposals to make it easier to assert rights. Historically the first efforts were to lower the cost of suit by establishing informal small claims courts.[43] Although many have noted that these courts serve more as a collection agency against the consumer than as a forum for him to present his grievances,[44] consumers who do go to these courts seeking justice often do very well. But even consumers who make use of these courts do not seek redress for misrepresentation, except in such small numbers that they are not separately classified in a major empirical study of small claims courts.[45] Moreover, it is impossible to tell whether those consumers who alleged misrepresentation were complaining about advertising or about point-of-sale inducements by sellers.

Another response to the problem of the high cost of dispute resolution has been to set up alternatives to courts, such as governmental arbitration and mediation services.[46] A recent study[47] of the workings of one very active Bureau of Consumer Protection, located in Illinois, remarked that only 18 percent of complainants mentioned misrepresentation, deception, or undue influence by the seller as the primary grievance. As might be expected, larger transactions (in dollar amounts) generated more complaints of this sort. Perhaps if false advertising is a problem, buyers still prefer to absorb their small losses rather than to invest in these proceedings.

Finally, some consumer advocates have argued for a system that provides incentives for private enforcement of consumer claims, such as multiple damage recovery, exemplary damages, and award of attorney's fees to a victorious consumer.[48] Along these same lines, others have urged that consumers (or their legal representatives) be able to sue in a class action as representatives of all consumers who have been victimized.[49] But the dynamics of litigation and its costs may shift the balance too far: groundless suits become too easy to bring and too expensive to defend against, offering the unscrupulous a kind of blackmail against legitimate business who may prefer to settle for some sum rather than to defend.[50]

Some state consumer legislation has attempted to build in safeguards against so-called "strike suits," while still encouraging private enforcement of meritorious claims. In Oregon, for instance, the defrauded consumer who proves a willful violation can collect his actual damages or $200, whichever is greater, as well as punitive damages and attorneys' fees and costs.[51] Even where generous bounties such as these are available, however, research discloses only two cases in which consumers complaining about false advertising availed themselves of the provisions of the act. Interestingly, in both cases, the goods would seem to be search goods. In one[52] the consumer wanted a tent for use in the winter, which requires special characteristics. Had the purchaser taken the precaution of inspecting a tent on display or opening the package in the store, he would have seen that the tent in question did not match the picture on the package and would not serve his purposes. In the other[53] the consumer bought an automobile engine at a gas station. The size of an automobile engine seems to be a matter that would be of sufficient importance to the purchaser to expect him to inspect before he buys. Regardless of whether these cases should have been brought at all, two reported cases in seven years indicate that even where consumers have been offered every inducement to come forward, no great flood of litigation seems to have engulfed the courts.

C. The Lanham Act

The Lanham Act, passed in 1946, greatly broadened rights of competitors to sue for misleading advertising.[54] A test of the hypotheses in this paper would be to examine cases under this Act in order to determine the efficiency effects of this broadened right of action. We have undertaken such an examination.

All 182 cases citing 15 U.S.C. K 1145(a) reported in Shepard's United States Citations 1970 edition and 1972 and 1975 supplements were read. The vast majority of these cases were simply standard trademark infringement actions, coupled with a claim of unfair competition under the Lanham Act.

Of the 182 cases cited, 16, or fewer than 10 percent, could be classified as complaints about a competitor's false advertising. (Excluded from this total were a number of complaints that a competitor's advertising used a picture of the plaintiff's goods, since such situations are merely variations of the tort of "passing off.")

Those 16 cases can be further subclassified. Perhaps most important, from an economic viewpoint, are those claims that consumers cannot easily verify by inspection or inexpensive experience (credence qualities), and where the amount of injury is so small that no individual purchaser will resort to the courts. In such instances, deceptive advertising may be profitable and result in harm to honest competitors, as well as misallocation of resources. At least 6 of the 16 cases arguably fall into this category.

Perhaps the clearest case for a competitor's remedy is *John Wright, Inc.* v. *Casper Corp.*[55] Two rivals in the sale of mechanical penny banks were the litigants. The plaintiff was the successor in interest to a firm that had gone to trouble and expense to produce authentically detailed reproductions of nineteenth-century banks. The defendant produced inexpensive imitations of the plaintiff's banks in Taiwan, yet advertised them as "authentic reproductions." Those consumers to whom authenticity and faithfulness to the original were important were being deceived, the true source of authentic reproductions was being deprived of sales, and yet no consumer would find it worth his while to sue.

Equally compelling is *Skil Corp.* v. *Rockwell International Corp.*,[56] where the plaintiff complained that the defendant falsely and extensively advertised the results of tests conducted by an independent testing concern that compared the defendant's power tools with the plaintiff's and those of two other manufacturers. The credence quality here was the impartiality of the investigator, since consumers might well place more faith in the result of a third party's testing than they would in a claim originating with the seller. If those test results were misrepresented, both the consumer and other manufacturers would suffer injury. Actual injury to any one purchaser would be too small to justify litigation, although the consumer would not be getting what he wanted.

A competitor's remedy also seems sensible in *Bohsei Enterprise Co.* v. *Porteous Fastener Co.*[57] In that case an importer of industrial fasteners complained that its rivals repackaged imported fasteners and either omitted the true country of origin or on occasion marked them "United States," thereby creating the false impression that these were domestic rather than imported goods. The complaint also alleged that consumers associate domestic manufacture with higher-quality goods.[58] If the allegations were true, the defendants were violating federal law[59] as well as misrepresenting their goods. In addition, they were diverting sales from other importers and those domestic manufacturers who would otherwise be preferred. Again, individual purchasers would have too small a stake to assert any claim.

A fourth case presents a slightly different situation. In *Cutler Hammer, Inc.* v. *Universal Relay Corp.,*[60] the defendant had allegedly bought surplus relays manufactured by the plaintiff and changed the part numbers to make it appear that they met current military specifications for aircraft use. In this instance, however, the court noted that reliance on the misrepresentation could cause death or personal injury. In a sense, the seriousness of the consequences mitigates against the need for a competitor's remedy, since the large potential liability to injured consumers should itself discourage representations of this sort.

A case that provides shakier support for a competitor's remedy is *Natcontainer Corp.* v. *Continental Can Co., Inc.*[61] The misrepresentation alleged was that Natcontainer's boxes conformed to minimum standards established by the Interstate Commerce Commission when in fact they did not. Here the boxes were sold to businesses, rather than consumers, in such quantities as to make a breach-of-contract action feasible, although no such action appears in the record. Indeed, the Lanham Act claim was asserted as a counterclaim by the defendant in an antitrust action brought by Natcontainer against one of its rivals. In this case, the Lanham Act complaint served as a weapon to discourage antitrust enforcement.

Perhaps the weakest case for a competitor's remedy, even where credence qualities were involved, was presented by *Ames Publishing Co.* v. *Walker-Davis Publications, Inc.*[62] There, one magazine publisher complained about another's attempts to launch a rival magazine. In the defendant's presentation to potential advertisers, circulation projections were asserted as facts, and verification of subscriber lists was claimed but never done. Although one would think that a competitor's remedy would be the only viable one here, the defendant was able to show that the plaintiff had engaged in exactly the same conduct when promoting its magazine. The court refused to recognize an "unclean hands" defense and granted an injunction. Ubiquity of the practice, however, may indicate that potential advertisers presented with these claims by all competitors would not be misled by one any more than by any other, and in fact might discount them all.

On the other end of the scale, several cases involve claims that would surely be verified by consumers before purchase. For instance,

Saxony Products, Inc. v. Guerlain, Inc.,[63] was part of a long-running battle between name-brand perfume manufacturers and those who market much cheaper perfumes as indistinguishable from them. When defeated in their claim that the copyists were impermissibly using their trademarks,[64] the name-brand manufacturers countered by alleging that the claim of similar scents was false and hence a Lanham Act violation. Consumers would clearly rely on their own olfactory sense and not on an advertising claim in this instance, since they were invited to make the comparison at the point of sale. Any falsehood would be immediately apparent, making proof of damage difficult and injunctive relief superfluous. The only possible explanation for such an action would be harassment of a cut-rate competitor.

In similar fashion, *Bose Corp. v. Linear Design Labs, Inc.*[65] involved complaints about statements that the defendant's stereo system produced the "most life-like reproductions" and the "most exacting reproductions ever heard." A potential purchaser of a stereo system will surely rely on his own ears, not on advertising copy, in such judgments. Any such statements, which can only be classified as seller's puff, can hardly produce harm to anyone, and litigation about them must be viewed as harassment of a newcomer.

What can we conclude from these cases? First, there have been extremely few of them, only 16 cases over a ten-year period. Part of the reason may be that competitors, rather than suing directly, would prefer to use the indirect, but free, remedy provided by complaint to the Federal Trade Commission. In the period from October 1977 to July 1978 there were 306 complaints filed with the FTC alleging deceptive advertising.[66] The FTC will not divulge the identity of complainants, so we are unable to determine whether these were filed by consumers or by competitors. Nonetheless, it is at least possible that this method is used. But for whatever reason, the small number of complaints filed with the Commission and the much smaller number of Lanham Act cases indicates that there was not, in fact, a huge demand for legal remedies for misrepresentation that the common law was restraining. Moreover, we have been charitable in deciding which cases might arguably have been efficient; none of the cases mentioned above seem to create large inefficiencies. The cases that we have not discussed (dealing with matters such as whether a hair rinse really rinses out easily[67] or whether a cigarette can advertise that it is "lowest" in tar and nicotine when in fact it is only tied for lowest)[68] also do not seem to be of significance. Those Lanham Act cases that do seem to involve substantial inefficiencies are generally passing-off cases, and remedies would have been available under common law.

Moreover, there is at least some evidence that firms have used the Lanham Act to harass new entrants. For example, in *Smith-Victor Corp. v. Sylvania Electric Products, Inc.*[69] the allegation was that a new type of photographic light would not, in fact, provide as much light as claimed. Since the two lights could be compared before purchase, this was clearly an attempt to harass a new competitor, who was at somewhat of a disadvantage since he did not have a long history of success with lights.

Defendants were clearly new entrants in seven of the sixteen cases selected for study. For instance, in *Saxony Products, Inc. v. Guerlain, Inc.*[70] it was the newcomer's frank and open imitation of plaintiff's "Shalimar" fragrance that led to the litigation. Cheap imitations were also the issue in *John Wright, Inc. v. Casper Corp.*[71] In *Ames Publishing Co. v. Walker-Davis Publications, Inc.*[72] the advertising attendant on launching a new publication led to the suit. Bose Corporation, an established manufacturer of stereo equipment, challenged the claims of newcomer Linear Design Labs, Inc.[73] Likewise, *H. A. Friend & Co. v. Friend & Co.*[74] involved a son who set up an unauthorized "branch" of the family business in California and began competing with it. The Potato Chip Institute took offense when General Mills began marketing its "Chipos," and tried to stop any advertising of the new product as potato chips.[75]

One interesting case involved Honeywell, Inc., a giant in the field of control systems, which was being sued by Electronics Corporation of America. Honeywell, in attempting to enter the market for replacement parts of Electronics Corporation equipment, was charged with misrepresenting the ease with which Honeywell parts could be substituted. Here Honeywell was trying to enter a new, although very limited, market and was advertising a "search" characteristic.[76]

Other cases, however, indicate that two already established brands may extend their competitive battle into the courts.[77] In *American Brands, Inc. v. R. J. Reynolds Tobacco Co.*,[78] instead of being used against the new entrant, the lawsuit seemed to be part of the challenger's campaign to launch a new low-tar cigarette. The new entrant charged in its Lanham Act complaint that advertising for the defendant's established Now brand falsely claimed that Now was "lowest" in tar when in fact the plaintiff's new cigarettes were as low. Defendant promptly counterclaimed for inaccuracies in the plaintiff's advertising (e.g., the plaintiff's Carlton brand was the "fastest growing"). As the judge remarked, actual tar content of cigarettes must be disclosed and is easily discovered by purchasers, making it unlikely that anyone had been misled. Nonetheless, an injunction was granted directing Reynolds to stop claiming its cigarettes were "lowest" in tar without some qualifying information.

In the remaining cases, it is difficult to ascertain the relative market positions of the plaintiff and defendant.[79] The foregoing suggests that although Lanham Act claims may be asserted to block new entrants, they are used at other stages in the competitive struggle as well. In any case, claims of misrepresentation seem to be used as a method of harassing rivals rather than as a method of encouraging truthful statements.

D. The German Experience

Rudolf Callmann[80] and Walter Derenberg,[81] two leading authorities on the American law of unfair competition, were strong advocates of strengthening the rights of competitors to sue for false advertising. Both had experience with the German system, which depends on competitor action and not government regulation, to prevent deception in the marketplace. More recently Warren Grimes[82] has studied the German system and holds it up as a model. Although we have not independently assessed the data summarized by Grimes, some observations based upon it follow.

In Germany, the Law Against Unfair Competition has governed the regulation of misrepresentation and false advertising since 1909. The important section of this law, section 3, "prescribes injunctive relief, [which is freely granted][83] against those who, in the course of competitive business activities, make deceptive assertions concerning business matters, specifically concerning the 'nature, origin, manner of manufacture or the value of goods or services,'" or "concerning 'price lists, the manner or source of acquisition of goods, . . . the receipt of awards, . . . the motive or purpose of the sale, or the amount of available supplies.'"[84] This law may be enforced by competing firms, by trade associations, or (since 1965) by consumer groups. In fact, consumer enforcement seems to be a small part of total enforcement.

The most influential group in enforcing this law is the Zentrale zur Bekampfung unlauteren Wettbewerbs e.V., an organization consisting of more than 1,100 members, mostly chambers of commerce, trade organizations, and larger business entities. In 1967 this organization handled about 3,000 cases.

Almost 93 percent of the complaints brought by this organization are directed against nonmembers. This is consistent with the argument that the larger, better-established firms who have invested in their reputations are less likely to practice deception. Indeed, in the United States, the worst offenders in consumer frauds are said to be the fly-by-night, door-to-door operators who strike once and disappear.[85] Nevertheless, an economist might question whether all the organization's energies are directed against such truly fraudulent practices. In fact "[t]he Zentrale has been accused of being a tool of the large and established firms."[86] Presumably, one use for such a tool might be to stifle competition by nonmembers, particularly smaller firms or new entrants. We have no direct evidence on this point, but in general the value of competition is less important in European jurisprudence. European law countenances anticompetive collusion by business rivals that would be per se violations of American antitrust laws.[87] Hence, an adverse effect on competition would raise fewer problems for German courts than in this country.

IV. SUMMARY

The major issue under discussion has been the common law treatment of suits by competitors for false advertising consisting either of untrue claims about one's own goods or about those of a competitor. In general the common law discouraged such suits, except in the special case of passing off. Although purchasers may have a right of action, in the general case consumers will not lose enough in any one transaction to bring legal action for misrepresentation. Competitors, however, may suffer enough loss to make legal action worthwhile, and commentators have urged that suits by competitors may be a better remedy for misrepresentation than government action. Thus, the common law ban on such suits has been considered puzzling and potentially in conflict with the view that the common law is generally explicable in terms of economic efficiency.

Except in the case of producer identity, our analysis casts doubt upon a need for any legal action for competitors premised on false advertising. We have shown that the economics of advertising, primarily as analyzed by Nelson, indicate that there generally will be little incentive to mislead in advertising.[88] Moreover, in only a few cases would there be competitors who were sufficiently damaged by misleading advertising to find it worthwhile to sue. The one situation where such suits are favored is in the case of the actual name of the manufacturer; this is a credence characteristic, whose truth consumers could not ascertain for themselves. If there is in fact little misleading advertising and if competitors would not usually sue, then there would be little loss if such private policing were discouraged. Furthermore, it is at least possible that allowing competitor suits for misrepresentation would give established firms a competitive weapon to use against new entrants. This is especially likely when we consider that new entrants advertise more heavily than established firms, and that it may be more difficult for new firms to establish the truth of advertising claims than for established firms to do so. Thus, if we did allow firms to sue easily for misrepresentation, there might be substantial costs in terms of reduced competition in markets. The economic argument indicates that there would be little benefit and substantial costs from allowing competitor suits.

In support of these arguments we have relied on several pieces of evidence. First, Posner has found that the Federal Trade Commission, in its attempts to police false advertising, has in fact accomplished little. Second, the evidence from Germany indicates that most suits for misrepresentation are undertaken by established firms. While there are other arguments that might explain this pattern, it is consistent with the hypothesis that such suits would be used to discourage competition, especially given the much lesser importance of competition as a value in Geman law. Third, and most persuasive, is the evidence showing the effects of statutory reversal of this position. Although the Lanham Act now allows competitors to sue for false advertising that damages them, there have been a trivial number of such suits. Of those that have been brought, moreover, only an extremely small number have been economically efficient, even with a broad construction of such efficiency. Many have been aimed at new entrants. This natural experiment with a statutory reversal of common law position has also served to buttress our theoretical arguments and to demonstrate that the common law was probably efficient in this area.[89]

Another consideration is the burden on advertisers if all advertising is scrutinized: even accurate advertising must run the risk of being charged as "misleading." If such burdens exist, the law may hinder efficient consumer choice since more information for consumers is better than less. The First Amendment to the United States Constitution clearly reflects that judgment when the information in question is political.

On the other hand, the Supreme Court only recently decided that commercial speech has any claim to First Amendment protection,[90] and then the Court took pains to note that "untruthful speech, commercial or otherwise, has never been protected."[91] In the terms developed here, however, competing political claims seem to exhibit more credence characteristics than most claims about goods or services, in that truth or falsehood is much harder for the consumer to determine. Yet even if the need to guard against falsehood is greater, the government is prohibited from intervening because of the dangers and distortions such intervention might cause. As both Ronald Coase[92] and Aaron Director[93] have pointed out, it is difficult to understand why governmental intervention in the marketplace for goods is regarded by many as a blessing, while its role as a regulator of ideas is so vehemently opposed. Market, not government, regulation in the realm of commerce, as well as ideas, may be a better idea. Moreover, when the nature of regulation was determined by litigation between firms, efficient results seemed to follow.

NOTES

1. In its Final Report the National Commission on Product Safety stated that it was impractical for consumers to press claims" . . . unless the claim is at least in the $5,000 to $10,000 range." D. Gould, *Staff Report on the Small Claims Court* submitted to the National Institute for Consumer Justice 16 (1972) [hereinafter cited as *Small Claims Report*]. See also Arthur Allen Leff, "Injury, Ignorance, and Spite: The Dynamics of Coercive Collection," *Yale Law Journal* 80 (1970): 21.

2. *See*, e.g., Milton Handler, "False and Misleading Advertising," *Yale Law Journal* 39 (1929): 22; Rudolf Callmann, "False Advertising as a Competitive Tort," *Columbia Law Review* 48 (1948): 876.

3. *See* Richard A. Posner, "The Federal Trade Commission," *University of Chicago Law Review* 37 (1969): 47, 66.

4. Phillip Nelson, "Information and Consumer Behavior," *Journal of Political Economy* 78 (1970): 311; Idem, "Advertising as Information," *Journal of Political Economy* 82 (1974): 729.

5. *See* Richard H. Holton, "Consumer Behavior, Market Imperfections, and Public Policy," reprinted in David Rice, *Consumer Transactions* (Boston: Little, Brown 1975), p. 57.

6. George J. Stigler, "The Economics of Information," *Journal of Political Economy* 69 (1961): 213, reprinted in George Stigler, *The Organization of Industry* (Ill.: *Richard D. Irwin*, 1968).

7. *See* Holton, "Consumer Behavior," p. 58.

8. The point is also made in chap. 3. *See also* Benjamin Klein and Keith B. Leffler, "The Role of Market Forces in Assuring Contractual Performance," *Journal of Political Economy*, vol. 89, no. 4 (Aug. 1981), for an argument that advertising can be used to guarantee quality to consumers. *See* generally Kristian S. Palda, *The Measurement of Cumulative Advertising Effects* (Englewood Cliffs, N.J.: Prentice-Hall, 1964), who demonstrates that advertising should be treated as an investment.

9. Michael R. Darby and Edi Karni, "Free Competition and the Optimal Amount of Fraud," *Journal of Law and Economics* 16 (1973): 67.

10. This may be another reason for allowing advertising by professionals such as doctors. The advertising will create an additional value in the brand name and hence provide additional incentives for quality service.

11. For any one purchase where credence qualities are involved, the consumer cannot be sure that he is getting a desirable good; i.e., there is a low probability of his finding out whether claims about any one good are true or false. However, if the consumer buys many goods from the same source, the probability of ascertaining that claims about one of those goods are false would be increased. Thus, if there are ten goods sold by a store and if there is only a

1 percent chance of finding out that any claim is false, the larger number of claims increases the chance of finding out that one or more of them are false. In this situation, claims about individual goods have credence characteristics, but the reputation of the seller of all of the goods is an experience characteristic.

12. Striking evidence is provided by a case brought by the state of Arizona against five manufacturers of rigid polyurethane foam insulation materials, charging a conspiracy to falsely advertise the flammability characteristics of the product. *State of Arizona* v. *Cook Paint & Varnish Co.*, 391 F. Supp. 962 (D. Ariz. 1975). If the allegations of the complaint are true, far from trying to keep one another honest, all the oligopolists banded together to deceive.

13. *See* Yale Brozen, "Entry Barriers: Advertising and Product Differentiation," in *Industrial Concentration: The New Learning*, Harvey J. Goldschmidt, H. Michael Mann, and J. Fred. Weston, eds., (Boston: Little, Brown, 1974), pp. 115–16.

14. The common law of sales has been largely replaced by statute, the Uniform Commercial Code. Given the unique drafting history of this statute, however, the fact that it is a "case-law code" makes it appropriate to include UCC provisions in this discussion. *See* Soia Mentschikoff, "The Uniform Commercial Code, An Experiment in Democracy in Drafting," *American Bar Association Journal* 36 (1950): 419; Grant Gilmore, "In Memoriam: Karl Llewellyn," *Yale Law Journal* 71 (1962): 813, 814. The next six paragraphs deal with provisions of the UCC.

15. *See* generally William L. Prosser, "The Fall of the Citadel (Strict Liability to the Consumer)," *Minnesota Law Review* 50 (1966): 791.

16. *See* William L. Prosser, *Handbook of the Law of Torts* (4th ed., 1971), sec. 105.

17. Ibid.

18. We make the same distinction between the consumer who complains he has been "taken," and the one who has received a defective product or "lemon," as do Page Keeton and Marshall S. Shapo in *Products and the Consumer: Deceptive Practices* (Mineola, N.Y.: Foundation Press, 1972). p. 3.

19. *Jacobson* v. *Art Storage & Moving Co.*, 16 N.Y.S. 2d 906 (N.Y. City Ct. 1939), appeal denied, 260 App. Div. 809, 22 N.Y.S.2d 928 (1940).

20. *See* Posner, "The Federal Trade Commission," pp. 47, 66.

21. 103 F. 281 (6th Cir. 1900).

22. 273 U.S. 132 (1927).

23. 7 F. 2d 603, 604 (2d Cir. 1925).

24. "Developments in the Law: Competitive Torts," *Harvard Law Review* 77 (1964): 888, 893.

25. Ibid., pp. 893–95.

26. This very rumor bedeviled McDonald's. *See Wall Street Journal*, Nov. 16, 1978, p. 14.

27. 251 F. Supp. 286 (E.D. Pa. 1966).

28. 129 F.2d 227 (ed Cir. 1941).

29. From time to time, it has been reported that dealers in illegal drugs have tried to use a trademark to guarantee the quality of their goods. Since such manufacturers cannot rely on the legal system to protect their trademarks, these attempts invariably fail.

30. 127 F. 2d 245 (7th Cir. 1942).

31. 86 F. 608 (7th Cir. 1898), cert. denied, 173 U.S. 703 (1899).

32. 162 F.2d 893 (2d Cir. 1947).

33. 2420 F.2d 1248 (7th Cir.), cert. denied, 400 U.S. 820 (1970).

34. 305 U.S. 111 (1938).

35. Richard A. Posner, *Regulation of Advertising by the Federal Trade Commission* (American Enterprise Institute, 1973), p. 31.

36. See, e.g., "Developments in the Law—Deceptive Advertising," *Harvard Law Review* 80 (1967): 1005, 1082-83.

37. See Note, *Baylor Law Review* 29 (1977): 559, 563–67.

38. Pub. L. 93-637, 99 Stat. 2183 (1975). Such power had been upheld as "implied," even without explicit legislative authority, in *National Petroleum Refiners Assn. v. FTC*, 482 F.2d 672 (D.C. Cir. 1973),

39. 15 U.S.C. § 57g (a) (2) (1976).

40. *Holloway v. Bristol-Myers Corp.*, 485 F.2d 986 (1973).

41. See John A. Sebert, Jr., "Enforcement of State Deceptive Trade Practices Statutes," *Tennessee Law Review* 42 (1975): 689, 698–704.

42. William A. Lovett, "State Deceptive Trade Practice Legislation," *Tulane Law Review* 46 (1972): 724, 743–49. These statutes are considered in Part III–B.

43. For the history of the small-claims-court movement, which dates back to 1605 in England, see Gould, *Small Claims Report*, p. 3. Efforts to reduce the cost of consumer suits continue: a bill to provide federal funds to states for establishing and promoting procedures for resolving minor consumer disputes passed the Senate but was defeated in the House. *Cong. Q. Weekly Report*, Oct. 21, 1978, p. 3082.

44. See, e.g., Note, *Stanford Law Review* 4 (1952): 237; Note, *Stanford Law Review* 21 (1969): 1657; Judge Tim Murphy, "Small Claims Court—The Forgotten Court," *D.C. Bar Journal* 34 (February 1967): 14.

45. John Montague Steadman and Richard S. Rosenstein, 'Small Claims' Consumer Plaintiffs in the Philadelphia Municipal Court: An Empirical Study," *University of Pennsylvania Law Review* 121 (1973): 1309. Their survey found that 18 percent of the 614 cases studied fell into a "miscellaneous" category, which included fraudulent advertising. (Ibid. p. 1327, note 133.) Fraudulent advertising was not separately mentioned as one of "the more prominent miscellaneous claims categories." (Ibid., Table B, p. 1347.)

46. See generally, David A. Rice, "Remedies, Enforcement Procedures, and the Duality of Consumer Transaction Problems," *Boston University Law Review* 48 (1968): 559, 588–95.

47. Eric H. Steele, "Fraud, Dispute, and the Consumer: Responding to Consumer Complaints," *University of Pennsylvania Law Review* 123 (1975): 1107.

48. See Rice, "Remedies, Enforcement Procedures," pp. 570–76.

49. The literature on consumer class actions is extensive. See the exhaustive report of Gould, *Small Claims Report*.

50. See, e.g., Note, "Consumers, Class Actions, and Costs: An Economic Perspective on Deceptive Advertising," *University of California Los Angeles*

Law Review 18 (1971): 592, 603–05. *See also,* Jonathan M. Landers, "Of Legalized Blackmail and Legalized Theft: Consumer Class Actions and the Substance-Procedure Dilemma," *Southern California Law Review* 47 (1974): 842. Landers also points out that the cost of resort to the courts means that businesses, too, cannot obtain legal redress for small injuries. Landers suggests that the legal system may reflect a social judgment that such small losses should lie where they fall, instead of using resources to reallocate the loss through the legal system. In other words, court time should be reserved for more weighty problems. *See also Hacket v. General Host Corp.,* 455 F. 2d 618, 626 (3d Cir.), *cert. denied,* 407 U.S. 925 (1972).

51. Or. Rev. Stat. secs. 646.638 (1971).

52. *Scott v. Western International Surplus Sales, Inc.,* 267 Ore. 512, 517 P.2d 661 (1973). The real bone of contention appeared to be the store's refusal to give a cash refund. The retailer offered the consumer a credit, which he claimed was worthless to him.

53. *Wolverton v. Stanwood,* 278 Ore. 341, 563 P.2d 1203 (1978).

54. Some courts have questioned whether the Lanham Act was intended to do any more than give a federal right of action "false descriptions of substantially the same economic nature as those which involve infringement or other improper use of trademarks." *Samson Crane Co. v. Union National Sales, Inc.,* 87 F. Supp. 218 (D. Mass. 1949). *aff'd per curiam,* 180 F.2d 896 (1st Cir. 1950). The Third Circuit gave the section a more expansive reading in *L'Aiglon Apparel v. Lana Lobell, Inc.,* 214 F.2d 649 (3d Cir. 1954). The controversy is reviewed in *Universal Athletic Sales Co. v. American Gym, Recreational & Athletic Equipment Corp.,* 397 F. Supp. 1063, 1071-73 (W.D. Pa. 1975), *aff'd mem.,* 556 F.2d 1171 (3d Cir. 1977).

55. 419 F. Supp. 292 (E.D. Pa. 1976), *aff'd sub nom., Donsco, Inc. v. Casper Corp.,* 587 F.2d 602 (3d Cir. 1978).

56. 375 F. Supp. 777 (N.D. Ill. 1974).

57. 441 F. Supp. 162 (C.D. Calif. 1977).

58. If "Made in USA" is perceived as a proxy for better quality by consumers, one may question the part of Posner's critique of the FTC that condemns devoting resources to combatting such deceptions. Consumers may not be xenophobic, as he points out, but they may prefer better-made goods. *See* Posner, "The Federal Trade Commission," p. 73.

59. 19 U.S.C. sec. 1304 (1976).

60. 285 F. Supp. 636 (S.D.N.Y. 1968). This case also points up the necessity of permitting a firm to guard its trademark. If the misnumbered part in fact caused a crash and blame could be traced to that part, injured parties would look to the original manufacturer, identified on the part, for redress. Although current law places the burden on the plaintiff to prove that the defect existed at the time the product left the manufacturer (*Restatement [Second] of Torts*) sec. 402A (1965), in fact the original manufacturer would have to put the intervening alteration of the part into evidence in order to put the plaintiff to his proof. On misuse of trademark grounds alone, the plaintiff may have had a good cause of action.

61. 362 F. Supp. 1094 (S.D.N.Y. 1973).

62. 372 F. Supp. 1 (E.D. Pa. 1974).

63. 513 F.2d 716 (9th Cir. 1975).

64. R. G. Smith v. Chanel, Inc. 402 F.2d 562 (9th Cir. 1968).

65. 467 F.2d 304 (2d Cir. 1972).

66. Letter from Carol M. Thomas, Secretary, Federal Trade Commission to authors (Nov. 22, 1978), in response to Freedom of Information Act request. One widely publicized instance of competitor complaint to the FTC occurred in the hotly contested beer-marketing battle between Miller and Anheuser-Busch. Miller complained that Anheuser-Busch's advertising its beers as "natural" was "misleading." See Wall Street Journal, Mar. 14, 1979, p. 48.

67. Alberto-Culver Co. v. Gillette Co., 408 F. Supp. 1160 (N.D. Ill. 1976).

68. American Brands, Inc. v. R. J. Reynolds Tobacco Co., 413 F. Supp. 1352 (S.D.N.Y. 1976).

69. 242 F. Supp. 302 (N.D. Ill. 1965).

70. 513 F.2d 716 (9th Cir. 1975).

71. 419 F. Supp. 212 (E.D. Pa. 1976), aff'd sub nom., Donsco, Inc. v. Casper Corp. 587 F.2d, 602 (3d Cir. 1978).

72. 372 F. Supp. 1 (E.D. Pa. 1974).

73. Bose Corp. v. Linear Design Labs Inc., 467 F.2d 304 (2d Cir. 1972).

74. 276 F. Supp. 707 (C.D. Cal. 1967).

75. Potato Chip Inst. v. General Mills, Inc., 461 F.2d 1088 (8th Cir. 1972).

76. Electronics Corp. of America v. Honeywell, Inc., 358 F. Supp. 1230 (D. Mass. 1973).

77. Skil Corp. v. Rockwell Int'l. Corp., 375 F. Supp. 777 (N.D. Ill. 1974); Alberto-Culver Co. v. Gillette Co., 408 F. Supp. 1160 (N.D. Ill. 1976) ("Tame" v. "Earth Born Creme Rinses"); American Consumer, Inc. v. Kroger Co., 416 F Supp. 1210 (E. D. Tenn. 1976) (Kroger's "Price Patrol" report); American Home Products Corp. v. Johnson & Johnson, 436 F. Supp. 785 (S.D.N.Y. 1977) ("Anacin" v. "Tylenol").

78. 413 F. Supp. 1352 (S.D.N.Y. 1976).

79. Universal Athletic Sales Co. v. American Gym, Recreational & Athletic Equipment Corp., 397 F. Supp. 1063 (W.D. Pa. 1975); Bohsei Enterprises Co. v. Porteous Fastener Co., 441 F. Supp. 162 (C.D. Calif. 1977).

80. Rudolph Callmann, The Law of Unfair Competition, Trademarks, and Monopolies, 3d ed. (Mundelein, Ill.: Callaghan 1965), sec. 8.2 (c).

81. See, e.g., Walter J. Derenberg, "Federal Unfair Competition Law at the End of the First Decade of the Lanham Act: Prologue or Epilogue," New York University Law Review 32 (1957): 1029.

82. Warren S. Grimes, "Control of Advertising in the United States and Germany: Volkswagen Has a Better Idea," Harvard Law Review 84 (1971): 1769.

83. Ibid., pp. 1789–90.

84. Ibid., pp. 1781–82.

85. See, e.g., David Caplovitz, The Poor Pay More (New York: Free Press, 1967), pp. 153–54.

86. Grimes, "Volkswagen Has a Better Idea," p. 1784.

87. Frederic M. Scherer, *Industrial Market Structure and Economic Performance* (Boston: Houghton Mifflin, 1970), p. 158.

88. What incentive there is will be strongest in the case of credence qualities. Consistently with its congruence with economic rationality, the common law most freely permitted private actions when such claims (as, for example, manufacturer identity) were at stake.

89. The law of false advertising discussed here is part of the general body of law called "unfair competition," which deals in general with torts committed by one business firm against another. Economic analysis has here been fruitful in examining one part of this law; Chapter 5 provides another example. Another example is the common law treatment of price competition. In fact, the common law said virtually nothing about such competition. *See* Edmund W. Kitch and Harvey S. Perlman, *Legal Regulation of the Competitive Process* (Mineola, N.Y.: Foundation Press, 1972) p. 193. Strictures on such behavior, which ban unfairly low prices, are clearly inefficient; such restrictions are creatures of statute, such as the Robinson-Patman Act. In this area the failure of the common law to interfere is a clear sign of its efficiency.

90. *Virginia State Board of Pharmacy* v. *Virginia Citizens Consumer Council Inc.*, 425 U.S. 748 (1976).

91. Ibid., p. 771.

92. Ronald H. Coase, "Advertising and Free Speech," *Journal of Legal Studies* 6 (1977): 1.

93. Aaron Director, "The Parity of the Economic Market Place," *Journal of Law and Economics* 7 (1964): 1.

PART III

THE GOVERNMENT AS LITIGANT

So far, we have dealt with firms as litigants. In this part, the government as a litigant is introduced. Government agencies do have long term interests in precedents, and therefore seek decisions that will fulfill their goals. However, these goals have no necessary relationship to efficiency. Firms sometimes find it worth organizing to respond to the initiatives of government agencies; this part also considers this response.

CHAPTER 7

Government Agencies
as Litigants

I. INTRODUCTION

In Part I, it was argued that private litigants, following their own self-interest, would tend to push the law toward efficient rules. In Part II, evidence on this point was presented. Here, we will examine litigation between government agencies and regulated parties. In brief, the conclusion is that regulatory agencies are motivated less than private litigants to seek efficient rules, but do have a long-range interest in asserting and expanding their own authority. Hence, the "principle" asserted by a decision may be of more value to them than the results of the particular case. The regulated party, on the other hand, is immediately concerned about his own case, and wishes to bargain to escape as cheaply as possible. Regulatory agencies can quite successfully trade leniency in the case at hand for acquiescence in assertions of new authority and powers. Furthermore, the agency's virtually complete monopoly on initiating litigation enables it to pick extreme cases that may result in sweeping kinds of "rules." The resulting rules, even if seldom enforced, serve as a fetter on those who wish to conduct their affairs in accordance with the law and also create the possibility for discriminatory enforcement. In short, while it may be completely rational for each respondent to trade a favorable finding today for burdensome and inefficient law in the future, such rules impose costs on society. Without some mechanism to aggregate the interest in efficiency of other regulated parties, inefficient rules may never be challenged. Even if other values, such as distributional equity or procedural fairness, eventually outweigh the claims for efficiency, society ought to recognize how much these other values cost in order to make informed decisions on how to allocate its resources.

In Section II the theory of litigation by agencies and by defendants is examined. The conclusion is that there is no incentive for efficiency in this litigation, but the agencies should seek their own goals and defendants should agree to give in on precedents in order to achieve lenient treatment. In Section III evidence from the behavior of the FTC and the SEC is presented that is consistent with this hypothesis. The last section summarizes this chapter.

II. THEORY

A. Administrative Agencies

The mechanisms described in Part I, which predict that the self-interest of litigants will push the law toward efficiency, operate differently in the context of agency-regulated party litigation. In litigation between two private parties, both engage in calculations to maximize the effect of dollars spent. Both are primarily concerned with effects on their financial position. The "bottom line" here has a well-recognized meaning, and both antagonists understand and share the same kinds of concerns. What distinguishes the dynamics of government agency-regulated party litigation is that the agency's bottom line is much more elusive and difficult to measure. Government litigators and the regulated do not share the same well-understood concern with efficiency, partly because an agency's statutory mandate and relationship with Congress induce the regulators to respond to other incentives. The legislation that creates the agency defines its powers and priorities, and sometimes mandates inefficient results. But the agencies themselves, responding to the desire to achieve congressionally-defined goals and their own goals, may exacerbate the inefficiencies of regulation by giving insufficient attention to the efficiency implications of their policies.

This section builds upon the work of William Niskanen[1], who hypothesizes that a rational bureaucrat will respond to those in control of his budget. Such a hypothesis seems plausible, inasmuch as the level of resources affects income, other nonmonetary rewards such as prestige, and also an administrator's ability to carry out the "mission" that may have attracted him to government service in the first place. But distortion is perhaps inevitable if the goals themselves are vague generalities. Agencies are often charged with producing "output" that is difficult to either define or measure. This problem of developing operational measures of success may cause them to concentrate on measures that are easily quantified and presented. For instance, it is much easier to keep track of cases won than to undertake an analysis of whether the agency's resources should have been devoted instead to other cases or to rule-making or other long-range planning. Hence, as C. M. Lindsay[2] has demonstrated in the case of the Veterans Administration, the need to compile a record that Congress can understand leads the VA to concentrate on producing visible and easily digested output.

There is some empirical evidence that supports this hypothesis. Richard Posner[3] studied the behavior of the Federal Trade Commission, and has commented that a rational administrator will choose to focus his litigation budget on precedent-setting cases he can win, thus enhancing the agency's present and future batting average. Posner demonstrates that a rational bureaucrat should concentrate on cases where the stakes for the defendant are sufficiently small so that the defense will not devote much effort to fighting the agency, thereby permitting the agency to stretch its budget. As Posner puts it, "The usual defendant is uninterested in whether the outcome of his case will have precedential significance."[4] He concludes that the behavior of the Federal Trade Commission, in concentrating on small cases, is "optimizing behavior rather than a manifestation of stupidity or timidity."[5]

The bureaucrat concerned about his budget also benefits if he can achieve results by imposing costs on others, rather than by devoting his own resources. Since costs borne by the private sector do not affect his balance sheet, the bureaucrat would be expected to resist taking direct action, funded by government, even if such action might in some cases be cheaper.

For example, consider the Consumer Product Safety Commission, charged by law to make more information about safety hazards available to consumers. The agency could undertake publicity directly, or it could require those it regulates to disseminate more information. Sometimes imposing the burden on the regulated is indeed efficient. For example, the manufacturer may be best able to disseminate existing information to each new purchaser at the time of sale at least cost. For safety hazards discovered after purchase, if purchaser records are maintained, recall notices directed to affected purchasers are an efficient way to disseminate information. In contrast, however, where a hazard becomes apparent in a very low-priced item, where purchaser records are nonexistent and too costly to maintain, publicity by the agency resulting in widespread news coverage might be by far the cheapest way to inform the public. Although the manufacturer could communicate via paid advertising, advertising does not command the same consumer attention as does news, and an advertising message would need to be repeated to achieve the desired impact. The source of the information affects its credibility as well, again arguing for governmental dissemination for the strongest possible impact.

Regardless of these efficiency considerations, however, when the Consumer Product Safety Commission became aware of a problem with a mechanic's trouble light, which could electrocute its user, the Commission's reaction was to try to shift the burden of informing past purchasers to the manufacturer.[6] We would expect the budget-conscious Commission to prefer an outcome that avoided a drain on its own budget, particularly a drain that would produce few measurable statistics to be included in its annual report to Congress. Furthermore, the Commission would have an interest in establishing its authority to order such advertising in the future. Therefore, the Commission sought a court order compelling the manufacturer to purchase prime broadcasting time and advertising space in 85 percent of the national newspaper circulation to give "public notice" of the light's dangers, as the act provides.[7] Although the Commission obviously had a long-term interest in the precedent being established, the immediate stakes in the case for the affected firm were so high that the manufacturer resisted the Commission's demand. The court instead ordered the Commission to hold a televised press conference to demonstrate the risks associated with the light. The resulting court-ordered news conference reached the average adult television viewer at least once, achieving the goal of transmitting the warning information to the affected audience at the least cost.

In sum, if a bureaucrat's concern is to use his budget to produce easily measured indicia of output, minimization of community costs will not be uppermost in his mind. Instead, he will try to shift costs to others, especially if the goal is to achieve an effect that is difficult to measure. Thereby, he can avoid a drain on his budget that does not produce statistics for his annual report to Congress.[8]

The bureaucrat's interest in achieving the goals of his agency coincides with an interest in increasing his budget. This combination may lead him to favor sweeping assertions of power and wide discretion. Hence, he can come to Congress complaining that he cannot keep up with the work load and needs more positions. Curiously, this strategy may fit neatly into each Congressman's own best interest: more administrative "red tape" allows him more opportunities to act as an "ombudsman" for his constituents, and client service looms large in the strategy of how to get reelected.[9] Hence, although the current public mood may indicate the results have become intolerable, creating more and more burdensome regulation may have benefited both the bureaucrat and the Congressman.

We argue then, that the bureaucrat seeking to maximize his budget is induced to favor expansive discretionary power. Such behavior is not checked by Congress, and in fact is rewarded, since Congressmen favor opportunities to intercede for constituents. If so, agencies that act to enforce rather vague and general statutes enjoy a great advantage: they can advance their interests by case-by-case adjudication.

As Robert Bork has pointed out, an agency concerned about shaping the law "can wait and select the best vehicles for their purposes"[10] from many possible cases. A rational agency will select cases whose facts are most extreme, since such cases will be easiest to prepare and win. Such cases are unattractive for the defense, and often lead to rather sweeping decisions. Even if in theory the resulting rule, rooted in the facts, may later be "distinguished," such fact-centered litigation is costly. The succeeding litigant must persuade the agency, whose finding of fact will not be disturbed on judicial review unless not supported by substantial evidence.[11] Therefore, if an expansive rule emerges from the litigation process, it is difficult to overturn, especially as time passes.

Recent changes in regulation have exacerbated these problems. Old-style regulation involved licensing in a particular industry: the FCC regulated communications, the ICC regulated trucks and railroads, the FDA regulated food and drugs. In contrast. the new regulation, as described by Murray Weidenbaum,[12] cuts across industry lines. For example, OSHA regulates workplace safety in all industries and EEOC regulates hiring practices in all firms. This changing pattern of regulation has several implications.

First, it means that regulatory agencies have large numbers of potential tragets among which to select. If, for example, OSHA is concerned with noise in the work place it might choose a relatively small firm and order this firm to use quieter equipment rather than the cheaper earplugs now being used. If the firm acquiesces, other firms have learned something about that firm's view of its chances of success. Even if this case is litigated, OSHA's interest in the precedential value of the decision might cause it to devote extra resources to win and thus obtain a precedent to use against other firms. Of course, each target firm can argue its own situation, but may find it difficult to force reconsideration of the entire strategy.

Second, the new pattern of regulation implies that there are fewer organizations that would aggregate the interest of all firms to oppose inefficient regulation at the outset. In the case of old-style regulation, the trade association would represent all firms with an interest in some type of regulation. To the extent that an agency regulates activities that cross industry barriers, no single trade association would have the same incentive to protest the regulations. Moreover, the sheer amount of information that regulated firms or their representatives would need to assimilate would be immense. In the past, railroads might have monitored the ICC and learned about all decisions that could affect them. Now, all industries must monitor the behavior of all regulatory agencies, which is a different and much more expensive task.

To be sure, there are associations such as the National Association of Manufacturers and the National Chamber of Commerce that do represent a large number of business firms, and thus that may be able to deal with the newer type of regulation. Moreover, new organizations have been formed in response to the new regulations. Among such organizations are the business-oriented legal foundations, discussed in Chapter 8. However, as the number of individuals affected by public action becomes larger, free rider problems become more severe. As the number of potential members of a lobbying group increases, we would expect a relatively smaller percentge of potential members to join the lobby.

B. The Regulated

We turn now to a consideration of the interests of regulated parties. We argued in Part I that a concern about the futue effect of a decision influences the choice of litigation tactics: whether to litigate or to settle, and what resources to devote to the litigation, once undertaken. Another critical and related decision is whether to argue broad legal principles, or instead to join issue about the particular facts of one's own case. A respondent facing an agency interpreting and applying vague statutory generalities has every incentive to fight hard for its own exoneration on the facts, instead of challenging the agency on new assertions of regulatory authority. The agency, on the other hand, always has an eye on its future cases, and may be willing to accede on the facts of this case in exchange for an affirmation of its authority. Even though the agency's new strategy may be most inefficient, the fact that is is facing one respondent more concerned with its short-term problem in this case than with the long-term effect on all similarly situated firms may mean it is not effectively challenged. If the agency chooses to focus its litigation budget on small cases, in terms of the stakes involved, the immediate monetary stakes in the case at issue may be very small, thus making it irrational for the target firm to devote enough resources to mount even minimal opposition. Posner argues that a rational agency will enhance its won-lost record by capitalizing on this fact of life.[13]

Second, the cost of mounting adequate opposition may be quite large, even in relation to considerable stakes, and such opposition may simply be beyond the reach of firms whose resources are small. The cost of a defense rises with the amount of factual data one must gather, analyze, and present, and also depends on the skill of advocates and their familiarity with cases of this sort.

Third, there may be cases, even when the stakes are large and resources apparently adequate, where the target of regulatory activity may be unable or unwilling to advocate a very broad principle, no matter how valid that principle may be. The target may prefer to concentrate on its own innocence rather than attempt to attack the entire proceeding, since the latter course could be interpreted as an admission of guilt. The target firm may also prefer to bargain with the agency, perhaps obtaining more favorable treatment in exchange for conceding the agency's view of the law. Affected firms often negotiate with the agency on the terms of the decree that will be entered. For instance, in exchange for a consent decree ITT succeeded in modifying a required "corrective advertisement."[14] The decree, as proposed in the complaint, would have required the firm to disclose that the FTC had accused them of misleading the public.[15] The compromise accepted by the FTC intimated instead that the company was taking voluntary action to correct an unforutnate possible misunderstanding of prior ads.

The benefits to be gained from establishing a broad-based limit on an agency's activity will accrue to all firms, including rivals. Hence, if the target firm can prevail by arguing the facts, it serves its own ends and fully captures the benefits; by contrast, if it makes the broad argument, and wins, all other firms enjoy a free ride on its efforts. Furthermore, any such altruistic behavior by large firms may be suspect. An immediate example is the much-ballyhooed complaint filed by Sears, Roebuck & Co.[16] asking for relief from inconsistent government directives in the employment area. The lawsuit was denounced as a public relations stunt to blunt the impact of an expected EEOC complaint against Sears.[17] Whatever the merits of its position, therefore, Sears' transparent private interest affected its credibility as a spokesman for the public interest involved.

Corporate counsel may also exhibit little enthusiasm for broad-based attacks. They may understandably view a client's chance of success as small, and counsel more attention to a more narrow defense. The risk of more broad-based attack is that a loss would establish a broad negative precedent. They may also see a virtue in maintaining a certain bargaining position with the agency itself, in their clients' interest, and may prefer to avoid antagonizing the agency and its staff.

Furthermore, an attorney's own relationship with the agency may act as a fetter on his willingness to mount frontal attacks. The agency may regulate or license those who appear before it,[18] and even if the sanctions for "misbehaving" are less obvious, those attorneys who represent varied clients before federal agencies may wish to maintain friendly relations with their counterparts on the agency staff in order to enhance their effectiveness in representing those clients.

Hence, there may be bounds that traditional attorneys will not over-step. While other lawyers may be willing to make broader arguments, they will lack experience before the agency.

Even if others affected by regulatory litigation can overcome the problems of organizing, communicating, and finding representation, they may face barriers. Although procedural devices exist to allow others to join on-going litigation (intervention), perhaps even as the representative of a much larger group (class action), those concerned solely with the future impact of a current agency position face problems of "justiciability."[19] Their claims are not concrete cases or controversies; they essentially raise hypothetical questions inasmuch as the agency may never choose to initiate action against those who assert concern. Even a trade association representing retail grocers was refused the right to intervene in an FTC proceeding against the A&P on the grounds that an interest that is confined to possible precedential effect will not support a bid to become a party.[20] Similarly, efforts to initiate a judicial test of FTC policy have foundered; courts have refused to entertain declaratory judgment action[21] on the grounds that such an action is premature or not ripe for resolution. If an individual or representative cannot assert his own justiciable interest, moreover, there is no way to employ another procedural device, the class action, which may sometimes serve as a way to aggregate small interests for litigation.

Although participation as a party or as class may be precluded, third parties interested in precedent have an alternative way to offer input to the decision. They may act as *amicus curiae*, presenting written or oral agrument for the agency's consideration. The *amicus* role is limited, however; *amici* may not present evidence, cross-examine witnesses, nor exercise any right to appeal.[22] *Amicus* participation may be a useful activity for legal foundations, which can devote the time and resourcs to becoming expert in matters no single firm could afford to research and present. Furthermore, participation as *amicus* ensures that the decision maker is aware that more than this case may be involved, especially when a question of first impression is under consideration.

II. CASE STUDIES

The thesis developed thus far is that bureaucratic agencies responding to the incentives they face will not take total costs into account and will not seek efficient rules. Furthermore, bureaucrats who seek to achieve higher budgetary levels have an interest in asserting new authority and more expansive powers. The individual respondent, on the other hand, will not make broad, generally applicable arguments if it can escape cheaply in its particular case, and the agency will not be effectively informed about the total cost of its policies. We offer as evidence the actions of two federal agencies, the Federal Trade Commission's regulation of advertising, particularly its advertising substantiation program, and the Securities and Exchange Commission's regulation of insider trading.

A. The FTC

The FTC, while a relatively old regulatory agency, nonetheless has many of the characteristics of newer regulatory agencies in that it has very broad authority over most firms, not merely firms in one industry. The FTC's litigation strategy is especially interesting, since the FTC had no explicit rule-making authority until 1975,[23] and so proceeded to give content to the law by adjudication. Its advertising regulation activities have been heavily criticized. Posner has studied the performance of the FTC and contends that much, if not all, of the advertising regulation by the FTC has been economically inefficient. Most importantly, each of the Commission's recent consumer protection initiatives followed the same pattern: a new assertion of regulatory authority was advanced against an individual respondent, which chose to focus on the facts of its own case.[24] In these test cases, the FTC consistently has asserted its power, but has opted not to exercise it. The individual respondent has nothing to appeal, and indeed may be satisfied by this outcome. Other individuals potentially affected are unlikely to take the trouble to register an opinion before the Commission. If these initiatives have efficiency implications, an organization such as a legal foundation would have two possible effects: to strengthen the cases of individual litigants before the FTC, and perhaps reduce the inefficiency imposed on the economy by this agency by asserting a broader and more general challenge to agency policy than any one litigant would have found worthwhile.

The Federal Trade Commission was established in 1914, and was given a very sweeping responsibility of proceeding against unfair methods of competition in commerce.[25] The Commissioners are charged with protecting competition and policing the marketplace, assignments that may at times pull in opposite directions.

The Commission has regulated advertising from the first year of its operation. Judicial review of Commission activities has traditionally been deferential, recognizing the Commission's expertise in determining what may be deceptive,[26] and giving the FTC considerable latitude in devising cease-and-desist orders,[27] which was the principal enforcement tool Congress provided. In other words, the Commission could declare the law with prospective effect only, and the only penalty the statute provided for was violation of the order. The order could be given only after the Commission issued a complaint, and afforded an opportunity to show cause at a hearing why an order should be issued. The statute also provides that "any person" may apply and "upon good cause shown" may be allowed to intervene in the proceeding.[28] Thus, any person or firm who believes his interests may be affected by the FTC's action against firm *A* may petition to become a party as well.

Intervention, by definition, refers to the process of joining an on-going proceeding as a party. In administrative law, commentators have noted a recognition of broad intervention rights before agencies, particularly in rate-making and licensing proceedings. Indeed, decisions according self-styled "public interest" groups a right to intervene in licensing proceedings before Federal Communications Commission[29] and Federal Power Commission[30] have been the subject of great interest.

The arguments for and against permitting intervention may be simply stated. Intervention by an interested party allows him to represent his own interests and present his point of view. It may assist the decision maker in reaching a better, more informed judgment. Against those advantages must be balanced the inevitable complication and delay that result when additional parties are added, each of whom wishes to argue, cross-examine, present evidence, and engage in discovery proceedings. The FTC argues that decisions about whether to permit intervention are committed to its discretion by the "good cause" limitation:[31] hence, there is no right to intervene, and the rules of the Commission make clear that intervention may be granted to limited terms only.

In one recent action, the FTC denied a motion to intervene made by a trade association, stating:

> [T]he possibility that an adjudicative proceeding may result in an interpretation of a law or regulation which may be applicable as a legal precedent to others not accused in the adjudicative proceeding, cannot be grounds for intervention in that proceeding by all who may possibly be affected in this way by it. . . .
>
> Participation as *amicus curiae* [is] . . . the traditional role accorded to those concerned with the precedential impact of adjudicative decisions.[32]

It may be that when only the long-range effects of a decision are of concern, an *amicus* brief is the preferred vehicle to place views before the decision maker. It is important to note that even if an agency succeeds in obtaining a ruling disadvantageous to the target firm, other similarly situated firms are not technically bound thereby.

Fundamental notions of due process, enshrined in the Constitution, demand that before a person (natural or corporate) can be deprived of liberty or property, government must give him notice and opportunity to be heard. Hence, if the FTC has issued an order against firm A, firms B-Z have learned something about the agency's view of the law, but are themselves not subject to any sanction even if they engage in same conduct unless, and until, the agency chooses to proceed against each one in turn. But this lack of immediate, binding effect does not mean that the decision about firm A is irrelevant when the agency turns its attention to firms B-Z. In any system where adjudication declares "rules of law," the doctrine of *stare decisis* is important. For reasons of administrative convenience, as well as concern for equality of treatment before the law, adjudicative bodies should treat like cases in like manner, and will follow their prior decisions unless they can be convinced not to do so. The more often a precedent has been applied, the stronger the claim for continuing to follow it: that rule of decisional law has become predictable and parties begin to rely on it. Indeed, courts have held that it is an abuse of discretion for an administrative agency to depart from its established precedents without explanation showing a reasoned change in policy.[33]

In 1975, Congress granted the FTC new authority to seek civil penalties for "knowing" violations of FTC caselaw determinations without the need for the Commission to first impose a cease-and-desist order. The possibility of civil penalties against nonrespondents greatly increases the precedential force of an FTC decision. Even though a defendant not subject to the original order is guaranteed a trial do novo on "issues of fact," issues of law are sometimes determinative of issues of fact. For instance, the FTC's substantiation theory provides a good example of how an opportunity to contest the facts will be of only limited value to a later defendant. Once the court accepts the Commission's view that it is the lack of prior substantiation, not the falsity of the underlying claim, that constitutes the violation, proof that the product did perform as advertised becomes irrelevant, although the subsequent advertiser may argue that it had a "reasonable basis" for making its claim. Obviously, it is easier to argue such a reasonable basis if the claim in fact turns out to be accurate.

This new rationale for FTC adjudicatory decisions may strengthen the claim of similarly situated parties that they should be permitted to participate in the original proceeding. In most cases the guarantee of a trial *de novo* on the facts may make participation as *amicus* sufficient. In other cases, however, particularly when a novel or expansive legal theory is proposed, those affected should be permitted to participate more fully, as intervenors, thus preserving a right to appeal and an opportunity to raise broader concerns than may affect the original respondent.

The FTC is charged with protecting the public, but all such protection has both costs and benefits. In the case of advertising regulation, the benefits to be gained are a reduction in resource misallocation caused by misinformed purchasing decisions. The costs include not only the obvious monitoring, investigation, and prosecution expenses, but also the burdens on conscientious and honest advertisers that agency action imposes. From an economic standpoint, the agency should consider both the costs and benefits of its action, and devote resources to the point where incremental expenditure equals incremental benefits. Sometimes the calculus is easy. The clearest case is the intentional fraud that produces no social value whatever. But even here, an imbalance between small harm and large administrative costs may argue against suppression. If the direct costs of federal enforcement far outweigh any possible injury, the matter seems inappropriate for FTC action.

In practice, the vast bulk of the Commission's work load deals not with outright fraud, but with charges of deception.[34] The Commission has been granted wide latitude to determine what might deceive, and need only show a capacity to mislead. This discretion makes critical the level of perception and skepticism the Commission assumes on the part of the audience. If the decision maker credits consumers with the intelligence of the hypothetical reasonable man, advertisers will enjoy more creative license for hyperbole. If, however, it is necessary to protect even the most unthinking and credulous[35] who might conceivably take such puffery literally, the societal costs of enforcement rise sharply. To the direct expense of enforcement must be added the loss of artistic, creative, and whimsical advertising, which may provide significant entertainment and aesthetic value, if the lowest common denominator is accepted as the regulatory norm. The benefits to be gained by insisting on more literal truth seem questionable: if the real world consumer more closely resembles the rational man than the fool, few have have been misled.

In borderline cases, however, the structure of incentives facing the agency will cause it to err on the side of too much, rather than too little, regulation. If the agency is too lenient and consumers do suffer injury, the error is visible and directly attributable to the agency. On the other hand, the benefits lost by more rigid rules are harder to demonstrate or to monitor.[36] Once the agency has decided to proceed, moreover, the individual respondent is at a disadvantage. His obvious concern is to be exonerated by the FTC; any advocacy of artistic freedom and lack of real harm are tainted by his self-interest in being permitted to continue with a course of conduct in which he had already invested. Such broad interests are realistically at stake, however, and should be presented to the agency. More detached public interest groups might credibly raise them, and, more importantly, prove them. The sophistication and perception of the consumer is empirically knowable and provable, although such proof is costly. In deception cases, studies of actual consumer attitudes could aid the Commission in choosing the appropriate base line. Additional spending by firms or organizations of firms could both make the arguments and provide the data to help the FTC adjust its intervention according to marginal costs and benefits.

Advertising's most important role is as information, not art. This is relevant in considering the history of the FTC's advertising substantiation efforts. The Commission asserts that unsubstantiated claims, regardless of their truth or falsity, are harmful to the customer, "unfair," and hence unlawful.[37] The FTC can point to four litigated cases in support of its position, but in none of them was the issue cleanly presented to a reviewing court. Indeed, in the strongest case for respondents, the Commission avoided a court test when it reasserted its theory, yet dismissed the complaint for failure of proof by its staff.

The earliest case in which the Commission discussed the need for prior substantiation was *Heinz v. Kirchner.*[38] In that case, the Commission recognized that the fool's test had its limits, and expressed the belief that no sizeable segment of the community would take literally a claim of "invisibility" for an inflatable swimming aid. In the Commission's view, claims that the device made a swimmer "unsinkable" were more serious, since some nonswimmers might rely on such a claim and endanger their lives. The Commission found the "unsinkable" claims to be untrue, and prohibited them.

The question of the need for prior substantiation was raised only tangentially. The Commission needed only to decide whether the respondent had been prejudiced because the hearing examiner had closed the record before he had been able to obtain test results to back up his claims. Since the facts conclusively showed that the respondent's predicament was entirely a result of his own dilatoriness in even seeking the information, it was an easy matter to affirm the exercise of the examiner's discretion. The opinion, however, laid the groundwork for the substantiation policy by asserting a special need for prior substantiation of health and safety claims. Without reasonable grounds for such claims, wrote Commissioner Elman, the advertiser demonstrates "a reckless disregard for human health and safety," which is "clearly an unfair and deceptive practice." Hence, although it seems unlikely that consumers would either understand the claim as more than "puff" or stake their lives on it, the respondent's delaying tactics combined with the strong public interest in preventing personal injury affected the Commission's dictum, if not its holding.

Robert Pitofsky has defended requiring prior substantiation of claims relating to significant health and safety concerns, asserting that justification for such a requirement is obvious.[39] It does not seem so obvious that Commission action is needed, at least where serious injury is possible. First, if danger is apparent, consumers can probably be trusted to discount advertising and take appropriate precautions. Moreover, false claims that lead to personal injury give rise to substantial liability. Injured consumers have ample incentive to sue if a misrepresentation causes harm, and any additional cautionary effect producd by FTC scrutiny seems superfluous. One might argue that compliance costs would be minimal if advertisers are already substantiating such claims. Nevertheless, if harm is unlikely, any resources expended by advertisers in responding to the Commission or by the Commission in verifying the data submitted appear to be wasted. Such a government-administered program ignores the efficiency with which the tort system can induce the appropriate level of caution without any bureaucratic intervention.

Whether or not additional governmental action would have the desired effect, Pitofsky points out that any reduction of personal injuries would be a clear benefit. He notes that it is less clear that substantiation produces benefits when all the consumer faces is minor economic injury. Exactly such a case was chosen by the Commission in its next foray into what advertisers may be required to do before disseminating claims. The Commission issued an order against Leon Tashof, a Washington retailer who advertised "discount" eyeglasses.[40] The store sold so few at the advertised price that an inference of bait advertising seemed unmistakable. The retailer also advertised "easy credit" without informing the purchaser that its collection policies were exceptionally rigorous. Although the hearing examiner recommended dismissing the charges, the Commission disagreed, and framed an order to closely regulate the retailer's future conduct. In particular, it ordered the respondent to take a statistically significant survey to demonstrate that prevailing market prices are substantially above his before he could advertise "discount" prices. Since violation of a Commission order subjects a respondent to civil penalties, the respondent could in theory be fined for making the claims without the survey even if the claims were true. On appeal, the Commission persuaded the majority of the reviewing court that in view of respondent's past record, its order was necessary to protect the public.

The Commission, in its zeal to fence in a retailer it viewed as exploiting the poorest members of the community, has set an unfortunate precedent when it went beyond prohibiting false or misleading advertising and undertook to specify what the retailer must do to ensure accurate information. For government to burden, and perhaps discourage, true commercial speech raises serious First Amendment concerns.[41] Truth may be a defense compelled by the First Amendment itself.[42]

In addition to constitutional implications, neither the FTC nor the reviewing court may have given enough attention to the role advertising can play in lowering the price that low-income consumers must pay for goods and services.[43] For such consumers, the cost of searching for price information is very high; indeed, the difficulty these consumers have in comparison shopping makes the information conveyed in advertisements especially important. These consumers may be less able to protect themselves from false claims, but they may also benefit more from accurate price information than those who can routinely seek out the best buy by checking several alternative outlets. In this case, the FTC arguably overstepped constitutional bounds and placed a burden on the dissemination of much-needed information by demanding a specified level of prior substantiation. Ironically, eight years later the Commission explicitly recognized the value of just this information to consumers. The Commission issued a trade regulation rule that purported to nullify state and local laws burdening advertising of information concerning opthalmic goods and services.[44]

In the case of the ghetto merchant, however, the retailor's history of charging more than other opticians while advertising "discount" prices weakened his equitable position and cast doubt on his ability to act as a spolesman for either honest retailers or consumers. Distaste for his past marketing practices persuaded two members of the reviewing court to uphold the full scope of the Commission's order. No other group or spokesman appeared to make the argument for free speech or more information. Furthermore, the case was valuable as a precedent for the Commission when it announced its substantiation rule in *Pfizer, Inc.*[45]

In that case, the Commission focused on the claims made by Pfizer, Inc. for its "Unburn" preparation, a low-cost, over-the-counter remedy for the pain of sunburn. In its complaint, the truth or falsity of the claims themselves were not even questioned; rather, the Commission took the position that the challenged advertisement represented that the manufacturer had conducted adequate and well-controlled scientific studies or scientific tests to back up its claims of fast pain relief and anesthetizing of nerves of sunburned skin. Inasmuch as

Pfizer had not conducted such studies or tests, the implied representation was therefore false, misleading, and deceptive. In addition, regardless of what was represented, the complaint charged that the act of making unsubstantiated advertising claims was itself an unfair practice and a separate violation of the act.

Pfizer is a reputable national marketer that could and did demonstrate that it had carefully tested its product to be sure no personal injuries would result. It also presented evidence that the main ingredients of its preparation were well-known and well-documented, and that it had gauged its claims by those of similar preparations already on the market. Pfizer could hardly be characterized as a hardened offender who had acted "in utter disregard of law"[46] and who thereby needed fencing in. Pfizer joined issue with the Commission on three levels. First, it denied that the ads made the representation alleged, arguing that the setting and the spokeswoman evoked fun in the sun, not science. Further, it denied that its marketing practice in any way violated the act. Third, it raised some affirmative defenses, including constitutional objections to the vague "fairness" standard the FTC espoused. After taking testimony, the hearing examiner recommended that the complaint be dismissed. The examiner found that the only claim made by the ads was that the product would work to relieve pain. Since it did work, the examiner saw no reason to proceed further.

In its opinion, the Commission took the opportunity to express its views of its authority to make advertising "fairer" by requiring that an advertiser have a reasonable basis for making affirmative claims. Commissioner Kirkpatrick pointed out that the manufacturer is better able than the consumer to bear the purely economic risk that the product will not perform as advertised. Hence, casting this risk upon the purchaser is itself an unfair practice. The opinion cited the Tashof case for judicial approval of this theory, even if the claims are true. Nonetheless, the FTC determined to affirm the hearing examiner's dismissal of the complaint, citing failure of proof by its staff.

In this case, then, the Commission wrote a lengthy opinion expressing a very expansive interpretation of "unfairness," and opened up a new area of regulation for FTC staffers. A respondent stood ready to contest that view, on the facts of its case, the law, and the wisdom of the policy. Serious objections were raised. By dismissing the complaint, the Commission avoided a court test, perhaps deciding to wait for a better case. By this strategy, the Commission achieved a way of setting out its views, yet deprived the respondent of any incentive or opportunity to pursue the question in the courts.[47] Even if Pfizer was not required to cease and desist from long-discontinued advertising, other advertisers might have been interested in pursuing a challenge if there had been some mechanism for them to present their views, but such a mechanism was lacking.

The final case that the Commission can use to illustrate court approval of its theory is *Firestone Tire & Rubber Co.*[48] Although false pricing, advertising, and misleading "safety" claims were charged, of interest here is the FTC's attack on Firestone's claim that its tire "stops 25% quicker." Firestone had conducted tests that supported the claim, but only against its own narrower tires and only on wet surfaces. In this case, however, Firestone did not contest the allegation of the complaint that its advertising represented a fully-tested claim. Since the FTC characterized that representation as false and deceptive, a category of speech that is outside the protection of the First Amendment, constitutional arguments were unavailable. Note that the truth or falsity of the underlying claim became irrelevant. As the reviewing court in Firestone remarked, "We are by no means sure that the Firestone Wide Oval tire does not 'stop 25% quicker.' But that is not our question."[49] The question was whether Firestone had conducted adequate tests to satisfy the substantiation requirement.

For products that do perform as advertised, requiring more and more testing obviously delays the introduction of a more desirable product and adds to its expense. As noted previously, substantial tort liability if the tire fails to perform and causes injury should be adequate incentive to substantiate safety claims.

One need not be callous about human health and safety to question the FTC's efforts. Rather, at some point, demanding more and more testing produces less benefit than cost and is not economically efficient. Furthermore, one may be most skeptical about the requirement for prior substantiation of claims which at worst may produce minor economic injury. Such an across-the-board requirement is likely to add little to consumer welfare. Pitofsky[50] observed that since false claims are already prohibited, one major effect might be to suppress truthful claims that are too expensive to substantiate fully. In the case of "Unburn," adding a requirement for double-blind scientific testing would add to the costs of this inexpensive sunburn remedy. As the case itself demonstrates, adequate market incentives probably already exist to deter false claims, since "Unburn" must satisfy customers if the product is to be purchased more than once and produce profit for the company. Furthermore, consumers might actualy lose information if sellers respond to stringent substantiation requirements by switching to noninformative "puffs" not subject to the requirements.

Nevertheless, individual respondents are now facing a Commission that is well-launched on its prior substantiation compaign and is unlikely to reconsider it without overwhelming proof of its deficiencies. Such proof may exist, but no single respondent is likely to devote resources to developing it. An organized group might have provided input as the policy-making stage and could be useful even now in challenging the Commission's use of its resources for this program.

The potential usefulness of public-interest intervention seems even more graphically illustrated by the Commission's formal advertising substantiation program. That initiative began when the FTC issued a resolution asserting authority to require advertisers to submit evidence to the Commission supporting claims for performance, efficacy, quality, and price comparisons before such claims were made to the public.[51] The first order to furnish documentation was issued three days later to seven major automobile manufacturers. Although the FTC has broad investigatory authority and responsibility for public information, orders under the act cannot be so oppressive or unreasonable as to raise possible Fourth and Fifth Amendment concerns.[52] Regardless of possible constitutional objections and doubts about the wisdom of the entire strategy, the automakers decided to comply with the order. In this instance, any refusal to comply could have been interpreted by the public as evidence that they in fact were making unfounded claims. Instead of contesting the order, therefore, they responded with massive documentation. An FTC staff report noted that the data received was in the main "data of a highly complex and sophisticated nature" or "set forth claims that are quite expensive and time consuming to verify."[53] The staff also noted that few consumers even sought access to the material.

The FTC has used the submitted information to build cases based on its "unfairness" theory. Complaints were issued against two automobile manufacturers and three air conditioning firms.[54] In one of those complaints, new ground was broken for General Motors entered into a consent order whose theory may serve as an attack on the primary goal of advertising—product differentiation. The complaint against GM charged that it had no reasonable basis for its claim that GM's 1971 Vega is the best-handling passenger car ever built in the United States. The challenged ad had used that exact language, but it was set off in quotation marks and clearly identified as a quotation from *Road and Track* magazine's report on its road test of the car. Nonetheless, General Motors agreed to a consent order requiring that further comparative handling claims, whether presented through testimonial or otherwise, must be supported by competent scientific tests.

Requiring independent substantiation for such claims seems pointless. Consumers may find it of interest that a testing group other than the manufacturer holds a high opinion of the car's handling abilities. Such independent comparative testing generates useful information for the public. GM's ad truthfully reported *Road and Track's* favorble opinion, clearly identifying the source. For the FTC to demand proof of a reasonable basis to believe that the opinion is true before the manufacturer can disseminate the information seems a poor way to produce a better-informed or better-protected populace.

Whether to avoid adverse publicity or to ward off a threat of required corrective advertising, GM determined to acquiesce in the Commission's view of the law. It agreed to a consent order requiring it to independently retest its cars, and in this case, all others, before claiming any comparative advantages. Other advertisers, and even consumer groups, might disagree with this new effort by the FTC, but there was no organized group to present their views or to provide data on the relative importance of automotive magazine testing in comparative decision making by consumers.

B. The SEC

Another example of regulatory inefficiency is provided by the history and growth of The Securities and Exchange Commission's Rule 10b-5[55] as a method of prohibiting trading on "inside" information. The SEC has succeeded in expanding a rather innocuous-sounding rule into a comprehensive federal law regulating trading in securities by those who are privy to "inside information."[56]

Rule 10b-5, which was adopted unanimously without discussion or debate by the Commission,[57] was viewed by the corporate bar as "just . . . another declaration against the man-eating shark."[58] The financial community took the SEC at its word that the new Rule was merely a weapon to extend the authority of the Commission over fraud in the purchase as well as sale of securities. In other words, the SEC was closing a loophole in the law and protecting sellers. In fact, ample precedent existed at common law to impose a duty to disclose on one party if his special relationship with the other would make nondisclosure a fraud.[59] The first case in which the SEC applied its new Rule[60] was one in which the same result would probably have been reached by common law courts: a corporation intent on buying its own stock to benefit the individual in control did so, without disclosing the true identity of the purchaser in order to get the shares as cheaply as possible.

One commentator has noted that "the development of 10b-5 into a potent weapon is due in no small part to the Commission's activities."[61] Besides promulgating the Rule in the first place, the SEC expanded its scope by rendering opinions as a judicial body, acting as a plaintiff in lawsuits in the federal courts, and appearing as *amicus curiae* in other cases.[62]

As a judicial body, the Commission is empowered to discipline brokers, dealers, and investment advisers registered with it. The Commission's decisions in this area are accorded great deference by the courts, as is common when discretion has been conferred on an agency. The regulated parties charged with violating Commission rules often settle with the Commission to avoid lengthy and expensive proceedings, as well as the possibility of harsher penalties and adverse publicity. Of special interest in the development of Rule 10b–5 jurisprudence, however, is the impact such internal disciplinary proceedings have had in private suits brought in the federal courts. In fact, one of the most influential and expansive early interpretations of the Rule came in a disciplinary proceeding, *In the Matter of Cady, Roberts,*[63] which was appealed no further because the SEC accepted the minimum penalty.[64] The benefit to the SEC, however, was the precedent thus created; interest was asymmetric. In that case, a registered representative, who was a director of a corporation, learned at a board meeting that the dividend was to be cut. He telephoned his firm, which sold the stock short from their discretionary accounts before the dividend news was made public. Although the language of the opinion was qualified, Henry Manne noted that "the general tone [of the opinion] as an attack on all insider trading is unmistakable."[65]

The *Cady, Roberts* decision expanded the category of insiders to include any person who possesses material nonpublic information, and also, for the first time, found fraud where the transactions were carried out over an organized, impersonal exchange. The SEC rejected the need for face-to-face transactions. Both expansions of the law vastly extended potential liability by including many more potential plaintiffs and defendants.

Others in the financial community, however, had neither a mechanism for learning about the SEC's view of insider trading nor a way to express their views on the desirability of greatly increased liability. Instead, the SEC unilaterally advanced its own notion of what the "public interest" required, concentrating on the need to assure the individual investor of the integrity of the capital markets. Accordingly, it has been criticized for using a disciplinary proceeding to announce a new and greatly expanded interpretation of the Rule.[66] Critics also point out that "Congress had rejected a suggestion that the *use* of inside information be made unlawful in view of the problems of proof involved."[67] By choosing to use a disciplinary proceeding, the SEC faced a broker concerned about his own license who accepted a slap on the wrist; no one internalized the broad impact of the decision on others.

The full effect of the SEC's expansive reading of Rule 10b–5 is difficult to document. Insider trading, if one includes as insiders all who have access to material undisclosed information, is by necessity a concealed practice. Many observers believe it is extremely widespread.[68] Even though recent scholarship by Michael Dooley points out that the SEC has brought very few cases, and settled almost all for minimal sanctions, it is clear that the SEC's activity against insider trading has had an impact on the securities industry. Market professionals are subject to the same sort of disciplinary action brought against *Cady, Roberts* and were the target of most of the SEC's enforcement.

Securities professionals trade in information and analysis, and play a role in the functioning of the nation's capital markets. It is their role to ensure that the stock of a company accurately reflects all available information, as quickly as possible. Such an efficient market works better to allocate capital, indicate attractive take-over candidates, and, in general, promote efficient use of resources.[69] If insiders (defined as those who successfully ferret out corporate information) are not permitted to profit from it, presumably there will be less incentive to seek out information, and corporations might be able to delay disclosures. Such incentives can complement government efforts to increase disclosure. In other words, for stock prices to accurately reflect the current and future prospects of a firm, there must be incentives to encourage the search for valuable information. To discipline securities professionals for making use of their information advantage is to discourage the diligent from seeking out information. Although insider trading prohibitions are defended on fairness grounds, stock prices that provide a correct indication of the company's worth as early as possible may, in fact, be fairer to all investors.

Furthermore, Henry Manne has articulated another advantage if insider trading is permitted. Manne would expressly permit trading by those who have access to corporate information by virtue of their employment status. Manne argues that allowing managers to profit from good news will encourage them to produce such news, and will provide appropriate rewards for the entrepreneur, whose innovation is necessary for economic growth.[70]

Regardless of these considerations, however, notions of unfairness and diminished investor confidence were cited by SEC Chairman Cary as reasons for prohibiting the use of inside information.

To a budget-conscious bureaucrat, moreover, this new kind of regulation presented an opportunity to expand. Insider trading is by necessity difficult to discover; once unusual news becomes fully disclosed, staff work is required to reconstruct who was buying and selling during the predisclosure period. Further effort must then be expended to discover who might have had access to a source of inside information. Building a case thus demands manpower and ever-increasing staff: indeed, since the SEC's efforts are almost wholly ineffective in controlling profitable use of inside information, this provides the agency with an argument for more staff and more resources. Since the practice seems slightly dishonest at first glance, and no politician wishes to become a champion of fraud, the offense of insider trading appears an attractive one for regulation.

Despite evidence that the volume of insider trading continued unabated after *Cady, Roberts* and *Texas Gulf Sulfur*,[71] and the incidence of trading based on tips by those not subject to reporting requirements is doubtless even higher,[72] it is clear that Rule 10b–5 has had an impact. To avoid the appearance of impropriety, securities professionals have set up elaborate systems to avoid improper use of inside information that they acquire.[73] All of this caution and effort seems misdirected if a market that quickly processes new information is the policy-makers' goal.

This case appears to be another example of how an expanding bureaucracy was able to bargain for acquiescence in its assertion of authority in exchange for minimal sanctions. The Cady, Roberts firm was understandably much more interested in its own license and continuing good relations with its overseeing agency than in mounting a full-dress challenge. Such a challenge might have been based on legislative history, or might have been couched in policy terms. Regardless of what all regulated parties might have done had there been a mechanism to aggregate their interests and put none of them out front on the firing line, the respondent in *Cady, Roberts* was content to swallow the minimum sanction and begin taking precautions to be sure the embarrassment would not occur again. Interests here between the SEC and the single respondent were clearly asymmetric, and the resulting inefficient rule now burdens the entire securities industry.

III. CONCLUSION

It was hypothesized that government agencies tend to seek more expansive rules and favor enforcement strategies that increase their ability to produce results. The bureaucrat neither bears the costs nor enjoys the benefits of his interventions. Unlike businessmen who innovate, however, the innovative bureaucrat does not get a reliable signal in the marketplace that his innovation is needed or desired. Regulated parties might be expected to provide information about the costs agency actions impose, but an agency does not get an accurate picture of its costs and benefits when it proceeds by case-by-case adjudication. Each individual respondent is understandably concerned about its immediate case, particularly when it is charged with engaging in conduct of which society disapproves. Since the respondent wishes to be exonerated on this charge, it will tend to put its energies toward contesting the agency's view of the facts. Any other strategy is nearly foreclosed; legal challenges are difficult to make, since courts have granted agencies like the FTC and the SEC almost limitless discretion both to decide what may mislead and to fashion an appropriate remedy. Even though commercial speech now enjoys some measure of First Amendment protection, speech characterized as deceptive and misleading may be regulated and suppressed by government. Therefore, so long as the agency is permitted to define deception, it may be able to immunize its activities from court review.

Hence, the FTC and SEC have been able to achieve regulation by consent decree. This situation seems more troublesome than the analogous practice of plea bargaining in criminal cases. There the governing law is defined in advance by the legislature. In contrast, when the same body is charged both with defining the law and enforcing it, some institutional mechanism appears necessary to be sure that burdensome and inefficient law does not become entrenched by default.

One might speculate whether the absence of a mechanism to present a business-oriented viewpoint has contributed to the current intense political backlash against the FTC.[74] Regulated parties have pressed Congress to rein in the agency, and some limits on its powers have been imposed. Without a way to combine forces during agency proceedings, business put its energies toward lobbying. Perhaps legal foundations to forcefully present the business-oriented viewpoint could have provided needed correctives and avoided the storm that now buffets the agency.

NOTES

1. William A. Niskanen, *Bureaucracy and Representative Government* (New York: Aldine Pub., 1971). For a recent discussion of this model see Dennis C. Mueller, *Public Choice* (New York: Cambridge University Press, 1979), Chap.

2. C. M. Lindsay, "The Theory of Government Enterprise," *Journal of Political Economy* 84 (1976): 1061.

3. Richard Posner, "The Behavior of Administrative Agencies," *Journal of Legal Studies* 1 (1972): 305.

4. Ibid., p. 311.

5. Ibid.

6. This account is taken from "Recent Decision," *George Washington University Law Review* 43 (1975): 1237, which analyzed *Consumer Product Safety Commission v. A.K. Electric Corp.*, Civil No. 74-1206 (D.D.C., Sept. 9, 1974) (unreported decision).

7. 15 U.S.C. sec. 2061 (b)(1). The district court is empowered to grant "such . . . relief as may be necessary to protect the public."

8. *See also* James T. Bennett and Manuel H. Johnson, "Paperwork and Bureaucracy," *Economic Inquiry* 17 (1979): 435.

9. David R. Mayhew, *Congress: The Electoral Connection* (New Haven, Conn.: Yale University Press, 1975): 108–10; Morris Fiorina, *Congress: Keystone of the Washington Establishment* (New Haven, Conn.: Yale University Press, 1977).

10. Robert Bork, *The Antitrust Paradox: A Policy at War With Itself* (N.Y.: Basic Books, 1978), p. 415.

11. *See, e.g.*, U.S.C.A. sec. 706(1); and *Illinois Central R. Co. v. Norfolk and Western Ry. Co.*, 385 U.S. 57 (1966). The FTC's findings of fact are "conclusive" if supported by "substantial evidence." FTC Act sec. 5(c), 15 U.S.C. sec. 45(c) (1970).

12. Murray Weidenbaum, *Business, Government and the Public* (Englewood Cliffs, N.J.: Prentice-Hall, 1977).

13. Posner, "The Behavior of Administrative Agencies," p. 211.

14. Trade Reg. Rep. par. 19,681 at 21,727 (FTC 1971) ("Profile Bread").

15. For an account of the changes from the proposed order to the one accepted for settlement, *see* Gerald J. Thain, "Corrective Advertising: Theory and Cases," *New York Law Forum* 19 (1973): 10–11.

16. *Sears, Roebuck and Co. v. Equal Employment Opportunity Commission*, 581 F. 2d 941 (1978).

17. *See, e.g.*, Kannar, "Sears Shall Overcome," *The New Republic* (March 10, 1979): 18.

18. The SEC has announced a "Market Access Strategy" of enforcement, which seeks to hold responsible the various professionals, such as attorneys and accountants, connected with a dishonest promotion. Rule 2(e) administrative disciplinary proceedings have been commenced against attorneys. *See In re William R. Carter and Charles J. Johnson, Jr.*, Admin. Proc. File No. 3-5464. For a critique, *see* Daley and Karmel, "Attorneys' Responsibilities: Adversaries at the Bar of the SEC," *Emory Law Journal* 24 (1975): 747.

19. "Justiciability" is a term of art that refers to limits on the business of federal courts designed to assure that the courts will not intrude into areas committed to other branches of government. The term also refers to questions presented in adversary context and in form historically viewed as capable of resolution through the judicial process. *Flast v. Cohen*, 392 U.S. 83 (1968).

20. *The Great Atlantic and Pacific Tea Co.*, 83 F.T.C. 1356, 1357 (1974), Order denying motion to intervene.

21. See, e.g., *Blue Ribbon Quality Meats, Inc.* v. *FTC*, 560 F.2d 874 (Cir. 1977); *Floersheim* v. *Engman*, 494 F. 2d 949 (D.C. Cir. 1973).

22. Holtzoff, "Entry of Additional Parties in a Civil Action: Intervention and Third Party Practice," *Federal Rules and Decisions* 31 (1962): 101.

23. The power to issue substantive trade regulation rules was explicitly granted by the Magnuson-Moss Warranty-FTC Improvement Act of 1975, Pub. L. No. 93-637, tit. II, 88 Stat. 2183. Prior to this time, the D.C. Circuit had held that such rule-making was within the authority of the Commission. *National Petroleum Refiners Ass'n.* v. *FTC*, 482 F. 2d 672, 683-84 (D.C. Cir. 1973), *cert. denied* 415 U.S. 951 (1974).

24. See *Campbell Soup* [1967–1970 Transfer Binder] Trade Reg. Rep. (CCHO) par. 19,261 at 21,424 (FTC 1970); *Firestone Tire and Rubber Company* 81 F.T.C. 398 (1972); *Pfizer, Inc.*, 81 F.T.C. 23(1972).

25. Federal Trade Commission Act, now 15 U.S.C. sec. 45 Unfair methods of competition unlawful. 341 et. seq. As originally enacted, this section provided: "Unfair methods of competition in commerce are hereby declared unlawful. The commission is hereby empowered and directed to prevent persons, partnerships, or corporations, except banks, and common carriers subject to the Acts to regulate commerce, from using unfair methods of competition in commerce." (Sept. 26, 1916, c. 311, sec. 1, 38 Stat. 717).

26. See *J.B. Williams Co.* v. *FTC*, 381 F. 2d 884 (6th Cir. 1967) which contains a history of case law on the FTC's authority to define what is deceptive.

27. *Sears, Roebuck and Co.* v. *FTC*, 258 F. 2d 307 (7th Cir. 1919).

28. 15 U.S.C. sec. 45(b) (1970).

29. *Office of Communication of the United Church of Christ* v. *FCC*, 359 F. 2d 944 (D.C. Cir. 1966).

30. *Scenic Hudson Preservation Conf.* v. *FPC*, 354 F. 2d 608 (2d Cir. 1965).

31. See McIntyre and Volhard, "Intervention in Agency Adjudications," *Virginia Law Review* 58 (1972): 230, 247.

32. In *Great Atlantic & Pacific Tea Co.* 83 FTC 1356, 1357 (1974).

33. See, e.g., *Greyhound Corp.* v. *ICC*, 551 F. 2d 414, 416 (D.C. Cir. 1977).

34. A study by Richard Posner of a year's output of FTC decisions and orders revealed about two dozen of the approximately 200 cases involved hard-core fraud. See Richard Posner, "The Federal Trade Commission," *University of Chicago Law Review* 37 (1969): 47, 77.

35. Courts agree that the FTC has been charged with protection not of experts, "but for the public—that vast multitude which includes the ignorant, the unthinking and the credulous." *Florence Mfg. Co.* v. *J.C. Dowd & Co.*, 178 F. 73, 75 (2d Cir.). See *Charles of the Ritz Dist. Corp.* v. *FTC*, 143 F.2d 676 (2d Cir. 1944).

36. Robert Reich, former Director of Policy Planning, Federal Trade Commission, recognized that consumer protection agencies will opt for "clean" (or nondeceptive) flow of information over "free" (or unimpeded) flow since the

costs of being misled are far more visible than the cost of *not* receiving information. See Robert Reich, "Preventing Deception in Commercial Speech," *New York University Law Review* 54 (1979): 775, 803–4. The tendency of the FDA to be overcautious is documented in Sam Peltzman, "An Evaluation of Consumer Protection Legislation: The 1962 Drug Amendments," *Journal of Political Economy*, vol. 81, no. 5 (1973): 1049.

37. See discussion in *In re Pfizer, Inc.*, 81 FTC 23 (1972). For commentary, see, e.g., "The *Pfizer* Reasonable Basis Test—Fast Relief for Consumers but a Headache for Advertisers," *Duke Law Journal* (1973): 563.

38. 63 F.T.C. 1282 (1963), *aff'd* 337 F. 2d 751 (9th Cir. 1964).

39. Robert Pitofsky, "Beyond Nader: Consumer Protection and the Regulation of Advertising," *Harvard Law Review* 90 (1977): 661, 682.

40. The facts are reviewed in *Tashof v. F.T.C.*, 437 F.2d 707 (D.C. Cir. 1970).

41. The Supreme Court has recognized that the First Amendment has some application to "commercial speech." *Virginia State Board of Pharmacy v. Virginia Citizens Consumer Council, Inc.*, 425 U.S. 748 (1976). Robert Reich, former Director of Policy Planning at the Federal Trade Commission, has analyzed the impact of the First Amendment upon the regulation of advertising in, "Preventing Deception in Commercial Speech," *New York University Law Review* 54 (1979): 775, and "Consumer Protection and the First Amendment: A Dilemma for the FTC?," *Minnesota Law Review* 61 (1977): 705.

42. Even before *Virginia Board*, courts were wary about suppressing truthful speech, commercial or otherwise. See, e.g., *Consumers Union of the U.S., Inc. v. Theodore Hamm Brewing Co., Inc.*, 314 F. Supp. 697 (D. Conn 1970), which protected a brewer's right to truthfully advertise its good rating from *Consumer Reports*. But see *Friedman v. Rogers*, 440 U.S. 1 (1979), which noted that even truthful information may have a significant potential to deceive, and deferred to the state's decision to prohibit practice of optometry under a trade name regardless of the value of the name as information to consumer. In *Friedman*, the Court noted that invalidation of state economic regulation on First Amendment grounds has been criticized as an unwarranted interference with the majoritarian political process, a resurrection of the "economic due process" doctrine. For a forceful expression of this viewpoint, see Thomas Jackson and John Jeffries, Jr., "Commercial Speech: Economic Due Process and the First Amendment," *Virginia Law Review* 65 (1979): 1, 30.

43. Several scholars have presented evidence that prices are higher when advertising is prohibited. See Lee Benham, "The Effect of Advertising on the Price of Eyeglasses," *Journal of Law and Economics* 15 (1972): 337; Robert Steiner, "Does Advertising Lower Consumer Prices?," *Journal of Marketing* (October 1973): 19.

44. *Advertising of Opthalmic Goods and Services*, 16 CFR 456 (1978). The D.C. Circuit Court of Appeals remanded most of the rule for reconsideration by the Commission in light of the Supreme Court's First Amendment invalidation of advertising restrictions. *American Optometric Association v. F.T.C.*, No. 78-1461 (D.C. Cir. decided February 6, 1980).

45. *In re Pfizer, Inc.,* 81 F.T.C. 23 (1972).

46. *F.T.C. v. National Lead Co.,* 352 U.S. 419, 129.

47. Commissioner Jones dissented on the disposition of the case, since it deprived respondent of an opportunity to seek court review. Ibid.

48. *Firestone Tire & Rubber Co.,* 81 F.T.C. 398 (1972), *aff'd* 481 F. 2d 246 (6th Cir. 1973).

49. 1973-1 Trade Reg. Rep, par. 74,588.

50. Pitofsky, "Beyond Nader." pp. 661, 682.

51. FTC Resolution-Advertising Documentation, 2 Trade Reg. Rep. par. 7573 (FTC 1971).

52. The current state of the law is set out in *American Motors Corp. v. F.T.C.,* 601 F. 2d 1329 (6th Cir. 1979), which concedes that corporations have constitutional rights, but must exhaust administrative remedies before seeking protection from the courts.

53. FTC Advertising Substantiation—Staff Report, 5 Trade Reg. Rep. par. 50,135 (FTC 1972).

54. [FTC Complaints & Orders] Trade Reg. Rep. par. 20,747 (Jan. 1975).

55. The Rule reads as follows:

> It shall be unlawful for any person, directly or indirectly, by the use of any means or instrumentality of interstate commerce, or of the mails, or of any facility of any national securities exchange,
> (1) to employ any device, scheme, or artifice to defraud,
> (2) to make any untrue statement of a material fact or to omit to state a material fact necessary in order to make the statements made, in the light of the circumstances under which they were made, not misleading, or
> (3) to engage in any act, practice or course of business which operates or would operate as a fraud or deceit upon any person, in connection with the purchase or sale of any security.

56. "Inside information" in securities law refers to nonpublic information material to the value of the securities traded. As Dooley points out, "It is assumed that the information is a significant factor in the decision to trade and that the trader is able to realize a gain or avoid a loss that he could not have if the information were publicly known . . . ." Michael P. Dooley, "Enforcement of Insider Trading Restrictions," *Virginia Law Review* 66 (1980): 1.

57. Mr. Milton Freeman, a drafter of the Rule, recounts that the only comment made in adopting the Rule was one question: "Well, we are against fraud, aren't we?". Freeman, "Conferences on Codification of the Federal Securities Laws," *Business Lawyer* 22 (1967): 793, 922.

58. *See* Halleran, "Symposium on Insider Trading in Stocks," *Business Lawyer* 21 (1966): 1009, 1021.

59. *See, e.g.,* A. Jacobs, "The Impact of Rule 10b–5," (New York: Clark, Boardman Co., 1978): sec. 2.01.

60. *Ward LaFrance Truck Corp.,* 13 S.E.C. 373 (1943).

61. *See* Shipley, "The SEC's *Amicus Curiae* Aid to Plaintiffs in Mutual Fund Litigation," *American Bar Association Journal* 52 (1966): 337.

62. Securities and Exchange Act of 1934 secs. 15(b)(4), 15(b)(6), 15 U.S.C. sec. 780(b)(4), (6) (1976); Investment Advisors Act of 1940 sec. 203e, f, 15 U.S.C. 80b-3(e), (f), (1976).

63. 40 S.E.C. 907 (1961).

64. Wm. L. Cary, "Insider Trading in Stocks," *Business Lawyer* 21 (1966): 1009, 1011.

65. Henry Manne, "Insider Trading and the Administrative Process," *George Washington University Law Review* 35 (1967): 473, 482.

66. Ibid.; K. David, *Administrative Law* (Supp. 1965): sec. 6.13 at 146–57.

67. *See* W. Painter, *Federal Regulation of Insider Trading* (Charlottesville, Va.: Michie-Bobbs, 1968), p. 118.

68. *See e.g.*, Robert M. Bleiberg, "Who's Afraid of 10b–5," *Barron's* (July 24, 1978): 7; *Wall Street Journal*, July 12, 1978, p. 1; ibid., June 2, 1976, p. 1.

69. See J. Lorie and M. Hamilton, *The Stock Market—Theories and Evidence* (Ill.: Richard D. Irwin, 1973); Vasicek and McQuown, "The Efficient Market Model," *Financial Analysts Journal* 28 (Sept.-Oct. 1972): 71.

70. Henry Manne, *Insider Trading and the Stock Market* (New York: Free Press, 1966).

71. 401 F. 2d 833 (2d Cir. 1968) (*en banc*) *cert. denied* 394 U.S. 976 (1969).

72. The evidence is summarized in a study of trading reports filed by insiders subject to the reporting requirements of Section 16(a) of the 1934 Act: officers, directors, and shareholders owning more than 10 percent of the outstanding share. Jaffe, "Special Information and Insider Trading," *Journal of Business of the University of Chicago* 47 (1974): 410.

73. The results of a survey of 100 randomly selected member firms of the New York Stock Exchange are reported in Lewis Solomon and Dan Wilke, "Securities Professionals and Rule 10b–5: Legal Standards, Industry Practices, Preventative Guidelines and Proposals for Reform," *Fordham Law Review* 43 (1975): 505.

74. *See* Ernest Gellhorn, "The Wages of Zealotry: The FTC Under Siege," *Regulation* (Jan/Feb 1980): 33.

CHAPTER 8

Business-Oriented Legal Foundations

I. INTRODUCTION

In Chapter 2, it was argued that when some groups organized to litigate, others would find counterorganization useful. In the last chapter, it was shown that government agencies would have more substantial interests in precedents than would firms, and that such agencies might seek inefficient rulings. It was shown that such was indeed that case for the FTC and the SEC. The theory would predict that firms might find organization for counterlitigation useful, and this is what is found. In particular, in recent years some business-oriented legal foundations (essentially, public interest law firms with a pro-market orientation) have come into being and have served largely to litigate inefficient rules promulgated by government agencies. In this chapter, the role of these foundations is considered. In Section II, several cases where such organizations intervened are examined, and it is shown that the intervention sometimes leads to increased efficiency. Section III summarizes this chapter.

II. CASES

We turn now to several cases where public interest law firms have contributed to a result consistent with economic efficiency.

A. *Marshall v. Barlow's, Inc.*[1]

Barlow, a plumbing contractor in Pocatello, Idaho, demanded that an OSHA inspector produce a search warrant in order to gain admittance to the nonpublic area of his business. The inspector did obtain a court order, pursuant to OSHA regulation,[2] but did not have to

143

demonstrate any "probable cause." Barlow again refused to admit him, and filed suit to test the constitutionality of the Act's warrantless inspection procedures. The American Conservative Union's "Stop OSHA" project supported Barlow as a test case, and several other business-oriented foundations filed *amicus* briefs.

Barlow's position was simple: he alleged that OSHA inspections were "searches" within the meaning of the Fourth Amendment, and therefore he could insist that government agents who wished to intrude into areas of his business not open to the public must respect his privacy unless they were able to convince a neutral judicial officer to issue a search warrant. The Supreme Court agreed with Barlow's position, rejecting the government's claim that such a warrant requirement was unnecessary and would hamper attainment of the legitimate goals of protecting the health and safety of American workers.

This case raised important issues about government power and individual rights. Its decision has had broad implications for all businesses subject to government regulation, as well as for other government agencies.[3] If the balance struck between privacy concerns and enforcement leads to efficient outcomes, and would benefit other firms, it is useful for legal foundations to provide resources to help Barlow press his case. The stakes for Barlow individually were small; the costs of inspection, even including fines and the cost of required compliance to correct violations, have been estimated at $1,000 for firms employing 100 to 200 workers.[4] Clearly, a local plumbing contractor would stand to lose far less in terms of management and employee time to accompany the inspector around a much smaller establishment. Hence, most small businessmen, no matter how outraged, would not initiate a lawsuit and press it to the Supreme Court absent support from some outside group.[5] Although the issue had been raised by other firms seeking to suppress evidence of violations found by inspectors,[6] it is the plaintiff standing on principle who presents the strongest case for respecting the constitutional guarantee. The agency, responding to Congress, would be expected to fight vigorously if challenges were raised, and interests here would be clearly asymmetric. In short, the small stake in the current inspection and the even smaller interest in any future change in policy, given the very low likelihood of future inspections, would suggest that Barlow would normally acquiesce in the inspection.

The Barlow decision was important to all businessmen facing government demands for access to their premises or records. In its decision, the Court took the opportunity to reaffirm its earlier position[7] that administrative inspections of commercial premises are "searches" within the meaning of the Fourth Amendment, subject to a warrant requirement. The Court's majority declined the government's invitation to read very broadly an exception to the warrant requirement for heavily regulated businesses on a theory of implied consent. Certain lower courts had read the exception so broadly as to threaten to swallow the rule.[8] In Barlow, the Court rejected the argument that knowledge of federal interest in health and safety meant that all business subject to the interstate commerce powers of Congress (virtually all business) had consented to warrantless intrusions. The Court's majority also refused to validate Congress's attempt to satisfy objections by legislative definition of reasonable searches, and held that the Constitution requires a warrant procedure. Although the majority held that a warrant for an administrative inspection could be issued on something less than the probable cause required for a criminal investigation, the Court recognized the importance of a neutral officer between the inspector and the citizen. Reaffirmation that businesses have a constitutionally protected claim to privacy is important, both to assure that government inspectors do not use their authority to harass law-abiding businesses and to underscore the importance of business privacy as a value in our society.

While this decision may appear to have little to do with allocative efficiency, one business-oriented local foundation pointed out in its *amicus* brief that enforcing a "cause" requirement could produce higher levels of occupational safety and health at lower costs.[9] While acknowledging worker safety as a valid concern, the brief pointed out that "a probable cause requirement would better protect employees by shifting the inspection emphasis to more serious violations." Several scholars who have studied OSHA point out that it is unlikely that reliance on safety standards enforced by random inspection will in fact reduce injuries. Walter Oi questions "whether safety inspections [which comprise the great bulk of OSHA inspections] are effective and desirable at all."[10] John Mendeloff cites available information that indicates that "only a minority of work injuries are caused by violations of safety standards and many of these are momentary violations which inspectors could rarely detect."[11] For these reasons, it is not suprising that OSHA's safety inspection program has had at most a small impact on injury rates. Economists agree that the costs of the current system outweigh its benefits. Robert Smith[12] and John Mendeloff[13] argue that an approach that incorporates features of an "injury tax," penalizing employers for accidents, would provide employers greater incentives to stress safety. Mendeloff suggests that OSHA's legal problems may make this shift attractive. Concentrating OSHA inspections on those establishments that report accidents would both give employers incentive to improve safety in order to avoid the costs and disruption of inspection, and satisfy constitutional objections that inspections should not be scheduled without probable cause.

Even if such a shift in enforcement strategy is desirable and more efficient, it may appear inappropriate to use constitutional litigation to compel it. One might argue that such considerations should be advanced to the agency itself or to Congress, rather than argued in constitutional terms. But Mendeloff demonstrated that any shift away from "safety standards" toward the "injury tax" favored by economists seems doomed to political defeat. He points out that business would oppose a tax, fearing ever-increasing levels motivated more by revenue-raising than injury control. Existing inspectors would be expected to resist diminution of their role, and most importantly, unions oppose philosophically any "license to maim" and insist on a "right to a safe work place" for every worker. If that right is to be enforced only by inspection, unless vastly more resources are to be poured into an inspection system, the promise will not be fulfilled. The symbolic value of maintaining a finite probability of inspection for every work place, no matter how good its safety record, diverts resources from more productive use and may be too expensive.[14] The foundations that urged the Supreme Court to recognize that the costs of a random inspection system include loss of employer privacy rights, protected by the Constitution, could help OSHA to explain to all groups that the agency must implement a more economically rational system even in the face of political opposition.

In a subsequent case, Pacific Legal Fondation again advanced the link between constitutional safeguards and a more rational OSHA inspection policy. PLF is acting as an *amicus* in a California case, *Salwasser v. Superior Court*, to support a businessman appealing criminal penalties imposed on him for refusing to honor a search warrant obtained by a California OSHA inspector. Mr. Salwasser asserted that the warrant was issued *solely* because he demanded a warrant. "Probable cause," even for an administrative inspection, must mean something more than this. In addition, Pacific Legal Foundation pointed out that the agency's resources would be better expended where there is probable cause to believe dangers are likely to exist.[15]

B. *Chrysler Corporation v. Brown*[16]

Legal foundations submitted *amicus* briefs urging the Supreme Court to recognize another aspect of corporate privacy. At issue was Chrysler's right to object to disclosure of confidential employment records and affirmative action compliance documents furnished to the Department of Defense.

As a condition of doing business with the federal government, Chrysler accepted an obligation to take affirmative action to ensure equal employment opportunity. Part of the obligation included submitting highly detailed information about Chrysler's employment patterns and pay scales. Chrysler objected when the Defense Department proposed to disclose that information in response to a Freedom of Information Act request. The information was concededly protected from mandatory disclosure; less clear was Chrysler's right to object to the agency's decision to voluntarily disclose information furnished in confidence.

From the standpoint of efficiency, Chrysler's position seems very strong. Collection of information is a valid function of government. Policy making and monitoring of current programs demand accurate information. Aggregation and dissemination of business information by government is undoubtedly useful, facilitating corporate planning and the efficient use of resources. Furthermore, the statistics are very important for academic research. One central information-gathering mechanism to serve both the public and private need for such information seem justifiable in economic terms. However, there are also valid arguments for preserving the confidentiality of the underlying raw data. Of most significance is the argument that firms must spend resources collecting information that is of value to the firm only if the firm can prevent others from benefiting from the information. If such information is subject to disclosure, firms will have less incentive to invest in producing the information.[17] The law of patents and trade secrets recognizes the need to encourage research by protecting rights in such valuable information.

Other information may be of little inherent value to the firm but might have adverse impacts if it is disclosed. Some information may be a source of embarrassment or of adverse legal action if made public. Indeed, some briefs pointed to the likelihood that firms would be less frank and candid in affirmative action self-evaluations if such information were to be disclosed to disgruntled employees or competitors.[18] Some information (such as line-of-business profit information or the detailed information about employment patterns and pay scales at issue in *Chrysler*) may give competitors advantages if it is released. In these cases, firms might be unwilling to supply such information if it is to be made public. The criminal law recognizes "informer's privilege" for this reason, and the confidentiality granted to census records is predicated on similar grounds. Although government may be able to force disclosure by subpoena or other legal discovery procedures, resort to such procedures is expensive and will increase the cost of economic planning. Furthermore, voluntary cooperation is often necessary to ensure that the information produced is of high calibre.

In sum, collection by the government of certain types of information is a necessary activity, but some of the information collected should be kept confidential. Chrysler was asking that information it had submitted to the government not be disclosed. Failure to maintain such confidentiality might have several ill effects: firms might avoid producing potentially embarrassing information, firms would refrain from voluntarily giving information to government bodies, thus increasing the costs of economic planning, or firms would reduce their investment in acquiring new information to inefficiently low levels.

One might expect the agencies themselves to be most acutely aware of problems in obtaining future information if assurances of confidentiality were not respected, and rely on them to strike the proper balance. Yet this ignores the structure provided by Congress designed to encourage disclosure, which induces the bureaucrat to decide doubtful cases in favor of disclosure.[19] The Act itself favors disclosure, sets up a rigid ten-day time limit for agencies to make their determination about whether to disclose, and provides a clear cause of action for the requester who is denied information. The submitter's rights are nowhere defined. Clearly, the path of least resistance is to disclose; Watergate and its aftermath make withholding of information look somewhat unsavory. The time limit makes it very difficult to undertake very careful review, especially given a large number of requests, and in many cases, the agency may lack expertise to judge how valuable the information is. Furthermore, the requester knows he has been denied information and is offered an expedited procedure in the courts. By the terms of the Act, the submitter need not even be notified and no procedure is specified to hear his claims. Hence, the agency is induced by Congress to make arguably inefficient decisions. Furthermore, although procedures had been provided to claim confidentiality at the time of submission, it is expensive and burdensome for the submitter to defend its claim or the agency to decide it unless, and until, the information in question is actually requested.[20] Affidavits indicated that the procedure was never utilized.

This issue clearly had broad ramifications for any organization or individual faced with requests or demands by government for information. Chrysler itself devoted considerable resources to the litigation, and many *amicus* briefs were filed, some by individual firms already involved in other litigation to resist disclosure,[21] some by various trade associations, such as the Chamber of Commerce and the

National Security Industrial Association (an association of defense contractors). In addition, the Mid-Atlantic Legal Foundation asserted the public interest in maintaining confidentiality, representing academics concerned about disclosures of personnel reports provided in confidence, as well as scientists and engineers who rely on assurances of confidentiality in submitting grant proposals to government. Such interests might not have been heard absent foundation support.

The Supreme Court's resolution of this important issue gave some comfort to submitters of information. The Court noted that Congress had provided protection to confidential material by making it a criminal offense for government officials to disclose it unless authorized by law.[22] The Court found no such authorization,[23] and hence admonished agencies and reviewing courts to observe the rights of those who furnish confidential information. Any agency decision to disclose information protected by the criminal statute would be agency action contrary to law, which a reviewing court could stop at the bidding of the adversely affected corporation.[24]

C. *Monsanto Company v. Kennedy*[25]

This case was a petition for review of a decision by the Commissioner of Food and Drugs banning the use of a substance, acrylonitrile copolymers, in plastic beverage containers.[26] The FDA cited evidence that some of the packaging material, residual acrylonitrile monomer (RAN), will migrate into the beverage under conditions of intended use and combine with the contents. If such migration occurs, the packaging material comes within the statutory definition of a "food additive."[27] Food additives are singled out for especially stringent regulation and FDA approval is required before any food additive may be used.[28] Furthermore, food additives are expressly subject to the Delaney Clause,[29] the Congressional determination that no additive may be approved if it is found to induce cancer in man or animal. The Clause is an explicit judgment that for carcinogens, no risk of exposure is to be tolerated, regardless of any benefits the substance may have, and regardless of exposure level.

The case of the plastic bottle was a difficult one. The plastics industry saw profit in containers that would be shatter-proof, light-weight, and refillable. Monsanto had succeeded in producing a bottle with very low levels of RAN. In fact, then-available analytical techniques were unable to detect any migration into the contents of the new bottles. The issue for the FDA was whether the substance "may reasonably be expected to . . . become a component . . . of any food."[30] If so, the substance would be classified as a "food additive" and, given disturbing animal test results,[31] should be banned. The manufacturers argued that if no migration could be detected, the regulation reserved for food additives was inappropriate. For the FDA, the problem was whether to risk as yet undetectable migration in the face of mounting evidence of toxicity. Some projections were made based on the "diffusion principle," a scientifically indisputable prediction that at some temperature and given enough time, there will be *some* migration of any two substances that come into contact.

For the Commissioner, the problem was what to do in the face of uncertainty. At higher RAN levels, this material would combine with the beverage. As a matter of theory, it was reasonable to project that migration would still occur at lower concentrations, even if chemical analysis was not yet sensitive enough to detect it. Based on these projections, and evidence of adverse effects on test animals, the material was classified as a "food additive," and was "not authorized to be used to fabricate beverage containers."[32]

The analysis just presented suggests that the FDA, responding to Congress, might be expected to opt to regulate in the face of uncertainty. Congress did expect regulation of food packaging as potential additives, expressly listing "packaging" in the definition of "additive." But the ramifications of this approach—regulating on the basis of the "diffusion principle"—are disturbing. If *any* two substances in contact can be expected to combine under some conditions, all packaging material would become "food additives" automatically subject to the strict scrutiny Congress intended for substances whose use might contaminate the nation's food supply. As Richard Merrill points out, "While application of the Delaney Clause to direct ingredients and animal drugs has proved controversial, its expanding application to indirect food additives is likely to prove the most disruptive." Merrill (p. 223) observes that the law disregards any showing of the material's special utility, and appears to make no allowance for the fact that the risk posed by migrating quantities of food-packaging materials, while not negligible, is likely to be considerably less than that posed by most direct food additives, which are used at much higher levels.

The problem of the inflexibility of the Delaney Clause may be laid at the door of Congress, which ruled out any cost-benefit analysis in the case of "food additives." Yet Congress did not dictate the regulatory response when new technology reduces migration to infinitesimal levels. Better technology has also enabled scientists to document more and more minute residues in foods. Peter Hutt concluded, "[Finding toxic substance in the food supply] is no longer the problem. We can now find them very easily. Indeed we have found that they are everywhere, and that one cannot eat any food at all without consuming some substances that have been shown to be carcinogenic in test animals. Now that we have found them, the problem is what to do about them."[33]

This case was seen as very important for the plastics industry. Questions have been raised about the toxicity and carcinogenicity of other plastics and this case would create an important precedent affecting all packaging. At issue was what burden of proof the industry would have to meet to satisfy the FDA. Several manufacturers and their trade association, the Society of the Plastics Industry, took part in the rule-making proceeding and appealed the Commissioner's decision. All of them were protecting their economic interest in avoiding stringent regulation based purely on the theoretical possibility of migration. Also at stake, however, was the interest in development of new, lightweight, more convenient containers that would reduce the risks of injury from exploding bottles. Pacific Legal Foundation filed an *amicus* brief with the D.C. Circuit Court of Appeals representing the broader interest in avoiding regulation that would be costly in terms of foregone benefits without more than theoretical evidence that the substance actually would become part of the food supply.[34]

The D.C. Circuit agreed that the FDA had to cite more than the "diffusion principle" to support a finding that a substance comes within the definition of a food additive.[35] In addition, the court advised the Commissioner that the statutory scheme permitted him latitude to ignore "*de minimis*" situations in deciding when to apply the statutory definition to a substance. The case was remanded to the Commissioner for consideration of new test results confirming migration from existing bottles. The court invited the Commissioner to consider announcing what level, if any, might be within the "*de minimis*" range.

Both parts of the opinion give the FDA greater leeway to decide that despite theory or even documented migration, the substance's use poses no significant risks and should not be treated as a "food additive." Such a decision appears to be consistent with both efficiency and the public interest. The presence of public interest *amici* highlights that more than economic harm to industry is at stake, and presents another facet of the public interest for the court's consideration.

D. *First National Bank of Boston v. Bellotti*[36]

Business-oriented legal foundations filed *amicus* briefs supporting a challenge to a law outlawing spending by corporations in connection with a referendum question. A group of five corporations filed suit to test the constitutionality of the law designed to prevent corporate advocacy against imposition of a personal income tax. This group had challenged an earlier similar statute, and clearly had a long-standing interest in this matter. Although the named plaintiffs would have defended their right to spend money to influence a referendum even without any *amicus* support, the attorney for the corporate plaintiffs has written that "[T]he mere presence of a number of *amici* would indicate that the issues are serious, have widespread ramifications, and should be addressed."[37] The Supreme Court held that the First Amendment's core concern with political speech would not permit governmental muzzling of one side of a controversy under the guise of regulating corporations. Hence, it was the character of the speech, not the corporate nature of the speaker, that was of constitutional significance. The *Bellotti* case is obviously important to corporations that wish to use corporate assets in order to influence the political process, and has raised questions about other restrictions on corporate spending in federal election laws.[38]

E. Reverse Discrimination Cases

Another group of cases in which legal foundations have played an important role is in the area of reverse discrimination, which tests the constitutionality of affirmative action programs. Legal foundations have supported challenges to the congressional determination to set aside 10 percent of federal public works money for minority-owned firms. Pacific Legal Foundation acted as counsel to general contractors, subcontractors, and four associations of contractors and subcontractors. A decision declaring the provision unconstitutional as a denial of due process and equal protection,[39] was vacated and remanded to consider mootness.[40] The case was held not moot, and the provision was held constitutionally impermissible. The Supreme Court has heard oral arguments in an appeal from another challenge to this provision in *Fullilove v. Kreps*.[41] The Mid-Atlantic Legal Foundation submitted an *amicus* brief in this case.

III. SUMMARY

It was hypothesized in that agency-regulated party litigation might provide a fruitful area for legal foundations to advance efficiency objectives. Five areas in which legal foundations have acted as *amicus* to support efficient outcomes when interest in precedent was skewed in favor of the agency were discussed. The foundations have served to reduce the cost of making effective arguments by becoming specialists in antiregulatory litigation, and are able to provide low-cost, effective representation to plaintiffs. Therefore, the foundations may bring more litigants into the type of "public law litigation" that increasingly concerns the federal courts.[42]

It should be noted, however, that foundations have tended to expend resources by submitting *amicus* briefs on cases where private parties were already organized and well-represented. One might question whether an *amicus* brief raising similar arguments has much impact on the outcome,[43] although it may help to demonstrate that a question is of importance to an even larger community. More research to specify the marginal cost/marginal benefits function of litigation expenditures would be useful to help the foundations allocate their own resources most efficiently. Until that research is available, the free market provides some assurance that the "right" amount will be expended: foundation officials sell their product in a very competitive market to potential contributors, and must satisfy them that their efforts are useful. Potential contributors should be able to sort out claims of effectiveness from superfluous efforts and support effective action. However, even where such foundations do serve to advance efficiency, that is clearly a second-best solution caused by the inefficiency of the rules sought by government agencies.

NOTES

1. 436 U.S. 307 (1978).
2. The Act itself contains no search warrant requirement. It does provide that an OSHA representative must present his credentials to the agent in charge and conduct inspections in a reasonable manner during regular working hours. 29 U. S. C. sec. 657 (a) (1)(2) (1970). Labor Department regulations contemplate that compulsory process may be sought if entry is refused. 29 C. F. R. sec. 1903.4(1976).
3. The Environmental Protection Administration has been sued by Dow Chemical Co. for choosing to employ aerial photography rather than seek a warrant when Dow refused to admit EPA engineers to one of its plants. The right to object to aerial photography by a competitor was upheld by the Fifth Circuit in *E. I. Dupont de Nemours & Co. v. Christopher*, 431 F.2d 1012 (5th Cir.), *cert. denied* 400 U.S. 1024 (1970). There the court noted that failure to respect a right to privacy would result in enormous wasted expense if companies felt compelled to build enclosures to guard confidential plant design from aerial snooping. Dow relied on the *Barlow* case to argue that government, too, must respect its privacy, and not make an end run around the Fourth Amendment. *Wall Street Journal*, Jan. 22, 1979, p. 1.

4. John Mendeloff, Regulating Safety (Mass.: MIT Press, 1979), p. 137.

5. The issues had been raised in at least one other case, which was litigated and appealed despite very small penalties. *See, e.g., Brennan v. Buckeye Industries, Inc.*, 374 F. Supp. 1350 (SD Ga. 1974). In that case, the manager of a small clothing manufacturer refused to admit an OSHA inspector unless his attorney could be present. The inspector did not want to wait, and OSHA sought a court order to compel admittance. Such an order was granted. Although the firm filed notice of appeal, it was unsuccessful in getting the court's order stayed. The appeal was abandoned. Following the inspection, the firm was fined a total of $140. We would predict that a small firm, facing very small penalties, would not devote resources to overturn an unfavorable decision. The firm renewed its constitutional objections before the OSHRC, challenging penalties imposed as a result of the inspection. When the penalties were imposed, the firm appealed to the Fifth Circuit. By this time, the Supreme court had upheld the firm's position in the *Barlow* case, changing the legal climate and making an appeal cheaper. Nonetheless, the Fifth Circuit held that Buckeye Industries, Inc. could not relitigate the point since it had failed to appeal from the original adverse ruling. *See Buckeye Industries, Inc. v. Secretary of Labor*, 587 F.2d 231 (5th Cir. 1979).

6. *See Wall Street Journal*, Jan. 22, 1979, p. 1.

7. The Supreme Court held the Fourth Amendment applied to administrative inspections of commercial property in the companion cases of *Camara v. Municipal Court*, 387 U.S. 523 (1967) and *See v. City of Seattle*, 387 U.S. 541 (1967).

8. *See* discussion in Charles & Barbara McManis, "Structuring Administrative Inspections: Is There Any Warrant for a Search Warrant?," *American University Law Review* 26 (1977): 942, 953–60.

9. Brief for *amicus* Pacific Legal Foundation at 4, *Marshall v. Barlow's, Inc.*, 436 U.S. 307 (1978).

10. Walter Y. Oi, "On the Economics of Industrial Safety," *Law and Comtemporary Problems* 38 (1974): 669, 698.

11. Mendeloff, *Regulating Safety*, pp. 127–28.

12. Robert S. Smith, *The Occupational Safety and Health Act: Its Goals and Its Achievements* (Orlando, Fla.: American Enterprise Pub., 1976).

13. Mendeloff, *Regulating Safety*, pp. 24 ff. *See also*, W. K. Viscusi, "The Impact of Occupational Safety & Health Regulation," *Bell Journal of Economics* 10 (1979): 117.

14. In a recent study, Richard Zeckhauser and Albert Nichol conclude that although they see this argument for appearances and equity, they would recommend that OSHA direct its resources in the most productive direction. Zeckhauser and Nichol, "The Occupational Safety & Health Administration—An Overview," IV Senate Comm. on Gov't. Operations, Study on Federal Regulation 169, 238 (1978).

15. Pacific Legal Foundation, *The Reporter* 5 (Jan.-Feb. 1979): 4.

16. 99 S. Ct. at 1705 (1979). For an exhaustive discussion of so-called Reverse Freedom of Information Act litigation, *see* Nancy Duff Campbell,

"Reverse Freedom of Information Act Litigation: The Need for Congressional Action," *Georgia Law Journal* 67 (1978): 103.

17. See Richard A. Posner, "The Right to Privacy," *Georgia Law Review* 12 (1978): 393. *See also* Anthony T. Kronman, "The Privacy Exemption to the Freedom of Information Act," *Journal of Legal Studies* 9 (1980): 727; and Frank H. Easterbrook, "Privacy and the Optimal Extent of Disclosure Under the Freedom of Information Act," *Journal of Legal Studies* 9 (1980): 775.

18. See, e.g., Brief for amicus Equal Opportunity Advisory Council at 3, *Chrysler Corp. v. Brown*, 99 S. Ct. 1705 (1979).

19. See Brief for *amicus* Mid-Atlantic Legal Foundation at 16, *Chrysler Corp. v. Brown*, 99 S. Ct. 1705 (1979).

20. See Walter Connolly and John Fox, "Employer Rights and Access to Documents Under the Freedom of Information Act," *Fordham Law Review* 46 (1977): 203, 211–12.

21. See, e.g., *Hughes Aircraft Company* and *Standard Oil of California*.

22. 18 U.S.C. sec. 1905 (1976).

23. 99 S. Ct. at 1718–1723.

24. Section 10 of the Administrative Procedure Act provides judicial review for "any person . . . adversely affected . . . by agency action." 5 U.S.C. sec. 702 (1976). The reviewing court shall hold unlawful agency action found to be not in accordance with law. 5 U.S.C. sec. 706(2)(A) (1976).

25. "Food Drug Cosmetic Law Report" (CCH) par. 38,010. (D.C. Cir. filed Nov. 6, 1979).

26. Acrylonitrile Copolymers. Used to Fabricate Beverage Containers, Final Decision, 42 Fed. Reg. 48528–48544 (1977).

27. 21 U.S.C. sec. 321(s) (1976) provides: "(s) The term "food additive" means any substance the intended use of which results or may reasonably be expected to result, directly or indirectly, in its becoming a component or otherwise affecting the characteristics of any food (including any substance intended for use in . . . packaging . . .).

28. It should be noted that the statute exempts substances generally recognized among experts as safe: pesticide chemicals, color additives, prior sanctioned ingredients, or new animal drugs. For an extremely lucid road map through the food safety provisions of the Food Drug and Cosmetic Act, see Richard A. Merrill, "Regulating Carcinogens in Food: A Legislator's Guide to the Food Safety Provisions of the Federal Food, Drug and Cosmetic Act," *Michigan Law Review* 77 (1978): 171.

29. 21 U.S.C. sec. 348(c)(3)(A) (1976).

30. 21 U.S.C. sec. 321 (s) (1976).

31. The Commissioner noted that interim reports from an ongoing chronic feeding study, as yet incomplete, "become increasingly alarming with the passage of time." 42 Fed. Reg. 48,536 (1977). The Commissioner concluded that acrylonitrile had been shown to be "a frank teratogen [cause of serious birth defects] in the rat, a tumorigin and probable carcinogen in the rat, a possible carcinogen in man, and a mutagen in several test systems." Ibid. p. 48,532.

32. *See* Acrylonitrile Copolymers, Final Decision, 42 Fed. Reg. 48,528 (1977).

33. Peter Hutt, "Food Legislation in Perspective," *Food-Drug Cosmetic Law Journal* 34 (Nov. 1979): 590, 598.

34. Pacific Legal Foundation, *The Reporter* 4 (June/July 1978): 3.

35. *Monsanto Company v. Kennedy*, "Food Drug Cosmetic Law Report" (CCH) par. 38,010. (D.C. Cir. filed Nov. 6, 1979).

36. *See, e.g., First Nat'l Bank of Boston v. Bellotti*, 435 U.S. 765 (1978).

37. Letter from Francis X. Fox to Ellen R. Jordan (February 1, 1980).

38. Roy Birnbaum, "The Constitutionality of the Federal Corrupt Practices Act after *First National Bank of Boston v. Bellotti*," *American University Law Review* 28 (1979): 149; O'Kelley, "The Constitutional Rights of Corporations Revisited: Social and Political Expression and the Corporation after *First National Bank v. Bellotti*," *Georgia Law Journal* 67 (1979): 1347.

39. *Associated Gen. Contractors of Calif. v. Sec'y of Commerce*, 441 F. Supp. 955 (C.D. Calif. 1977).

40. 438 S. Ct. 909 (1978), on remand 459 F. Supp. 766 (C.D. Calif. 1978).

41. 584 F. 2d 600 (2d Cir. 1978) *cert.* granted 99 S. Ct. 2403.

42. *See* Abram Chayes, "The Role of the Judge in Public Law Litigation," *Harvard Law Review* 89 (1976): 1281.

43. The same question has been raised about "public interest" resources to obtain greater enforcement of occupational safety and health laws. "To the extent that PIL resources merely substitute for union resources, doubt is raised concerning the efficiency of such resource allocation." Russel F. Settle and Burton Allen Weisbrod, "Occupational Safety and Health and the Public Interest," in *Public Interest Law: An Economic and Institutional Analysis* by Weisbrod, Burton A., Handler, Joel F. and Komesar, Neil K. (Berkeley, Calif.: U. of Calif. Press, 1978) p. 303.

PART IV

IMPLICATIONS AND CONCLUSIONS

In Chapter 9, an important implication of the efficiency of law is examined: if the law is economically efficient, then decisions can be made without the decision maker knowing the law. In Chapter 10, criticisms of the economic approach are addressed. The argument is then summarized, and policy implications are derived.

CHAPTER 9

The Law and Decision Making

I. INTRODUCTION

It has been the argument of this book so far that in many circumstances the law will tend toward efficiency. Efficiency deals with the way in which resources are used; if resources are used efficiently, then in some sense society is achieving its goals. However, there is another less obvious implication of efficiency in law. The argument, which was developed in response to a paper by Mario Rizzo[1], is that when the law is efficient, then costs of making decisions are greatly reduced. In this chapter, this argument is developed in some detail.

If the law is economically efficient, disputes that arise will be settled in such a way that future actions will be guided by economic criteria. The purpose of law, from an economic viewpoint, is to guide behavior, not to settle disputes—a point that needs little justification. There is, however, another aspect of law that has not been as well examined and in which the argument that the law is economically efficient is of potentially great importance. The law not only governs behavior but also the planning of behavior. Planning (managing) is an important economic activity: many resources are devoted to it. Thus, rules that reduce the costs of planning are potentially important sources of gains in efficiency, just as are rules that reduce the costs of production. To date, the economic analysis of law has focused on the latter types of rules (for example, arguments that law allocates fault to the lowest-cost avoider say that legal rules reduce the costs of producing safety). But the implication of the analysis presented here is that, to the extent that rules are economically efficient, so the costs of decisions will be reduced, and that this gain in efficiency is important.

The arguments in this chapter rely on certain aspects of economic theory that may not be familiar to noneconomists. The first section, therefore, explores the relationship between knowledge of

159

economics by agents and the usefulness of economics in explaining the behavior of agents. In the second section, applications of economics to efficient law are discussed. The third section applies the analysis to the evolutionary models of law. Next, I examine the implications of the analysis for discussions of statutes, where economic efficiency is not generally held to be relevant, and show that the costs of inefficient statutes may be much higher than the simple consideration of their inefficiency would indicate. The last section is a summary of this chapter.

II. ON KNOWLEDGE OF ECONOMICS AND BEHAVIOR

Economic theory starts with the assumption that economic agents are rational maximizers. Consumers maximize utility, and firms maximize profits. From these assumptions, detailed sets of predictions are derived. The predictions are in general about derivatives of functions, predictions about responses of agents to changes in parameters. The methods used for deriving the predictions are mathematical -- the rigorous application of formal tools to the assumptions of rational behavior.

Obviously, individuals do not behave in exact conformity to economic theory. No individual, not even the most passionate believer in the economic model, draws a set of indifference curves and a budget line to derive his utility-maximizing set of purchases before going grocery shopping. No firm knows the details of its production function and the associated isoquant map. Consequently, noneconomists sometimes criticize economic analysis since, they argue, people do not behave in the way that economics hypothesizes.

Such arguments are, of course, completely erroneous and based on fundamental misconceptions about economic theory.[2] Economists assume that people maximize and derive the implications of this behavior from formal models. But the behavior does not depend on knowing the details of the models. Rather, the models are used by economists to predict what the behavior of the maximizing agents will be. Milton Friedman uses the example of a billiard player. A physicist must use the laws of physics to predict the results of the behavior of an expert billiard player, but the player himself need not go through the detailed calculations to make his shot. More recently, economists studying the behavior of laboratory rats as consumers found that in their consumption choices, the animals behave as the theory of consumer behavior, based on assumption of rational calculation, would predict.[3] It is not essential to assume that a rat can invert a bordered

Hessian or perform other sophisticated mathematical procedures in order to explain its behavior. Presumably, what is involved is an evolutionary mechanism that has selected animals (including humans) for essentially rational behavior, independent of the understanding of the rational actor.[4]

Similar arguments apply to firms. Armen Alchian has shown that, even if firms do not understand maximizing behavior, selection pressure will, nonetheless, lead to extinction (bankruptcy) of firms that do not behave in a way that approximates profit maximization, so that it will be possible to assume that surviving firms behave as the economic model would suggest.[5] Thus, the results of consumer and producer theories are that we expect firms and individuals to behave as economics predicts (as rational, maximizing agents) even if they understand nothing about economics. Gary Becker has argued that even random behavior will often be explicable in terms of economic models.[6]

We may say that economics explains and predicts the behavior of agents without their necessarily understanding the engine that motivates them. A biological analogy may be instructive: species evolve in ways predicted by the Darwinian theory of natural selection even though only humans have recently come to understand the theory. The model can explain the behavior of actors without their knowledge of it. Similar results apply in economics. The significance of this analysis for the economic approach to law will be clarified below.

III. EFFICIENT LAW

Assume now that, as argued by Posner, Rubin, and others, the common law is economically efficient: the rules used in the resolution of disputes are those an economist would use if he were concerned solely with achieving efficiency. That such rules would enable society to best utilize scarce resources goes without saying, for that is the definition of efficiency. But such rules woul have other implications.

It might be useful to clarify the distinction between the use of "rational" and "efficient." An individual is rational if he calculates costs and benefits of actions and equates these at the margin. Economic analysis is performed assuming that all decision makers are rational in this sense. A set of rules will be efficient if it leads decision makers to consider all relevant costs and benefits in making their decisions. A set of rules is economically efficient if it requires decision makers to include the relevant external and internal costs in deciding on levels of economic activities. If the law is economically efficient, then the costs and benefits included in the calculations will be correct economic costs and benefits.

Economically efficient rules enable rational decision makers to disregard the legal implications of their actions and consider only the economic implications. (Not that decision makers may disregard the effects of their actions on others, but they need not worry about the legal rules governing responsbility for actions; calculation of the economic effects is sufficient.) This surprising and powerful result follows immediately from the aforementioned discussion. If people behave, for whatever reasons, as economically rational agents, and if the law punishes only behavior that is economically nonrational (inefficient), then the law will not affect people's actions. Whatever activities people would choose would be economically rational and, therefore, legal.

Consider, as an example, a firm thinking of introducing some potentially dangerous product. The decision maker must decide how safe to make the product. Presumably, the danger from using the product is affected both by the product design (the amount of resources the firm devotes to safety) and by the behavior of the user (the amount of resources the user devotes to safety). In deciding how much to devote to safety, the firm need only consider the most efficient way of producing it, not the law of unsafe products. If the firm considers only this aspect of safety, and is correct in its calculations, then it will be judged by the legal system to have acted correctly if any accidents should occur. Exactly the same analysis would apply to any legal decision. If, for example, a firm is contemplating breach of contract (perhaps because some costs have changed), then the decision as to whether breach should occur is purely an economic one: the firm merely calculates costs and benefits of breach and decides whether the action pays. There is no need to consult lawyers in determining the legal status of the decision.

This result, moreover, is quite general. The driver of a car need not know the relevant accident law. How closely should I follow the car in front? Knowing that I will be liable if I am following at a distance that is economically unsafe (a distance for which the costs are greater than the relevant benefits) is sufficient. I need merely calculate the distance that is safe, and may be confident that it is the legally mandated distance. For another example, in many situations legal responsibility follows a "reasonable man" standard. A decision maker need not know that he should behave reasonably to avoid liability, for a truly reasonable (economically rational) man will behave reasonably and will thus not be liable. Thus, to the extent that all activities are governed by legal rules and legal rules are economically efficient (rational), decision makers in all walks of life and engaged in all activities need not be informed about the law.[7]

Note carefully that this does not imply that decision makers must understand the economic analysis of law. As in the general economic analysis of behavior, there is no presumption that the decision maker must understand the analysis in order for the analysis to explain behavior. The complicated mathematical analyses by economists of optimal tort liability, for example, may be viewed as attempts to deduce from outside how fault is allocated. If the law is economically efficient in allocating fault, then the rules in use will be the rules deduced from the models. It is, of course, possible that the analysis by economists of efficient legal rules will be more sophisticated than the analysis by courts or decision makers. For example, some economists, in analyzing the rational behavior of firms, have developed better decision rules than those used by firms. The contributions by economists to programming theory may be viewed in this light. Nonetheless, in general, the economic analysis will merely model the behavior of the maximizing individuals.

This analysis has very important implications about decision making: individuals can make decisions without considering their legal implications. There is, for example, no reason to consult lawyers in making most decisions. The lawyer can tell the decision maker what the legal implications of the decision would be, but if the law is economically rational, the advice is not needed. In drawing up a contract, a businessman needs a lawyer to draft the contract that does what the businessman wants, but to the extent that contract law is rational, the lawyer does not need to advise him on the terms of the document.

What would the world be like if most laws were based on something other than economic rationality? Decision making would itself be a very costly activity. Individuals would need to consult lawyers or law books before making any important decision; this would add substantial costs. Two decision makers would be needed rather than one, and communication would be very expensive. The decision maker would see the world in terms of economic categories. The lawyer, however, would view the world in other terms that might be internally consistent, but would, nonetheless, be different from those used by the decision maker. Thus, there would be losses in information, and incorrect decisions would sometimes be made.

Such behavior would be especially expensive in the case of new, untried activities. For old, established activities, a lawyer could codify relevant laws and advise the decision maker, but the law would not have been established for new activities. The businessman would need to communicate to the lawyer the nature of contemplated activity. The lawyer would then need to explain to the businessman the legal rules governing it. The categories used by the parties would not be the same, and communication would be expensive.

Return to the example of an entrepreneur who has invented some new, potentially unsafe product—say a new type of power saw. He must now decide what safety devices to put on the saw. If the law follows economics, the entrepreneur must calculate the cost of various devices that he could install and compare these costs with the cost to buyers of taking certain precautions. The decision rule is simple: for a given degree of safety, presumably that which other, similar products exhibit, use that combination of methods and rules that is most efficient, that is, cheapest. For an entrepreneur, this would be a relatively straightforward calculation, since the essence of entrepreneurial ability is the ability to make good calculations of potential costs and benefits. The decision about optimal safety equipment would be very similar to the decision as to whether to produce the new product. For the product, the question would be, are the benefits of this product, as measured by the willingness of consumers to pay for it, greater than the costs? If the answer is yes, the product would be produced. For each potential safety feature, essentially the same question would be asked. Thus, decision-making ability, the essence of entrepreneurship, is, in this case, the ability to make determinations about safety features, if the law is economically rational.

If some other criterion is used in the legal setting, the problem is entirely different and much more difficult. The businessman must attempt to ascertain from a lawyer what the rules governing fault are and try to relate these presumably rather abstract rules to the decison at hand. The task would not be impossible but would greatly complicate decision making, especially when new products and processes were involved.

Consider the strict liability regime.[8] In this world, the rules are clearly lawyer's rules, however logical and consistent they may be. The entrepreneur must approach a lawyer and try to determine just what will happen under various possibilities. Communication may well be imperfect and difficult (expensive); the entrepreneur and the lawyer consider different aspects of the problem and define the world in different ways. The entrepreneur might have some difficulty explaining to the lawyer all of the events that might occur. He might then receive incorrect legal advice that would lead to incorrect decisions.

To see what is involved, let us briefly examine Richard Epstein's discussion of assumption of risk as a defense in a strict liability regime. The potential defendant must ask whether the potential plaintiff is in contractual relationships with the defendant, for various issues hinge on this relationship. Another issue is whether he forced the plaintiff either to take the risk or abandon his right of way. The defendant may then ask if the plaintiff chose the least-cost way of going through the barrier raised by the defendant. There are then potential counterpleas, which we need not elaborate here. The point is that these questions and their potential answers are purely lawyers' questions, since, by hypothesis, Epstein's rules are not economic rules. In an ongoing situation we might expect businessmen to be familiar with the various alternatives that could affect their business, but in a situation involving a new technology entrepreneurs would not likely think in the categories Epstein sets forth, and thus would not ask lawyers the correct questions. In fact, in a recent article Professor Epstein has allowed his principles of strict liability to be modified in order to account for utilitarian considerations.[9] While preferring not to discuss this modification in detail, it is nonetheless an additional complication and would make the discussion of fault and liability much more complicated than would be surmised from the earlier analysis. It would appear that, not only would decision makers need a lawyer to instruct them in liability, but that also some economic constraints would be operative. The extent to which utilitarian (economic?) considerations would override other considerations is somewhat unclear, and thus decision making would seem to be greatly complicated by this modification.

This same argument is made by Robert Bork in his discussion of antitrust law. Bork argues that the exclusive goal of antitrust law should be the maximization of consumer welfare—essentially, the goal of efficiency as defined and defended by Richard Posner and as used in this book. Bork defends this goal as leading to desirable results. More relevant here, he also defends the goal of welfare maximization because it will lead to low-cost decision making by businessmen. "He [the businessman] can know what the law is when the goal of the law is consumer welfare, because the major distinctions of such a system run along the same lines in which the businessman thinks, making lawful his attempts to be more efficient and making unlawful his attempts to remove rivalry through such means as cartelization, monopolistic merger, and deliberate predation."[10] This is exactly the point made in this chapter.

IV. APPLICATION TO EVOLUTIONARY MODELS OF LAW

Recently, economists and lawyers have explained the efficiency of law by using an evolutionary approach, as exemplified in Chapter 1. In the models proposed, the driving force is generally that inefficient laws will be litigated more than efficient laws and hence will more likely be overturned. The model in Chapter 1, and that of Landes and Posner argue that some litigants will be concerned with changing precedent so that inefficient laws will more probably be challenged than efficient laws. George Priest[11] argues that the disputes under inefficient rules will be over larger amounts than those under efficient rules and therefore are more likely to be litigated. The analysis presented here can explain why inefficient rules are more apt to be litigated than efficient rules in a way related to Priest's argument, but from a different perspective.

Assume that most laws are efficient. Decision makers will then be less likely to know the law and be able to proceed assuming its efficiency. Some laws are, however, inefficient. Since most laws are efficient, decision makers will assume that all laws are efficient; that is, it will not pay to hire an attorney to advise on behavior if most efficient behavior is legal. Then individuals are most likely to violate those rules that are inefficient since they will probably be ignorant of those rules. When a rule is violated, there is a potential for a dispute. When rules are disputed (litigated), there is possibility for the rule being overturned. Thus, inefficient rules are more likely to be violated than are efficient rules and more likely to be litigated and overturned. The mechanism is not the amount under dispute (as postulated by Priest), but rather the number of disputes arising under inefficient as compared with efficient rules. Inefficient rules generate more disputes. The mechanism proposed here gives an alternative explanation of why inefficient rules are more heavily litigated than are efficient rules and, hence, why the law would evolve toward efficiency.

V. STATUTES

Statutes are sometimes passed because the common law is unable to correct certain problems of externalities in markets. Thus, statutes may be economically efficient in the sense in which the term is being used here. There are, however, other explanations for the passage of many statutes. George Stigler and Sam Peltzman have argued that statutes are commonly passed because some interest groups obtain sufficient political power to get a law passed that provides particular benefits for them.[12] In this situation, the results of the law will have no relation to economic efficiency; rather, the law will effect a pure wealth transfer. James Kau and Paul Rubin have tested this theory and have found that special interests are important in influencing legislation.[13]

This inefficiency of statute law would be expected to impose substantial costs on the economy, and indeed, this does seem to be the case.[14]

The inefficiency of statutes has another cost that has not been analyzed. When legally binding rules are not economically rational or efficient, decision makers can no longer rely on their intuition about costs and benefits to make decisions. It becomes necessary to consult attorneys or other experts on the law in order to determine what behavior is acceptable and what is illegal. Inefficient statutes not only impose direct costs on the economy by the very nature of their inefficiency, but also indirect costs, for they increase, perhaps substantially, the actual costs of making decisions. If the law is efficient, managers must rely on attorneys only to draft contracts that are economically useful: when inefficient laws govern, attorneys may be needed to make sure that actions of firms are legal and efficient. Some examples will help to clarify this point.

The case of the relationship between automobile manufacturers and the franchised sellers of automobiles is interesting. Economic analysis indicates that franchise contracts would generally be expected to maximize the joint profits of the franchisor and the franchisee by giving each party property rights in those aspects of behavior that the party controls.[15] Once such a contract is signed, however, the franchisee would have an incentive to modify the terms of the agreement to benefit him more, since part of the efficiency gains from the contract would go to future franchisees who would not be represented directly at any given time. For example, if the franchisor has rights to terminate franchises easily, the value of the contract for all parties will be increased because of the easy policing of quality that this right implies. However, part of this value will accrue to future franchisees; all those who already have contracts would have an incentive to use political actions to change the terms of the contract. In fact, this is what seems to have happened. Starting in the 1950s, a federal law and many state laws have substantially modified the terms of franchise contracts between manufacturers and dealers.[16] These laws are clearly inefficient; some of them, for example, require that existing dealers approve the granting of a franchise to new dealers, a law not unlike the professional licensing statutes that have been much studied by economists. This chapter, however is not directly concerned with the inefficiency of the laws, but with the effect of the laws on decision making.

Again, the hypothesis in this chapter is that, before the passage of the statutes, decision making would be by managers and based on the pertinent economic issues. Conversely, after passage of statutes that are economically inefficient, lawyers would become involved in decision making as well as in mere drafting of contracts. The evidence seems to be quite consistent with these arguments. Referring to the contract used in the 1930s (before the advent of statutes) Stewart Macaulay writes: "This document typically was relatively short; it required, in effect, that the dealer keep the company satisfied with his sales, service facilities, and personality; it carefully said that the company was not promising to fill any of the dealer's orders for cars or parts that the dealer was not an agent for the company; and it allowed either party to terminate at will."[17] This contract would seem to have desirable efficiency properties, and it would seem to be a businessman's contract, with the legal input primarily in the drafting.

As a result of the passage of the law, contracts have become much more complex. For example, the Ford contract, as reported by Macaulay, begins with a three-page preamble; other clauses in the contract clearly indicate that lawyers have had a hand in drafting the contract in such a way as to minimize the impact of the legislation.[18] Lawyers had a part in decision making as well as in drafting. Similar results occurred in the functioning of the businesses. Macaulay argues that the company's legal staff could " . . . even influence the company's business practices—such as record keeping—so that it would be ready for suit."[19] The prediction advanced above, that the influence of lawyers on decision making would increase as a result of economically inefficient rules, has clearly been confirmed in the case of automobile franchising. Moreover, if records are normally kept in such a way as to make decision making more accurate and effective, then changes in such procedures in order to facilitate litigation would be a clear cost of legislation, but one which normal economic analysis would be likely to neglect.

Much economic activity is now controlled by statute, and the amount of statutory control has been increasing. The Securities and Exchange Commission, a relatively old agency, controls the terms on which firms are able to raise funds. The Consumer Product Safety Commission regulates safety features of products. The Occupational Safety and Health Administration regulates work-place safety and health. The Equal Employment Opportunity Commission and other agencies regulate nondiscrimination by employers. The Employee Retirement Income Security Act regulates pensions. Regulatory agencies also affect particular industries: the Interstate Commerce Commission regulates trucking and railroads; the Food and Drug Administration, foods and drugs; and the Federal Motor Vehicle Safety Commission, automobile safety. Multiple examples could be discussed. We will consider primarily those regulatory commissions that affect all businesses—the SEC, CPSC, OSHA, the EEOC, ERISA, and similar agencies.

First, note that none of these agencies affect the types of decisions a firm must make. With or without the SEC, firms must raise capital. Firms must also decide levels of product and work-place safety and which employees to hire. All of these decisions have legal implications. The existence of these agencies has no implications for the types of decisions that must be made, but does have profound ones for the costs of making decisions. Murray Weidenbaum has documented some of these costs. Firms must fill out huge numbers of forms; top managers must spend much more time worrying about the legal implications of their activities; company staffs dealing with matters subject to regulation have been greatly expanded and given much more say in managing companies.

This pattern of behavior is exactly what the theory advanced here would predict and is evidence for the view that the common law, which controlled these activities, was itself economically efficient. If, for example, the common law of product safety were economically efficient, management would be able to decide on optimal levels of safety without consulting lawyers. The economic intuition of managers would itself be adequate for deciding on optimal and, hence, legally mandated levels of safety. Imposition of an economically irrational statute would then indicate that managers' intuition was not sufficient for making such decisions, and thus additional personnel would need to be hired to make the required determinations. Conversely, if the common law of product liability were economically inefficient, then firms would already employ staffs of lawyers to make such decisions; the imposition of a (different) irrational law would require retraining of legal advisers, but not an increase in their numbers. Thus, the tremendous increase in costs of decision making and in the power of advisory staffs in making decisions is strong and persuasive evidence for the theory advanced here: since the common law was economically efficient, entrepreneurs and businessmen could make legally correct decisions by considering only the economic aspects of the decisions. The recent increase in inefficient statutes means that such decisions must now be made by experts in the law since economic rationality is no longer a sufficient criterion for making legally correct decisions.

One cost imposed by statute on business is the filling out of government forms. For example, the Occupational Safety and Health Administration (OSHA) as of 1970, required " . . . virtually all employees to keep three separate records: A log of occupational injuries and illnesses, a supplementary record of each occupational injury or illness; and, a summary sheet of injuries and illnesses (OSHA Forms Number 100, 101 and 102, respectively). A supplemental quarterly survey was also required (OSHA Forms 102F and 102FF)."[20] Presumably, the information in these forms was relevant for the firm decision making even before OSHA. However, as Friedrich Hayek pointed out long ago,[21] one advantage of a market economy is that it is informationally efficient. In the case of employee safety, the important information would be contained in the price demanded by workers for additional safety and the price of achieving this safety. This knowledge would enable employers to make economically rational, and hence legally correct, decisions about optimal amounts of safety. The information required by OSHA would be economically irrelevant and would exist only because of the inefficient statute. To the extent that the law was economically efficient, there would be a saving in costs of information since employers would use prices in decision making and prices contain the relevant information. The imposition of additional information requirements would serve no economic purpose; rather, it would be another example of the increase in decision costs imposed by inefficient statutes.

VI. SUMMARY

The argument advanced here is straightforward, but the implications of the argument have not, to my knowledge, been pointed out in the literature. Individuals and firms, in making economic, and perhaps all, decisions behave in economically rational ways; that is, decision makers calculate the expected costs and benefits of their actions.[22] All actions have potential legal implications that must be taken into account. If the law is economically efficient, however, decision makers can proceed without knowing the actual legal rules, for the legal rules will take into account costs and benefits of actions. Inefficient rules are more likely to be violated, hence litigated and overturned. This presents an alternative explanation for the efficiency of law. Conversely, when the law uses mechanisms other than economic rationality, decision making becomes much more expensive, for agents must determine what legal rules are binding in any given situation. As more economic activity is governed by economically inefficient statutes, decision makers must consult lawyers and other experts in the law before taking actions. The substantial increase in the costs of decision making as a result of an increase in statutes, documented by Murray Weidenbaum, is consistent with the theory advanced here. Moreover, the lower cost of decisions before an increase in statutes is further evidence for the economic efficiency of the common law. Adding a noneconomic standard of liability, as proposed by Richard Epstein and defended by Mario Rizzo, would also substantially add to decision-making costs.

NOTES

1. Mario Rizzo, "Law and Flux: The Economics of Negligence and Strict Liability in Tort," *Journal of Legal Studies* 9 (1980): 291.

2. The arguments in this section are from Milton Friedman, "The Methodology of Positive Economics," in *Essays in Positive Economics* (Chicago: U. of Chicago Press, 1953), p. 3.

3. John H. Kagel, et al., "Experimental Studies of Consumer Demand Behavior Using Laboratory Animals," *Economic Inquiry* 13 (1975): 22; *see also* Gordon Tullock, "The Coal Tit as a Careful Shopper," *American Naturalist* 105 (January 1971): 77.

4. For a discussion of the evolution of economic behavior, *see* Paul H. Rubin and Chris W. Paul II, "An Evolutionary Model of Taste for Risk," *Economic Inquiry* 17 (1979): 585.

5. Armen A. Alchian, "Uncertainty, Evolution, and Economic Theory," *Journal of Political Economy* 58 (1950): 211.

6. Gary S. Becker, "Irrational Behavior and Economic Theory," *Journal of Political Economy* 70 (1962): 1, reprinted in Gary Becker, *The Economic Approach to Human Behavior* (Chicago: University of Chicago Press, 1976), p. 153.

7. Actually, the point is somewhat overdrawn. One goal of law is to reduce costs of legal decision making. Thus, in many situations the law will not attempt to measure the costs of, for example, accident prevention for the particular individuals involved, but use instead some average standard of care. This means that an individual who is an extremely good driver will not be able to follow more closely than average (as pure efficiency would indicate) since he will, nonetheless, be subject to the same standard of care as the average driver, and will therefore need to know this standard of care. Although this point weakens the argument, it does not cancel it. The businessman, for example, in deciding on safety in new products, may correctly use the standard of the average consumer as the correct measure of safety precautions to build into the product. For a discussion of this point, *see* Richard A. Posner, *Economic Analysis of Law*, 2d ed. (Boston: Little, Brown,, 1977), p. 125.

8. *See* Richard A. Epstein, "A Theory of Strict Liability," *Journal of Legal Studies* 2 (1973): 151; idem, "Defenses and Subsequent Pleas in a System of Strict Liability," *Journal of Legal Studies* 3 (1974): 165; idem, "Intentional Harms," *Journal of Legal Studies* 4 (1975): 391; idem, "Nuisance Law: Corrective Justice and Its Utilitarian Constraints," *Journal of Legal Studies* 8 (1979): 49; idem, "Causation and Corrective Justice: A Reply to Two Critics," *Journal of Legal Studies* 8 (1979): 477.

9. Epstein, "Defenses and Subsequent Pleas in a System of Strict Liability," p. 177.

10. Robert H. Bork, *The Antitrust Paradox* (New York: Basic Books, 1978), p. 81.

11. George Priest, "The Common Law Process and the Selection of Efficient Rules," *Journal of Legal Studies* 6 (1977): 65.

12. George J. Stigler, "The Theory of Economic Regulation," *Bell Journal of Economics and Management Science* 2 (1971): 3; Sam Peltzman, "Toward a More General Theory of Regulation," *Journal of Law and Economics* 19 (1976): 211.

13. James B. Kau and Paul H. Rubin, "Self-Interest, Ideology, and Logrolling in Congressional Voting," *Journal of Law and Economics* 22 (1979): 365; *Congressmen, Constiuents, and Contributions* (Boston: Martinus Nijhoff, 1982).

14. For a discussion of the recent increase in statutes and some of the costs of this increase, see Murray L. Weidenbaum, *Business, Government, and the Public* (Englewood Cliffs, N.J.: Prentice-Hall, 1977).

15. See chap. 3.

16. The history of the legal relationships between automobile manufacturers and dealers is presented in Stewart Macaulay, *Law and the Balance of Power: The Automobile Manufacturers and Their Dealers* (New York: Russell Sage, 1966).

17. Ibid., p. 79.

18. Ibid., pp. 86–87.

19. Ibid., p. 100.

20. Weidenbaum, *Business, Government, and the Public*, p. 148.

21. Friedrich A. Hayek, "The Use of Knowledge in Society," *American Economic Review* 35 (1945): 519.

22. Gary S. Becker, *The Economic Approach to Human Behavior* (Chicago: University of Chicago Press, 1976).

CHAPTER 10
Summary, Conclusions, and Implications

I. SUMMARY

The analysis in this book is based on evolutionary models, described in Part I. These models have the implication that, under certain assumptions, the law will move toward efficiency. These assumptions essentially are that parties to disputes have symmetric interests in the rules under consideration. If this condition is satisfied, then inefficient rules will be litigated more frequently than efficient rules, and more will be spent on litigation by parties with an interest in having the efficient rule prevail. Thus, the models would predict efficiency in certain classes of disputes.

In particular, a class of disputes that should be efficient are those in which firms are litigants on both sides of the dispute. Under these circumstances, firms would have an interest in precedents and, in general, firms would also expect themselves to be on either side of a dispute in future cases. For example, firms sign contracts to buy and also to sell, therefore, a firm that at one time is disputing a contract in which it is a buyer might expect to be involved in the same sort of dispute in the future, but from the side of the seller. In this circumstance, the efficient rule should come to prevail. Part II of the book provides some tests of this claim by examining in some detail specific legal rules dealing with firms. The conclusion reached is that there are at least plausible arguments about magnitudes of transactions costs such that the claims may be true. The sort of testing provided in this part is not sufficiently empirical to guarantee the conclusions, but the claims do provide some hypotheses that should be suitable for econometric testing.

Part III of the book addresses the issue of government agencies as litigants. Here, the argument is that such litigants would have continuing long-term interests in precedents and, therefore, should use litigation strategies in order to achieve these goals. However, there is no strong reason for expecting the goals of such agents to be consistent with effeciency. Both hypotheses are borne out: government agencies (specifically, the FTC and the SEC) do appear to be concerned with precedents and do seem to use litigation strategies to achieve desired goals; these goals do not seem to be related to efficiency. Another prediction of the model is that it will sometimes pay for groups to organize in order to internalize some gain from litigation. This is especially likely to occur when inefficient rules are being promulgated. There is some evidence, in Chapter 8, that this too is occuring: business firms are contributing to market-oriented legal foundations that sometimes serve to litigate and obtain precedents that are relatively more efficient than those obtained by government agencies.

The argument in the book is based on the assumption that laws will evolve toward efficiency. There are, in the literature, two criticisms of this claim. Some claim that efficiency is not a meaningful characterization of the law; there are also assertions that evolution will not occur, or will not occur in the process analyzed here. The next section addresses these claims, while the last section provides some policy implications of the analysis.

II. SOME CRITICISMS OF THE APPROACH

One issue that has come up repeatedly in the literature is the definition of efficiency.[1] Here, efficiency is used in the standard economic sense, that a situation is efficient if it is Pareto optimal. In partial equilibrium analyses of law, efficiency in all rules but one is assumed; if this is so, then using a wealth-maximization criterion will guarantee efficiency in that rule as well. It is not correct to argue, as Posner does,[2] that wealth maximization can be used to determine the initial allocation of property rights, but once this determination is made, then wealth maximization can be used for marginal adjustments. This point is discussed at some length by Donald Keenan.[3] Since the analysis here has been partial equilibrium analysis, there is little cost to assuming efficiency in the rest of the system.

Mario Rizzo has also criticized the notion of efficiency as used by Posner and by Rubin.[4] He prefers a system of strict liability as developed by Epstein.[5] Rizzo argues first, that the type of economic efficiency of the common law discussed by Posner and others is unachieveable and thus not a meaningful goal for any system of strict liability. The hypothesis underlying Rizzo's analysis is that evolutionary models of efficiency in the law such as those proposed by

Rubin, George Priest, and John Goodman, and discussed by Landes and Posner, will not be able to achieve and maintain economic efficiency. I reject this hypothesis, but in the following discussion I will grant Professor Rizzo his assumptions and analyze his arguments as if the evolutionary mechanism would indeed not be sufficient.

Economists who have studied tort law worked out rather elaborate systems of conditions that must be met for such law to be economically efficient.[6] Rizzo does not directly address these arguments; rather, he claims that, because of incomplete markets, differing potential time frames for decisions, second-best considerations, and the trading that may occur at disequilibrium prices, it is impossible to determine whether a particular law is efficient and to say what a law should be if it is to achieve efficiency.

If we grant these arguments, Rizzo's contention, that it is impossible to tell if the law is efficient in any given situation, is correct. But these objections are not merely objections to the view that the law is efficient, but objections to the view that any economic transaction is efficient. Should we have rent control laws? If we accept Rizzo's viewpoint, it is hard to say: the market price of rental property relative to other goods may be a disequilibrium price and, anyway, second-best considerations must also apply. The futures market for contingent rental claims is also not sufficiently complete. Thus, Professor Rizzo's argument not only applies to the impossibility of achieving efficiency in legal allocations, but also to the impossibility of achieving efficiency in any market transaction.

This result is not surprising, since the economic approach to liability law is to use marketlike processes to establish a price for tortious conduct that approximates, as closely as possible, the market price that would obtain if market transactions were possible. Thus, any argument that criticizes the economic approach to law is implicitly a criticism of the economic approach to value determination in general. Epstein's system of liability rules would impose an essentially arbitrary (from an economic viewpoint) system of prices on accident-causing behavior. Any defense of these arbitrary (nonvalue-maximizing) prices in the legal realm would equally be a defense of arbitrary prices in other realms—tariffs or minimum wages could not be shown to be inefficient in this world. Perhaps Professor Rizzo is willing to accept the economic and political implications of these sorts of arguments, but they might well be costly.

What are the other alternatives? One alternative is to simply ignore most of the problems that Professor Rizzo raises, which is what most economists do implicitly in their policy analyses. We essentially assume that the world is close enough to equilibrium so that it is desirable to achieve efficiency in as many markets as possible. Another option is simply to refrain from making any normative pronouncements at all. Some economists do indeed take this approach, although it is not one that I find congenial, nor do most economists who have chosen to study the economics of law.

Having said this, I would now like to discuss in more detail Professor Rizzo's argument that the evidence for the efficiency of the law is often based on "looking at a situation and guessing what the underlying efficiency considerations might be."[7] As Professor Rizzo rightly indicates, this is only a first step and the conjecture must be empirically tested. The criticism is vaild but is not as damaging as might appear.

First, a possible test for a theory is the economy with which it organizes a large body of data. The economic approach as developed by Richard Posner does indeed meet this criterion; from what seems a large and confused mass of random data, Posner has been able to abstract a consistent set of principles and organize this body of data. It is impossible to tell whether this abstaction process is correct without hard empirical testing, but its organizing force is such that we might want to use it unless, and until, it is proven incorrect. Similar arguments may apply in biology. Here, the assumption is that features of living organisms are adaptive and much effort is aimed at determining the adaptive features of particular structures. In any given case the hypotheses are not formally testable, but the organizing power of the Darwinian paradigm is sufficiently powerful so that it is maintained.[8]

Second, saying that a theory has not been adequately tested is not an argument for rejecting the theory. It is rather an argument for seeking tests of the theory. Arguments that particular legal structures are economically efficient are difficult for economists to prove. They require measurements of magnitudes of effects as well as directions, and the statistical techniques generally used by economists are not well-suited to making measurements of magnitudes. Nonetheless, I do not think that the problem is hopeless, and it does not seem desirable to give up on the efforts. For example, in Chapter 6 the common law of false advertising was examined and qualitative arguments indicating that this law might have been efficient were presented. In this case, the common law bas been changed by statute, and we were able to examine the effects of this statute on behavior of parties. The results of this natural experiment in changing the common law indicated that the common law was probably efficient in this case, since the statutory reversal had virtually no effect on behavior and did add some costs. Other examples of tests of the theories are discussed in Chapter 2. These tests are imperfect, however, and until some more quantitative data are available, we must give Professor Rizzo the potential validity of his argument.

Third, a criticism that we cannot determine the efficiency of the law is no more valid than a similar argument about the efficiency of markets. It is impossible to be sure that private transactions are efficient. We generally assume, however, that such transactions are efficient because we know something about the mechanisms that lead to them. We assume that such transactions are undertaken by utility-maximizing individuals and thus presume that voluntary transactions are value maximizing. It is, nonetheless, impossible to prove in any given case that a particular transaction is efficient. I developed my model of efficient evolution of law for precisely this reason: to propose a mechanism that would lead to efficiency and thus create a presumption that observed rules were efficient. Professor Rizzo has assumed that my mechanism and related mechanisms would not work, and I do not wish to dispute that contention here. Evidence on that point has been presented throughout the book, and the reader may judge its strengths.

In addition to the criticisms of efficiency, there are also in the literature some criticisms of the evolutionary approach. One recent and fairly detailed criticism of this type of argument is that presented by Lewis Kornhauser.[9] Kornhauser presents several arguments against evolutionary models; these arguments will be addressed seriatim.

First, he argues that the strong form of the evolutionary claims rely on an argument that efficient rules are never litigated. In the model presented in Chapter 1, this was true; but that model is obviously an oversimplification. It would not be difficult to demonstrate that, in the context of that model, the results would carry through if litigation were random except that the bias toward excess litigation of inefficient rules persisted. Economists who assert the law of demand do not claim that no one behaves perversely, but only that, net, the results should hold.[10] That is the claim here as well.

A more serious criticism is that litigants are concerned with their own wealth rather than with the efficiency of the law, and that therefore some litigants might choose to litigate efficient rules if the overturn of these rules would increase their own wealth position. But most of the evolutionary arguments only apply to a class of disputes—those in which there are symmetries on both sides of the issue. Where these conditions are not met, then the form of the evolutionaly model considered here will not imply efficiency. This argument has been made briefly in Chapter 1 and in more detail in Chapter 2, and need not be repeated here.

The other issue addressed by Kornhauser is the issue of the settlement process. The assumption in the models presented here is that individuals are sufficiently rational so that when there is a net gain from settlement, this gain will be appropriated. That is, litigation has costs and will therefore only be pursued when the benefits of litigation are greater than the costs. This can occur only if there is some cost of the current rule to the parties involved that is greater than the cost of litigation. Kornhauser questions this assumption, and argues that sometimes irrationality will govern. Some economists generally assume that individuals are rational and efficient in their pursuit of self-interest; others claim that this is not so, and that errors and irrationalities govern. This dispute seems to be fundamental in the literture, and it may not be resolvable. (After all, most legal cases are settled, but some are litigated. Does this provide evidence for the rationality argument, since most cases are settled, or for the irrationality argument, since some are not settled?) This argument within the economics profession seems to indicate a difference in paradigm, in the sense used by Thomas Kuhn,[11] and may not be capable of being settled, for it may come down to a question of taste. I believe strongly that rationality will govern, and that scientific progress in economics will be maximized by assuming that this is so, although Kornhauser and others dispute this claim. Perhaps the ultimate test will be for each side to proceed using its favored assumption and observe the extent to which it can gain adherents, so that eventually one paradigm or the other may govern.[12] Science does not advance, however, by merely criticizing claims: implications must be deduced and tested for progress to occur.

III. POLICY IMPLICATIONS

The claim pursued throughout this book has been that when interests are symmetrical, then the litigation process will lead to efficient rules being adopted. This is an extension of the basic Coase Theorem. Ronald Coase[13] argued that when parties had property rights in valuable resources, they would be able to allocate these resources efficiently between themselves. Posner[14] pointed out that the legal rule was not always irrelevant, since sometimes the costs of changing the rule would outweigh the gains. Here, the argument is made that rule itself is endogeneous and, under the right set of circumstances, the correct (efficient) rule will be chosen. In the Coase world, the rule does not matter. In the Posner world, the rule matters and should be chosen correctly. In the world discussed here, it is the parties to disputes who matter, for if the parties are chosen correctly, then the correct rule will occur. (Presumably there is some metaprocess that chooses the parties; this issue was addressed somewhat in Chapter 2, but will be ignored here. Policy implications are not useful if no one has the power to make policy.)

In most of the preceding analysis, the parties were naturally chosen. The disputants in a contracts case, for example, are those who have signed the contract; since in many circumstances these parties have the correct set of interests, the rule will be efficient with no intervention. However, one entire class of property disputes has been almost entirely ignored throughout. This is the case where parties are not symmetrical in their interests and where there are no contractual agreements between them. The paradigm case is of course pollution, where one party (generally the polluter, though more recently groups of consumers) has an ongoing interest and the other does not, and where there are no contractual relationships between them. As discussed in Chapter 2, there is no presumption for efficiency in this situation.

Economists have generally proposed two potential solutions to the pollution problem.[15] One solution is to use a Pigouvian tax (that is, a tax based on the amount of pollution) in order to achieve optimality; the other is to create marketable rights in pollution and allow parties to trade these rights. Since both solutions would create property rights where such rights do not now exist and would require parties to internalize the costs of their actions, economists generally are indifferent about which should be chosen. However, the argument here is that it is not only rights that must be defined efficiently, but also rules, and the that nature of institutions will lead to more or less efficient rules. Given this argument, it becomes clear that the solution based on creating marketable rights is preferred to the tax solution. When a tax is used, then some government agency will be needed to enforce the tax. There will also be disputes about interpretations of the rules governing the tax, and litigation about the meaning of these rules will result. But, as shown in Part III, government agencies as litigants have no incentive to seek efficiency in precedents. Therefore we may predict that the tax solution will lead to inefficient rules about the allocation of property rights. On the other hand, if rights are created and sold on the open market, then we will have a situation in which firms are arrayed on both sides of the issue, and the firms will have roughly symmetric interests in future cases. In this circumstance, we may predict that the rules that will govern the rights will be the efficient set of rules

Thus, to the extent that the analysis presented here does lead to a policy implication, it is this: In order to have efficiency in the use of resources, there must be efficient rules; efficient rules are likely to result from having parties with symmetric interests on both sides of disputes. Where intervention is necessary to change the definition or ownership of a property right, this intervention should take the form of creation of some party with the correct interest, rather than of a government agency to enforce a regulation. The party with the interest will not only use the right correctly, but will also have the proper incentives to generate the correct rules to control the right.

NOTES

1. This issue has recently been addressed at some length in a special symposium issue of the *Hofstra Law Review*, vol. 8, (Spring, 1980).
2. Richard A. Posner, "Utilitarianism, Economics, and Legal Theory," *Journal of Legal Studies* 8 (1979): 103.
3. Donald Keenan, "Value Maximization and Welfare Theory," *Journal of Legal Studies* 10 (1981): 409.
4. Mario J. Rizzo, "Law Amid Flux: The Economics of Negligence and Strict Liability in Tort," *Journal of Legal Studies* 9 (1980): 291; "The Mirage of Efficiency," *Hofstra Law Review* 8 (1980): 641.
5. *See* Richard A. Epstein, "A Theory of Strict Liability," *Journal of Legal Studies* 2 (1973): 151; idem, "Defenses and Subsequent Pleas in a System of Strict Liability," *Journal of Legal Studies* 3 (1974): 165; idem, "Intentional Harms," *Journal of Legal Studies* 4 (1975): 391; idem, "Nuisance Law: Corrective Justice and Its Utilitarian Constraints," *Journal of Legal Studies* 8 (1979): 49; idem, "Causation and Corrective Justice: A Reply to Two Critics," *Journal of Legal Studies* 8 (1979): 477.
6. For a recent example, *see* Janusz A. Ordover, "Costly Litigation in the Model of Single Activity Accidents," *Journal of Legal Studies* 7 (1978): 243.
7. Rizzo, "Law Amid Flux," p. 291.
8. For a discussion of this point in the context of biological theory, *see* Michael Scriven, "Explanations and Prediction in Evolutionary Theory," *Science* 130 (Aug. 28, 1959): 477. Scriven also claims that similar arguments apply in the social sciences, including economics. For a similar discussion, *see* Richard A. Posner, "Some Uses and Abuses of Economics in Law," *Chicago Law Review* 46 (1979): 281.
9. Lewis A. Kornhauser, "A Guide to the Perplexed Claims of Efficiency in the Law," *Hofstra Law Review* 8 (1980): 591; *see also* Robert Cooter and Lewis Kornhauser, "Can Litigation Improve the Law Without the Help of Judges," *Journal of Legal Studies* 9 (1980): 51.
10. For the standard statement of the argument that even without rationality, the results of economic theory will apply, *see* Gary S. Becker, "Irrational Behavior and Economic Theory," *Journal of Political Economy* 70 (Feb. 1962) reprinted in Becker, *The Economic Approach to Human Behavior*, (Chicago: University of Chicago Press, 1976): chap. 8.

11. Thomas S. Kuhn, *The Structure of Scientific Revolutions* (Chicago: University of Chicago Press, 1962).

12. The extent to which this problem has parallels in biology is interesting. There, the issue is the adaptiveness of traits. In many cases, more than one gene will exist in some population. Some biologists view the various genes as being adaptive; others view them as the result of randomness. Those who claim adaptation would make arguments similar to economists who argue for the rationality of behavior; those who claim randomness would make arguments similar to economists who argue for irrationality. In both cases, it is not clear how the disputes will be settled. For an accessible discussion of the biological point, *see* Richard C. Lewontin, "Adaptation," *Scientific American* 239 (September 1978): 212.

13. Ronald Coase, "The Problem of Social Cost," *Journal of Law and Economics* 3 (1960): 1.

14. Richard A. Posner, *Economic Analysis of Law*, 2d. ed. (Boston: Little, Brown, 1977).

15. *See*, for a recent example, Larry E. Ruff, "Federal Environmental Regulation," in Leonard W. Weiss and Michael W. Klass, eds., *Case Studies in Regulation* (Boston: Little, Brown, 1981). Ruff argues that either method might be optimal in some cases, and that generally a combination of charges and marketable rights will achieve the optimal solution.

Index

of 1975, 97; Pfizer, Inc., 129-130; power of, as regulator, 123-133; *stare decisis*, 125; substantiation theory, 125, 127, 132-133

feudal land tenures, 20

First National Bank of Boston v. *Bellotti*, 151-152

franchise contract, 39-49; antitrust implications, 47-48; capital market explanations, 41; franchisee behavior, 46; franchisor behavior, 46-47; institutional structure, 40-41; interactions, 47; policing, 43-44; profit sharing, 42; sales monitoring, 45

franchise interactions, 47

franchisee, behavior of, 46

franchisor, behavior of, 46-47

freedom of contract, 21

Friedman, Lawrence, 20

Friedman, Milton, 160

Friend & Co., H.A. Friend & Co. v., 103

Galanter, Mark, 23

Germany: false advertising, 104-105; Law Against Unfair Competition, 104

Goetz, Charles, 55

"good cause" limitation, 124

Goodman, John, 18, 175

Gould, John, 3, 12

Grand Rapids Furniture Co. v. *Grand Rapids Furniture Co.*, 95

Grimes, Warren, 104

Guerlain, Inc., Saxony Products, Inc. v., 102

H.A. Friend & Co. v. *Friend & Co.*, 103

Hayek, Friedrich, 17, 170

Heinz v. *Kirchner*, 127

Hirsch, Werner, 25

Hirshleifer, Jack, 18

Homestead Acts, 20

Horwitz, Morton, 22

human capital, 65-70; acquisition of, 70-71; as collateral, 66; courts role in, 68-69; enforcement of convenant, 68-69; general training, 68; noncompetition clause, 67; privacy regulation, 67; specific training, 65-66

Hunt, Shelby, 45

Hutt, Peter, 150

insurance companies, 5-7, 26

interactions, franchise, 47

interest groups, influence of, 28-30

intervention, 124

Jensen, Michael, 42

John Wright, Inc. v. *Casper Corp.*, 100, 103

Karni, Edi, 88

Kau, James, 28, 166

Keenan, Donald, 174

Kellogg Co. v. *National Biscuit Co.*, 96

Kennedy, Monsanto Company, 149-151

Kirchner, Heinz v., 127

Kornhauser, Lewis, 177-178

Kronman, Anthony, 51, 56, 59

labor contracts, 66, 68

Landes, William, 3, 18, 24

landlord-tenant law, 25

Lanham Trade-Mark Act Congress, 85

Lanham Act, 27; and false advertising, evidence of, 99-104

Laseen Savings and Loan Association, Tucker v., 29

law: efficient, 159-165; evolutionary models of, 165-166

legal analysis, 70-72; contracts of adhesion, 70; employee, 70-71; employer, 71-72; standard form contract, 70

legal foundations, 143-156; *Chrysler Corporation* v. *Brown*, 146-149; *First National Bank of Boston* v.

property law: exclusivity, 20; feudal land tenures, 20; nineteenth-century statutes, 19-21; transferability, 20; universality, 20
public good problems, 13; statute law, 13
purchasers, new remedies for, 98-99

R.J. Reynolds Tobacco Co., American Brands, Inc. v., 103
restrictive covenant, 63-79; customer lists, 72-74; enforcement of, 68-69, 75-76; human capital, 65-70; legal analysis, 70-72; nature of, 64-65; sale of business, 76-78; trade secrets, 74-76
risk aversion, 9
Rizzo, Mario, 159, 174-177
Rockwell International Corp., Skil Corp. v., 100
Rubin, Paul, 28, 47, 161, 166, 174-175
rule creation, 58

Saginaw Manufacturing Co., American Washboard v., 92
sale of business, 76-78
sales monitoring, 45
Salwasser v. Superior Court, 146
Saxony Products, Inc. v. Guerlain, Inc., 102
Scott, Robert, 55
search goods, 92, 94, 99
Security Exchange Commission (SEC): v. Cady, Roberts, 135-136; non-disclosure, 133-135
self-enforcing contracts, 51-55; cost to society, 53-54; role of courts, 53-55
settlement costs, 12
Skil Corp. v. Rockwell International Corp., 100
small claims courts, 98
Smith, Robert, 145
Smith-Victor Corp. v. Sylvania Electric Products, Inc., 103

specific performance, 59-60
standard form contracts, 70
stare decisis, 125
statue law, 13, 17-33; asymmetric interests, 27-30; contractual interests, 25-26; efficiency of common law v., 19-22; monopoly, 21-22; property law, 19-21; symmetric interests, 26-27; unconscionability, 21
statues, 166-170; regulatory agencies, 168-170
Stigler, George, 47, 63, 166
strict liability regime, 164-165
substantial interest, 7, 23
substantiation theory, 125, 127, 132-133
Superior Court, Salwasser v., 146
Sylvania Electric Products, Inc., Smith-Victor Corp. v., 103
symmetric interests, 26-27; automobile accidents, 26; business torts, 26-27; false advertising, 27; Lanham Act, 27

Telser, Lester, 51-53, 58
Testing Systems, Inc. v. Magnaflux Corp., 94
Tollison, Robert, 22
trade secrets, 74-76; Orkin Exterminating Company, 75
trademark identification, 94-96
transferability, 20
Tucker v. Laseen Savings and Loan Association, 29
Tullock, Gordon, 3, 18, 31

unconscionability, 21, 56
unenforceable contracts, 51-61; penalty clauses, 51, 52, 55-59; self-enforcing contracts, 51-55; specific performance, 51, 52, 59-60
Unico v. Owen, 29
Uniform Commercial Code, 90

About the Author

Paul H. Rubin has been professor of economics at Baruch College and the Graduate Center, City University of New York since 1982. Previously he was professor of economics at the University of Georgia. He served as a Senior Staff Economist on the President's Council of Economic Advisers in 1981–82.

Dr. Rubin has published widely in the area of economics, particularly in the fields of Law and Economics, and Public Choice. He has published in the *American Economic Review*, the *Journal of Political Economy*, the *Quarterly Journal of Economics*, the *Journal of Law and Economics*, the *Journal of Legal Studies*, and numerous other journals. He is also coauthor of a book, *Congressmen, Constituents, and Contributors*, with James B. Kau, published by Martinus Nijhoff in 1982.

Dr. Rubin received his B.A. in Economics from the University of Cincinnati and his Ph.D. from Purdue University.